LESSONS FROM A MATERIALIST THINKER

Cultural Memory
in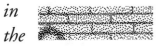
the
Present

Mieke Bal and Hent de Vries, Editors

LESSONS FROM
A MATERIALIST THINKER

Hobbesian Reflections on Ethics and Politics

Samantha Frost

STANFORD UNIVERSITY PRESS

STANFORD, CALIFORNIA

Stanford University Press
Stanford, California

©2008 by the Board of Trustees of the Leland Stanford Junior University.
All rights reserved.

Chapter 1 appeared in an earlier version with the same title, "Hobbes and the Matter of Self-consciousness," in *Political Theory* 33, no. 4 (2005): 495–517; reprinted, in slightly revised form, with the permission of Sage Publications. Chapter 4 is a revised version of "Just Lie," an essay that originally appeared in *Theory and Event* 7, no. 4 (2004). Chapter 4 also includes a passage from "Faking It," an article published in *Political Theory* 29, no. 1 (2001); amended and reprinted with the permission of Sage Publications.

Printed in the United States of America on acid-free, archival-quality paper

Library of Congress Cataloging-in-Publication Data
Frost, Samantha.
    Lessons from a materialist thinker: hobbesian reflections on ethics and politics / Samantha Frost.
        p. cm. — (Cultural memory in the present)
    Includes bibliographical references and index.
    ISBN 978-0-8047-5747-8 (cloth : alk. paper) — ISBN 978-0-8047-5748-5 (pbk. : alk. paper)
    1. Hobbes, Thomas, 1588–1679. 2. Ethics. 3. Political science—Philosophy. 4. Materialism. I. Title.
B1248.E7F76 2008
192—dc22

                                                                                                    2007037546

Typeset by Bruce Lundquist in 11/13.5 Adobe Garamond

For Simon and Madeleine

Contents

Acknowledgments

Borrowing insights from the venerable Thomas Hobbes, I must acknowledge that although I am the author of this book, I am not the sole origin of its arguments and insights. Over the years, conversations and exchanges with many colleagues and friends have shaped and sharpened my thoughts, and various institutions have provided the material conditions for my work. What is good in this book, then, is the product of many fine people (although I claim the errors and infelicities as my own).

First and foremost, I would like to thank Melissa Orlie, whose intellectual engagement and support have been critical to the conceptualization and writing of this book. Her enthusiasm, generosity, and theoretical acuity have been indispensable to the development of this project. Indeed, I am certain this would have been a lesser book without her conversation.

At the project's bare inception, I was lucky to be able to work amidst the curiosity and challenge provided by my colleagues at Rutgers University, particularly Benjamin Barber, Dennis Bathory, Mark Button, Susan Craig, Debra Liebowitz, Anne Manuel, Gordon Schochet, and Manfred Steger. Both at Rutgers and beyond, the indomitable Linda Zerilli shaped my critical thinking and served as a model. I can only hope that this work begins to serve as an acknowledgment of all that I have learned from her.

In the years subsequent to my time at Rutgers, pieces of the project were given audience by faculty at Amherst College, the University of California–Santa Cruz, the University of Chicago, Johns Hopkins University, the University of London, and the University of Illinois, as well as by colleagues at the annual meetings of the American Political Science Association and Western Political Science Association. I am grateful for the exchanges and insights generated on each occasion.

Wendy Brown and the late Iris Marion Young both made critical interventions at early stages that helped me to refashion the direction and tone of the arguments. Early drafts received critical feedback from Cliff Christians, C. L. Cole, Bill Connolly, Diana Coole, William Corlett, Jodi Dean, Tim Dean, Thomas Dumm, Peter Euben, Jason Frank, Wayne Martin, Kirstie McClure, Sara Monoson, Richard Samuels, Richard Schacht, Morton Schoolman, Jacqueline Stevens, John Tambornino, Paula Treichler, Elizabeth Wingrove, Yves Charles Zarka, and a slew of anonymous reviewers. I am grateful to all these valuable interlocutors.

As the project developed into a book, I was fortunate enough to have the following people read and offer critical comments on various chapters: Jane Bennett, Kinch Hoekstra, Bonnie Honig, Patchen Markell, Ted Miller, George Shulman, Siobhan Somerville, Miguel Vatter, Stephen White, and Linda Zerilli. The criticism and encouragement offered by these generous souls were tremendously helpful as I sought to clarify my arguments.

Richard Flathman read the project in its entirety at its fresh beginning as well as at its more bookish end. In both cases, his commentary and insights have been invaluable. Richard Boyd, James Martell, and Melissa Orlie also read through the entire manuscript in its final stages and offered comprehensive and extraordinarily helpful reflections. I used their suggestions and queries as prompts for thinking and revision even if I could not answer adequately the provocative questions they posed.

As the project progressed, I received institutional support from Rutgers University, the University of California at Santa Cruz, and the University of Illinois at Urbana-Champaign. I am grateful for the material and intellectual resources provided by each. At the University of Illinois, in particular, I want to acknowledge the encouragement and support of faculty and staff in the Gender and Women's Studies Program, the Department of Political Science, and the Institute for Communications Research. Funding from the Research Board at the University of Illinois allowed me time away from teaching to complete Chapter 1. Research leave provided by the College of Liberal Arts and Sciences at the University of Illinois enabled me to complete the manuscript. Cheers to Jim Park and Roswell Quinn for research assistance. Many, many thanks to Carolyn Brown for shepherding the book through the production process at Stanford University Press, to Rosemary Wetherold for copyediting that clarified my words, and to Jessie Baugher for checking the accuracy of my text and saving me many an embarrassment.

Throughout the arduous process of reading, thinking, composing, and revising, I had the pleasure and good fortune to be sustained by the love and friendship of all my kin. For years of unwavering support and love, many thanks to Mum and Joe, Dad and Carole, Nanna and Bampa (in memoriam), Emma, Pete and Rebecca, Kim, the entire Williams crew (plus Susan and Toby), and Michele, Tom, and Colin. Big hugs, snuffles, and kisses to my precious Simon and Madeleine. Thanks (again) to Melissa for believing when I could not. For being a loving presence as well as cheerful sounding-boards, thanks to Julie and Jodi, Tim and Ramon, Lisa and Karen, Debbie, and Luanne and Bob. Particular thanks to Jessie, whose diligent care of my children gave me the freedom to write the book to completion. And, finally, thanks to Kris, whose love and friendship have made the windup to the end of this project an unexpected pleasure.

LESSONS FROM A MATERIALIST THINKER

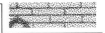

Introduction

A *picture* held us captive. And we could not get outside of it, for it lay in our language and language seemed to repeat it to us inexorably.

LUDWIG WITTGENSTEIN, *Philosophical Investigations*

Thomas Hobbes is not who we think he is. Or, to make the point more precisely, his work does not say what we have thought it says. I make this claim not in the guise of an expert exhorting the generalist to attend to the marvelous complexities revealed by careful study of Hobbes's philosophy. There are plenty of rich and detailed studies of Hobbes's work; what is at issue is not whether people read his texts closely or carefully enough. Nor do I offer this claim as an intrepid archeologist having unearthed precious gems of text that heretofore have been passed over by other professional excavators of Hobbes's oeuvre. The texts I draw on are those of Hobbes that are widely read and generally drawn upon by experts and nonexperts alike; what is at issue is not a (re)introduction of a new or forgotten piece of writing. Rather, I forward the proposition about our collective misrecognition of Hobbes and his thinking as a provocateur who has realized that we have a particular way of seeing and reading Hobbes's political theory that we do not yet recognize *as* a particular way of seeing and reading.[1] In fact, one of the central claims of this book is that the habits of apprehension that frame and constrain our encounters with Hobbes also shape and delimit how we make sense of personhood and ourselves more generally. In making these habits explicit and visible, I hope to effect a

gestalt shift in the way we look at and understand both Hobbes and ourselves and thereby to elucidate intriguing possibilities for thinking about
ethics and politics.

So one of the tasks of this project is to unmask the iconographic
Hobbes—the Hobbes, that is, who articulates a distinctively modern
brand of calculating, self-interested individualism and who paints such
a dismal portrait of the inevitability of violent conflict that his political
theory is seen as justifying or even as appealing for unsavory authoritar-
ian forms of governance. This Hobbes and the "Hobbesian individual"
who is seen as having sprung full-formed and ugly from the philosopher's
head have gripped public and scholarly imaginations for centuries, serving
as easy references for any pundit or serious thinker who seeks to deplore
the violence of war, analyze the causes of conflict, criticize the destruction
wrought by the instrumentalist, consumerist mind-set, or champion the
virtues of broad-based citizen action. One of the arguments I put forth in
this book—most specifically in the first three chapters—is that underneath
the vision of self and politics conjured by the mere mention of Hobbes's
name is someone else, *another* iconic figure, namely, the Cartesian subject. It is René Descartes's rendering of the self as split into two ontologically distinct but practically related entities of mind and body that gives to
the iconic Hobbes his hard-core individualism and the accounts of rationality, desire, and political absolutism that are its corollary. Indeed, if we
read Hobbes's work through his materialist metaphysics, which is to say
through a philosophy resolutely opposed to that articulated by Descartes,
we not only see that the iconic Hobbes is something of an impostor born
of Descartes's imagination and philosophical categories. A materialist reading of Hobbes's philosophy also undermines what we have taken to be the
centrality of the individual for his thinking about politics and brings into
focus the pacifism that drives his ethical and political work. Put differently,
what emerges through this way of seeing Hobbes is a thinker whose appreciation of our embodiedness or materiality issues in a complex portrayal of
our profound interdependence and a compelling account of the ways and
means to peace.

Related to the interest in recasting Hobbes and his work, an addi-
tional aim of this book concerns the habits of self-perception and understanding that accompany our implicit and unavowed adoption of the terms

of Descartes's ontology. For a good while now, thinkers in the West have been held captive by a Cartesian picture of the human subject: a person split internally into mind and body. To be sure, many theorists and philosophers have rejected the mind/body dualism that has come to serve as the abridgment and signature of Descartes's philosophy. Yet, even as scholars have redescribed the relationship between mind and body, refiguring what it is to be an embodied person, we have not yet been released from the captivity of the dualist picture. This is not to say that we have fallen short in our portrayal of the imbrication of mind and body in a human being, as if what is at issue is the accuracy or fullness of our representations. Rather, although we have largely transfigured the subject from mind-in-a-body to embodied-mind, we have not yet changed the broader picture or framework through which we recognize or understand what being a subject or a person means. That is to say, even as theorists and philosophers might offer different claims about what a person is—"we are embodied minds"—the constellation of concepts we generally use to talk about personhood remain profoundly Cartesian. And when we repeat this language in our discussions of subjectivity, ethics, and politics, we are recaptured by Descartes's picture of the subject even as we think we have left it behind.[2] This book represents an effort to trace the outlines of an alternative picture or framework for understanding the thinking, rationality, desire, and action of a non-Cartesian subject.

In many respects, then, this project is an experiment in reading. That is, it is an attempt to satisfy a curiosity about what might happen were we to grant to Thomas Hobbes his materialism. What I mean by the term "grant" here is not the mere acknowledgment that he develops a materialist philosophy, an allowance that requires the periodic gesture to the mechanistic worldview that is presumed generally to go along with a materialist metaphysics. What I mean, rather, is a thoroughgoing concession, a giving-over in which Hobbes's materialism is articulated in all its depth and breadth, in which its implications for our conception of ourselves and our world are elaborated as fully and as trustfully as a generous imagination can accommodate.[3]

As is intimated in the opening paragraphs, the reason such an experiment requires a generous imagination is that to give oneself over to Hobbes's materialism is to have to face serious challenges to our conception of what it is to be a person. What confronts us here is not the prospect that his materialism figures people as something akin to automata—at this point in time, such a figuration is hardly credible enough to pose much of a challenge. Rather, when spun together into a coherent argument, Hobbes's materialism compels us fundamentally to rethink our conceptions of self-consciousness, reasoning, desire, and action, of what an "individual" is, and of what collective ethical and political life might and should be.[4] In other words, taken seriously, Hobbes's materialism calls into question what Sheldon Wolin has called our "tacit political knowledge," the "complex framework of sensibilities built up unpremeditatedly" that we draw upon in our reflective inquiries, the broad tradition of understanding that "tells us what is appropriate to a subject and when a subject matter is being violated or respected by a particular theory or hypothesis."[5] In fact, we could say that in calling into question the commonplaces that orient our thinking, Hobbes's materialism—or this reading of it—violates the "norms of minimal intelligibility" that Jacques Derrida claims serve as the ground upon which exegesis, analysis, and criticism take place and make an interpretation recognizable to others as a commentary on a common text.[6] So one must be generous in order to be open to apprehending the sensible in a train of thinking that we might at first be inclined to presume will lead to utter nonsense.

Of course, it is important to note here that, as a metaphysical orientation, Hobbes's materialism was neither strange nor incomprehensible to his contemporaries: materialisms of different kinds were gaining intellectual currency and attracting critical attention in the early modern period.[7] Like many other philosophers in seventeenth-century Europe, including Descartes, Pierre Gassendi, and Marin Mersenne, Hobbes reconsidered and responded to the political, moral, and theological problems posed by ancient thinkers.[8] In doing so, he drew on the atomism of ancient skeptics such as Epicurus to formulate the mechanistic account of the movement of matter at the heart of his materialism.[9] Similarly, Hobbes was far from alone in having his thinking shaped by the broadly influential if bitterly contested mechanistic natural philosophy developed by Galileo.[10] Further, in his moral and political work, Hobbes leaned heavily on the insights of Hugo Grotius, for whom the principle of self-preservation served as a bulwark against skeptical moral relativism and as scaffolding for theories of state.[11] In addition to this broad philosophical context, the proliferation of Reformation Christian doctrines provided the conditions for the development and intelligent reception of his materialist accounts of the self. That is to say, Hobbes's materialism had affinities with strands of Lutheran and Calvinist Protestant Christian denominations that denied the soul outlived the flesh, that affirmed the materiality of the spiritual world, and that subscribed to deterministic doctrines of predestination.[12] In other words, the philosophical priority Hobbes gives to the materiality of the world, his effort to describe the self and human action "according to the principles of matter in motion,"[13] and the ethical and political significance he attributes to the living human body share antecedents and common philosophical ground with other arguments developed in the period in which he wrote. Indeed, it was precisely because his materialism was intelligible to his contemporary audience that Hobbes was excoriated for the religious, ethical, and political entailments of his arguments.[14]

So although Hobbes's materialism was not widely accepted in the seventeenth century, it was not deemed incomprehensible. From our perspective, the intelligibility of Hobbes's metaphysics and its entailments can be ascribed to the fact that he wrote his materialist philosophy before the remarkable ascendancy of Descartes's philosophy—or to be more precise, *during* what Jonathan Israel calls the "Crisis of the European Mind," the period of intellectual upheaval in mid-seventeenth-century Europe in which the Cartesian "mechanical philosophy" rose and spread.[15] To make the point more precisely, Hobbes formulated a materialist account of self, society, and politics both against and before the Cartesian framework for conceptualizing what it is to be a person had become so thoroughly dispersed and entrenched as to stand as an unacknowledged commonplace in our thinking about consciousness, desire, and action.[16]

Read through the ubiquitous penumbra cast by Descartes's philosophical system, Hobbes's materialism has (somewhat understandably) been dismissed as illogical, incoherent, wrong, or irrelevant.[17] However, as the ontological status of mind/body dualism has been called into question by developments in feminist and contemporary political theory, philosophy, science, and cultural studies,[18] as the constellation of concepts we use to figure subjectivity and social interaction have been critically analyzed and reformulated,[19] and as other materialist philosophies from the early modern period have come to be reassessed,[20] it has become possible to think beyond the panoply of concepts that together compose the Cartesian picture of the self. That is, the contemporary intellectual context is such that we can read Hobbes's materialism and receive the complex and extraordinary insights about subjectivity, ethics, and politics that he offers.

The analytical starting point of Hobbes's entire philosophy is the axiom that "the World, (I mean not the Earth onely, that denominates the Lovers of it *Worldly men,* but the *Universe,* that is, the whole masse of all things that are) is Corporeall, that is to say, Body."[21] Everything that exists is matter: there is nothing else. Such a thoroughgoing materialism has generally been thought to entail a crude mechanistic account of action that condemns us to a deterministic behaviorism or to some such mode of acting that makes us unrecognizable to ourselves.[22] That is, in saying that matter is all there is, Hobbes is thought to have jettisoned the immaterial soul or mind and to have left us with a body whose features are inadequate to account for the extraordinary complexity of what it is to be a thinking, feeling, choosing person.[23] However, as I argue in the chapters ahead, the sense that the material body alone cannot give us a sensible account of what it is to be a person derives from an implicit adherence to the terms of Descartes's philosophy. What we imagine Hobbes to have done in articulating his materialism is to have attempted to account for how a self might be conjured from essentially unthinking matter. But of course, as Stanley Cavell points out in his own meditations upon the ways in which Descartes's dualism continues to haunt philosophy, to proffer a materialist account of the subject by pasting the attributes of mind onto matter is to shift the weight of the "self" to the inert "matter" side of Descartes's dualism—which is not to reject the terms of dualism at all but rather merely to make a conceptual move within the confines of those very terms.[24] To put the problem a little differently, because we are (sometimes unwittingly) bound to a Cartesian-type conception of matter, we cannot very easily recognize—or even see—the alternative understandings of self and society Hobbes proposes. In spite of ourselves, we tend to be Cartesian in our understanding of what a wholly material self might be.

Hobbes eschews a Cartesian understanding of matter. Instead, he formulates what, in the first chapter of this book, I call a "variegated materialism." According to this materialism, matter is varied rather than uniform in its characteristics: whereas some matter is inert, other forms of matter are animate and thinking. In these latter cases, of course, Hobbes is referring to people. In his view, liveliness and thinking do not need to be added to otherwise inert matter to make a person, for they are essential aspects of what some matter simply is. In making such a claim, Hobbes obviates many of the conjuring exercises presented by materialist portrayals of the subject that are founded on the "matter" side of the Cartesian binary: how can we figure blank, indurate, mute matter as capable of thought, feeling, and self-movement? Starting with the presumption that there are indeed such things as "thinking-bodies," Hobbes develops a complex account of thinking, desire, and action.[25] And unsurprisingly, the conception of the self that he develops from this notion of animate, thinking matter is radically different from the conception of the self we get through relying on either side of the Cartesian binarism.

As will become clear as the argument of this book unfolds, what is at stake in Hobbes's materialism is the concept of the self-sovereign individual we generally associate with his political work—the selfish, calculating "possessive individual" of political theory lore.[26] When Hobbes elaborates the processes that constitute thinking, desire, and action in a being composed of "matter in motion," he produces a figure whose orientation to time and whose relationship to the material world have a profound effect upon its sense of self as well as upon the tenor and course of social interactions. To state the point briefly, Hobbes's subject is not an autonomous, self-defining, integrated, and internally unified individual. Indeed, in many respects, the very concept of the individual is displaced as a central unit of his political analysis. For the self that emerges through Hobbes's materialism, thoughts do not spring from some well within; likewise, desires are not, as Jean Hampton claims, "*intrinsic* properties."[27] Rather, thoughts and desires are constituted and reconstituted intersubjectively and in relation to the material environment. In fact, for Hobbes, to speak of the intersubjective nature of our existence is not enough. In his analysis, the patterns of our reasoning and desire and our very capacity to act are such that we must speak of action and interaction in terms of our interdependence. We could say, then, that with his materialist metaphysics Hobbes gives us an account of self and society that has at its center the principle of heteronomy.[28] So Hobbes's materialism challenges not only our sense of how to imagine what a person is. It also challenges the habits of thinking that are operative in our use of the autonomous individual as the central figure in our theorizing about ethics and politics.

The habits of thinking broached and challenged in this effort to recast the substance and implications of Hobbes's materialism are as follows. First, we tend to think that matter, in itself, cannot be self-aware. In other words, self-consciousness is difficult to imagine if we confine ourselves to the realm of matter.[29] In Chapter 1, I draw out Hobbes's accounts of sensation and perception to suggest that, for him, some forms of matter can be self-aware and that this self-awareness takes the form of memory. This figuration of self-awareness as memory disrupts the immediacy implicit in the Cartesian model of the self-conscious subject and instead portrays the subject as able to know itself only through a longer temporal frame than the present moment. In other words, Hobbes's argument suggests that a subject's self-consciousness—and its broader sense of self—must be thought in connection to the past and the future. As will become clear in the pages ahead, this temporal shift at the very center of the conceptualization of the individual subject has implications for our imagination of the subject's relation to others as well as its engagement with the world more broadly.

Second, we tend to think that thinking and reasoning are activities undertaken by an active agent of thought, an agent who is sovereign of or who has direct control over the thinking process. However, this model of the thinking-self's self-mastery rests upon the presumption of the thinking-self's incorporeality. According to Hobbes's materialist accounts of perception, thinking, desire, and reason, we are not and cannot be masters of our thoughts as they occur. As I explain in Chapter 2, in his view, the processes that constitute our thoughts and that move us from one thought to another are so complicated and fast that we can only say that "thoughts happen" without our immediate awareness and direction. This is not to say that we do not have any control over our thoughts whatsoever. For Hobbes, a complex combination of desire, language, and habit enables us to recognize, organize, and give sensible structure to our thought patterns. To acknowledge this aspect of his argument, however, is to have to give up the notion that reason is a source and sign of our autonomy and instead to see the process of reasoning itself as conditioned by desire, language, and habit—and the various social, cultural, and political forms that shape them.

Third, as is intimated in its disruption of our presumption of the autonomy of reason, Hobbes's materialism compels us to rethink what we mean by the concept of determinism. Although in all likelihood not many contemporary theorists would claim that our thoughts, desires, and actions emerge solely from a source within us—a true self, a pure soul—there is a general theoretical reluctance to think about determinism because our habits of thinking and our conceptual vocabulary make determinism something of a thief: it seems to steal our agency, our sense of our personal effectiveness, or our ability to proclaim, "It is *I* who did this."[30] In other words, a deterministic materialism such as Hobbes's is presumed to position subjects as utterly passive objects of forces that are unilinear in their movements, totalizing in their effects, and beyond any one person's control. As I argue in Chapter 3, however, Hobbes's materialism is irreducible to the deterministic, mechanistic models of it.[31] In fact, his account of determinism disrupts the binarism of free will and determination that is central to the Kantian formulation of the problem of freedom and necessity that in many respects conditions our aversion to deterministic theories of willing and action.[32] What distinguishes Hobbes's determinism from the kinds of determinism to which many theorists feel allergic is his attention to the temporality of the subject. To preview the argument, for Hobbes, each particular person embodies a particular lived history, the causal trajectory of which is distinct from the history and series of historical determinants in the world in which he or she moves. Action occurs at moments when these temporal and causal trajectories coincide. According to Hobbes's analysis, although each of these trajectories is determined by prior causes, the conjunctions or points of contact between them that produce action are unpredictable and indeterminable. So, although each action is, in fact, determined, each is also distinctive and creative.

As the formulations in the sketch of determinism begin to indicate, Hobbes's arguments about willing and action displace the notion that the individual is the single origin of his or her action. Instead, they foreground the combined effects of memories, other people, and contexts upon individuals' plans, desires, and actions. Importantly, such an analysis of the thoroughly intersubjective and material constituents of our selves entails a fundamental rethinking of the relationship between self and others and more particularly of the ethical imperatives that should guide our interactions. Hobbes's ethics is generally read through the presupposition that the subject is a rational, autonomous individual.[33] In some cases, Hobbes is seen as having portrayed ethical activity as selfless compliance with rationally derived principles. His ethics is understood here as a precursor to a Kantian deontic account of duty.[34] In other cases, Hobbes is seen as having portrayed ethical activity as obedience to imperatives that are the product of a reasoned and self-interested consideration of a structure of disincentives. In this view, prudential advisories are elevated to the status of moral dictate on the command of the sovereign.[35] However, Hobbes's materialist portrayal of thinking, desire, and action both displaces the individual and makes it impossible to isolate reason as a single determinant of action. Accordingly, his ethics entails neither that individuals adhere in their actions to rational rules nor that they consider their own advantage as if in opposition to that of others. Rather, as I elaborate in Chapter 4, Hobbes's ethics enjoins people to attend to their relations with others through time. More precisely, he calls on us to consider how our relations with others bear on the prospects for peace. For him, the pursuit of peace is, or at least should be, our primary ethical concern.

Hobbes's portrayal of the intersubjective and material conditions of thinking, desire, and action also requires that we rethink his account of power. We generally conceive of Hobbesian power as a brute capacity for exploitation and domination, a resource in a zero-sum game in which gains to one's advantage are necessarily a loss to another's disadvantage. The political story entailed by such an understanding of power—a story that is not coincidentally the iconographic Hobbesian story of conflict—is one in which the scramble to acquire power produces splintering chaos, war, and the need for a superior power to quiet and quell the anxious and violent tumult. However, as I argue in Chapter 5, with his materialist portrayal of thinking, desire, and action, Hobbes refigures power not as something that an individual might have or acquire to the detriment of another but rather as the conditions for action. At once drawing upon and affirming his analysis of the intersubjective nature of our thoughts and passions, Hobbes portrays power as arising from as well as consolidating our interdependence. Giving a social and political elaboration of the heteronomous character of action, Hobbes proposes that power is the conjunction of the individual, social, and contextual causes that both prompt an action and enable the realization of a person's initiative in the form of an effect.[36] In other words, power conceived as the conditions for action comprises not only people's particular capacities but also their relations with one another through time and the material environment in which together they act and interact. In fact, Hobbes's various discussions of power suggest that, in his view, neither individuals nor the sovereign can act except with the assistance or cooperation of others. His insight into this profound interdependence reinforces his claim that the effort to foster the conditions for peace must be at the center of everything we do.

Before moving ahead to elaborate the argument of this book in its detail, let me address a set of questions that inevitably will press because of the book's focus on embodiment. In contemporary theoretical scholarship, and especially in feminist, critical race, and queer theory, a focus on embodiment involves careful attention to the norms, institutions, and discursive practices through which gendered, racialized, and sexualized subjectivities are produced. That is to say, the body is considered to be a node in a network of power relations in and through which identities are specified, reiterated, and contested. For theorists engaged in such work, the body is rarely considered as simply "the body," as if there were a singular and generic phenomenon about which general statements could be made. Rather, a body is construed as knowable or conceivable only in terms of its political specificities: a body is always a particular kind of body, a product of historically specific relations of gender, racial, and sexual power. For political theorists, this emphasis on the specificity of bodies has entailed analysis of the ways in which explicit statements as well as ideas implicit in a text's logics, paralogisms, silences, and asides produce forms of embodied subjectivity that instantiate, explain, and justify social and political inequalities. Given such theoretical practice, to read Hobbes's arguments about materiality and bodies without searching for their gender, racial, or sexual implications seems to be a sign of political obtuseness and naïveté if not willful stupidity. One might ask: does one not elide a history of rich political insight in reading Hobbes's claims about "body" at face value and without suspicion? Shouldn't one presume, as some feminists have done, that Hobbesian "body" is figuratively female? that what Hobbes says about embodiment might well serve as a signpost to the gendered, racial, and sexual presumptions that underwrite his political vision?[37]

These are important questions. But my sense of Hobbes's materialism is that to use such categories of analysis in reading his work is actually to circumscribe rather than to open up the possibilities for political insight. It is quite clear that for Hobbes the category "body" is not implicitly feminine or racially marked for exclusion: for him, the entire universe—and everything in it—is body, or matter. To presume out of habit that this broad claim is best read as a clue to uncover his production of sexualized or racialized forms of subjectivity seems to me to reaffirm the very associations that critical theorists seek to challenge.[38] Indeed, Hobbes's materialist insistence on every subject's thoroughgoing embodiedness, his dismantling of the myth of the self-sovereign individual, and his account of the complexities of social relations and political action suggest that we might learn more about power, inequality, and the pernicious effects of dualistic thinking by reading his claims about embodiment as broadly ontological rather than as surreptitiously and narrowly normative.

To put the point another way, this book does not take the body as the target of representation and the repository of symbolic meaning nor does it analyze the panoply of forces and the forms of violence that produce identities and make particular bodies socially or politically intelligible (or unintelligible). Rather, this book takes the body as it lives, experiences, negotiates, creates, and rejects different aspects of the social and material world in which it exists. It is concerned with the phenomenology of material subjectivity, with the possibility of providing a coherent account of how a wholly material organism perceives, engages, and moves around in a wholly material world.[39]

As we shall see, what emerges from this rereading of Hobbes's philosophical and political work is a radically different picture of this notorious thinker. Because the figure of the autonomous, rational individual is not at the center of his theory, his work cannot really be counted as liberal or even protoliberal. This is not to say that in Hobbes's thinking, individuals and their identities are subsumed to and merely a precipitate of an organic community.[40] Hobbes acknowledges the singularity—or what Richard Flathman calls the "unicity"—of each individual.[41] The issue is that, in his view, individuals are not discrete actors. To the contrary, his work demands that we think of individuals—and their thoughts, desires, and actions—in terms of their relation to and effect upon the collective of which they are inevitably a part. Indeed, Hobbes's analysis of our intersubjectivity and our interdependence points to the dailiness of the actions through which we affirm and reaffirm the extant political order—and through which we might disrupt it.[42] In other words, his materialist analysis of power prompts us to think of him not as giving us an origins story but rather as giving us an anatomy or a constitutional analysis of a peaceful polity. This very anatomy foregrounds the complex networks of mutually transformative relations between the material environment, the social and political contexts of our actions, and ourselves. In so highlighting the relationships that are both the condition and the consequence of our actions, Hobbes's work pushes us to reject the narrow instrumentalism in relation to natural and social resources that he has heretofore been thought to advance. To the contrary, through his materialism, Hobbes provokes us to consider carefully the extent to which our current actions will nourish or destroy the economic, political, and environmental conditions of possibility for our actions in the near as well as the distant future.

1

Hobbes and the Matter of Self-Consciousness

In a fascinating comment to the Dutch Protestant minister and scientist Andreas Colvius, René Descartes explains what he himself understands to have been the point of his famous argument for the cogito.[1] Dismissing the significance of having provided proof for "the certainty of our existence," Descartes highlights instead his claim that "this *I* which is thinking is *an immaterial substance* with no bodily element."[2] In other words, he characterizes as his distinctive achievement the development of an account of the thinking subject as an incorporeal entity, an account of thinking as essentially separate from the workings of matter. If we shift the terms of emphasis, we might also characterize it as the development of an account of matter as essentially unrelated to thought. Indeed, if we conceive of Descartes's achievement as the articulation of a distinctive account of matter, then we can appreciate anew just how profound an effect his philosophy has had on our thinking about thinking. For when we reject his argument for the incorporeality of the cogito (which many of us are wont to do) and turn our attention to bodies, more often than not we find ourselves face-to-face with mere lumpish matter, at a loss about how to explain just how it is that something that is essentially matter has the capacity to think.[3] Even if we can muster a fairly basic account of perception, the mechanics of matter make it difficult to imagine how a theorist of a wholly material subject might contrive the internal distance necessary for the thinking self to observe itself: matter seems to be stupid to the kind of turning upon oneself that makes the Cartesian thinking subject's self-perception an "intuition" or "an intellectual cognition of the simplest and most direct kind."[4] It seems to me, however, that to puzzle about matter in this way is not only to accept from the start the essential unthinkingness of matter and to try to account—rather hopelessly—for the possibility of thought. It is also to demand that matter imitate the movements and turns that Descartes uses to figure the subjectivity of the incorporeal thinking self, the self that ostensibly has been rejected.

That the terms of Descartes's dualism continue to haunt our conceptions of both matter and self-consciousness might be of little concern to political theorists were it not for the fact that the introspective trope that Descartes uses to portray our self-knowledge structures our conceptualization of our self-mastery.[5] That is, a corollary of the trope of introspection is the presumption that we determine and direct our own thoughts and that we use our thoughts to control and constrain our passions and desires—a presumption that also underlies a whole range of different conceptions of what it is to be a political actor. Consequently, to extricate ourselves from Descartes's account of the incorporeal self is not only to have to formulate an alternative account of the nature and form of our relation to ourselves. To reject Descartes's dualism is also to have to develop different ways to imagine the thinking, feeling, and action involved in ethical and political activity. In other words, to disentangle ourselves from the terms of Descartes's philosophy, we must give up (on) and replace the individual conceived as a discrete, self-sovereign, autonomous actor. In this book, I argue that Thomas Hobbes gives us the reasons and resources to do this and much more.

It is well known among political theorists that Thomas Hobbes formulated a materialist metaphysics. Likewise, it is no secret that he was one of Descartes's great challengers—in his *Objections* to Descartes's *Meditations* as well as in the correspondence coordinated by Marin Mersenne.[6] Yet the greatness of Hobbes's challenge to Descartes has not really been fully appreciated. Or perhaps it is better said that we have not yet taken full measure of the possibility that a significant part of Hobbes's greatness is in his challenge to Descartes's philosophy. As I shall elaborate below, when Hobbes repudiates Descartes's dualistic conception of the subject, he does not offer in its stead the mechanistic materialism we generally attribute to him—this latter, I will argue, is a specifically Cartesian mechanistic materialism that is alien to Hobbes's philosophy. Rather, Hobbes articulates a distinctive materialism that not only refuses the possibility of the Cartesian incorporeal thinking self but also refuses the very terms under which matter is conceived of as unthinking. Indeed, we can find in Hobbes's philosophy and political theory an account of what it is to conceive of subjects as "thinking-bodies."[7] In this chapter, I will read Hobbes's accounts of sensation, perception, and thinking to argue that, for a wholly embodied subject, self-consciousness, or self-knowledge, takes the form of memory. I will also begin to suggest that when we take memory to be the key to our relationship to ourselves—when we transfigure the temporality of our self-awareness—our theoretical sense of the relationship between the individual and the world and political collective also undergoes a profound shift. In fact, as I argue in the course of this book, Hobbes's materialist theory of the subject requires (rather surprisingly for our habits of interpretation) that we take as the unit of political analysis not the single individual but rather the unavoidable relationships of interdependence that constitute the conditions that make each individual's actions possible.

Before consenting to venture forth into the thick of Hobbes's metaphysics, the busy reader might well ask: Why Hobbes? Why should we revisit old Hobbes (yet again) when we could instead turn to the many contemporary efforts in philosophy of mind, neuroscience, and even political theory to rethink the implications of our embodiedness? The short answer, which is at least implicit in the paragraphs that open this chapter, is that we do not yet have an adequate framework to conceive of the relationship between the fact that we are bodies—flesh—and the fact that we are thinking selves.

Of course, developments in neuroscience suggest that we are on the way to acquiring the kinds of information and insights that might help us make the conceptual shifts and acquire the conceptual vocabulary necessary to rethink our materiality. Antonio Damasio, for example, has presented popular versions of scientific findings that the physical perturbations we know as emotions and the mental gymnastics we know as thinking are inextricably linked.[8] "Descartes' error," as Damasio calls our collective difficulty in thinking well about the body and thinking, consists in "the separation of the most refined operations of the mind from the structure and operation of a biological organism."[9] Neuroscience tells us, to the contrary, that every perception, thought, and judgment involves not simply the elegant patterns of thoughts, images, and representations that we ordinarily depict as the work of reason and the intellect but also neurochemical reactions and complex physiological adjustments throughout the body and brain. Indeed, the former cannot happen without the latter.

However, even though Damasio's research gives us fascinating insight into the marvelous complexity of the human organism's mental and emotional activity, what his work tells us about self-consciousness is not yet clear: some among his more philosophically oriented readers complain that the philosophical musings he undertakes as a result of his scientific findings give us an inadequate theory of thinking and subjectivity. More specifically, Colin McGinn and Ian Hacking are concerned that his apparent reduction of thinking to the neural activity of an organism striving for homeostasis misses the intentionality of our thoughts and emotions—the fact that they are "of" objects, persons, and situations in the world and not just representations of bodily states—and also fails to account well enough for the subjective experience of being a thinking person, an "I" or a self.[10] I am not well-enough versed in the complex debates in the philosophy of mind to evaluate their judgments of Damasio's work. But given both the extraordinary resonances between his and Hobbes's descriptions of what perception, thinking, and judgment are like in a thinking-body, I am not convinced that Damasio is not at least in range of his philosophical target. And even if he does not get the philosophy quite right, his work is important, for it signals both that a scientific picture of a wholly embodied subject is emerging and that we need to redouble our efforts to imagine thinking and self-consciousness in non-Cartesian terms. Only a little tongue-in-cheek, perhaps I could say that Damasio's problem in his effort to refigure self-consciousness is that he turns to the notoriously cryptic Spinoza for philosophical assistance rather than to Hobbes. But of course, in looking to Spinoza rather than Hobbes for a philosophical elaboration of our materiality, Damasio is in good company.

When contemporary theorists plunge back into seventeenth-century philosophies of materialism to explore the political implications of our embodiedness, many of them join Gilles Deleuze in his rejection of the rationalist Spinoza, focusing instead on the movements of body and affect in the world that Spinoza spins from the threads of his metaphysics.[11] In concurrence with Jonathan Israel's recent portrayal of Spinoza's philosophy as the touchstone of what is radical in the Enlightenment, they scoff at the stodgy English authoritarianism of Hobbes's political theory and align themselves instead with the political radicalism they see unfolding from Spinoza's philosophical rejection of Cartesian dualism.[12] It is interesting to note, however, that the gesture to an unfavorable portrait of Hobbes by which such neo-Spinozistic projects rather frequently orient themselves is often made without sufficient attention paid to the striking similarities between Hobbes's and Spinoza's metaphysics and theories of subjectivity, without thought, that is, for the very real possibility that the metaphysics upon which Spinoza's radical politics is built may be influenced by, or at least have strong affinities with, the metaphysics authored by Hobbes.[13] Or to make the same point differently, when people use Hobbes as a foil for the radical Spinoza, they do so without considering the ways in which our understanding of Hobbes's political theory might be modified by his materialism.

Interestingly, in his review of recent neo-Spinozistic works, William Connolly tries to leaven the persistent invocation of the iconic "Hobbesian individual" by speculating that there may be a Hobbes "who could enter into productive dialogue with Spinoza on the topics of diversity, ethics, and generosity."[14] Connolly's marking of such a possibility opens the space to reconsider the affinities and differences between the ethical and political insights that Hobbes and Spinoza draw from their respective materialist philosophies. For his part, Connolly draws on the developments in neuroscience mentioned above, as well as the Spinozistic strains in a range of political theorists, in order both to elucidate the visceral and affective dimensions of reasoning and judgment and to reanimate the ethical and political demands of pluralism. More specifically, he elaborates various techniques and practices that we might undertake to coax our embodied selves to "acknowledge the comparative contestability" of the "theo-ontologies" that undergird our orientation toward the world—the aim here being to foster "agonistic respect across difference."[15] However, as Stephen White has remarked, the practice of "critical responsiveness" that Connolly would have us cultivate to facilitate the emergence of a true pluralism presumes that we possess, even as we must work upon and refine, the virtue of generosity.[16] Although I would not argue with the claim that some among us are graced with Connolly's Spinozistic openness to openness, I suspect that for many there may be issues, beliefs, or forms of action to which we simply refuse to be open. At a time when the world is wracked by violence that seems only to escalate as people clutch maniacally to fundamental beliefs, I am intrigued by the possible insights we might gain from a materialist thinker like Hobbes, who, apparently less hopeful (or less generous) than either Spinoza or Connolly, presumes the intractability of hostile conflict at the very same time that he searches for a way to peace.

Recasting Hobbes's Materialism

We commonly understand Hobbes to have offered a Cartesian mechanistic materialism as an alternative to Descartes's depiction of the thinking self as an "immaterial substance."[17] That is, we tend to perceive him as having articulated a materialism that, in refusing the ethereal character of Descartes's thinker, shifts the "self" to the "matter" side of Descartes's dualism, thereby reducing people to a mere sum of material particles—to "dehistoricized bit[s] of matter-in-motion," as Sheldon Wolin once put it.[18] Rather predictably, when we approach Hobbes's philosophy with a Cartesian mechanistic materialism in mind, the possibility of thinking itself becomes a problem: at the same time that some contemporary Hobbes scholars are developing increasingly nuanced accounts of the role of our passions and bodily desires in the process of reasoning, yet others stumble over Hobbes's account of thinking and reasoning itself, worrying that what he calls thoughts cannot be attributed the status of real thoughts because their sensorial quality—their derivation from sensory experience—prohibits the kind of abstraction and complexity that we generally think thoughts have.[19] For these latter scholars in particular, thinking within Hobbes's materialist account of the subject is rendered a futile activity: lacking the capacity for abstraction and self-reflexivity, we cannot use our thoughts to direct ourselves in our actions.[20]

Now, the huge range of text that Hobbes devotes to thinking, reasoning, abstraction, and philosophy suggests a couple of things: first, that he simply does not see thinking as futile or impossible; and second, that in finding thinking an impossibility within his materialism, we might be reading into Hobbes's philosophy a view of matter that he rejects. Indeed, if we read Hobbes's work alert to the possibility that his materialism differs in kind from that developed by Descartes, a different, non-Cartesian materialism does indeed come into view. We could call what emerges a variegated materialism, a materialism that acknowledges that matter can take distinctive forms and be organized in varied and particular ways—a materialism in which some such distinctive forms and organization of matter can think.

To propose that we qualify our attribution of a mechanistic materialism to Hobbes is, admittedly, to ask that we stir up some of our most settled understandings of Hobbes's philosophy. So let me clarify just what it is I want to hold up for reconsideration. I do not dispute Hobbes's adoption of the new mechanistic science as an explanatory framework. As many scholars have noted, the turn by early modern thinkers to a mechanistic understanding of the workings of the material world served as a repudiation of the blind and politically dangerous superstitions fostered by the obfuscations of scholastic or neo-Aristotelian philosophies.[21] Like many of his contemporaries, then, Hobbes rejects the idea that material objects have an intrinsic purpose or a final cause, subscribing instead to the mechanistic principle that "[t]here can be no cause of motion, except in a body contiguous and moved" (DCO 9:124). What distinguishes Hobbes's materialism, I think, is the manner in which the science of mechanism is used to explain or understand human behavior.

To be sure, Hobbes's contention that any movement in or action by an object can come only "from the *action* of some other immediate *agent* without itself" suggests that Pheng Cheah might be correct when he characterizes Hobbes as a modern mechanist par excellence.[22] Such a propensity for perceiving Hobbes as describing people as machinelike automata is only fueled by the famous metaphor that opens the *Leviathan:* "For what is the *Heart,* but a *Spring;* and the *Nerves,* but so many *Strings;* and the *Joynts,* but so many *Wheeles,* giving motion to the whole Body."[23] It is understandably tempting to read this machine metaphor as evidence that Hobbes's materialist rejection of Descartes's philosophy entails that subjects be little more than machines. However, to succumb to the temptation of such a reading is to let ourselves be duped by the terms of Descartes's materialism.[24]

Admittedly, when Hobbes says that "life is but a motion of Limbs," he does seem to reduce the complexities of organismic life to the mechanics of motion. However, he goes on to make what turns out to be a crucial distinction, stating that the source of such life, the "begining" of it, is not "artificiall" (as in an automaton) but rather "is in some principall part within" (L intro.: 81). We might well characterize this "principall part within" as the soul. But in doing so, we must recognize that Hobbes vehemently rejects the conceptualization of the soul as something distinct from the body, as an immaterial entity ontologically separate from but housed somewhere within the material body (L 46:693). According to Hobbes, the soul is a characteristic of the body or, to put it more precisely, is a characteristic of a particular kind of body. As he says in his admittedly idiosyncratic reading of Scriptures, "The *Soule . . .* signifieth alwaies, either the Life, or the Living Creature; and the Body and Soule jointly, the *Body alive*" (L 44:637–38). For Hobbes, then, the soul that is the source of the "motion of Limbs" is quite simply the very liveliness of the living creature.

It is important to dwell for a moment upon this notion of a "body alive," for in specifying that the distinction between automata and human bodies lies in the fact that the motions in and the movement of human bodies derive from the very liveliness of the body, Hobbes suggests that there are forms of body or matter that are distinguished by their aliveness. When Hobbes declares in *Leviathan* that "[t]he World, (I mean not the Earth onely, that denominates the Lovers of it *Worldly men*, but the *Universe*, that is, the whole masse of all things that are) is Corporeall, that is to say, Body" (L 46:689), he claims that we cannot describe ourselves as more than or as something in addition to "body." But in contending that the only thing we can take ourselves to be is "body," or matter, he is not making the claim that we humans are "mere" body, "mere" matter, resolvable aggregates of uniformly indeterminate, basal, elemental particles. As the notion of a "body alive" suggests, there are some forms of "body" that are distinguished from others by their being alive: they are animated by what Hobbes calls a "Vitall Motion" that is "begun in generation, and continued without interruption through their whole life; such as are the *course* of the *Bloud,* the *Pulse,* the *Breathing,* the *Concoction, Nutrition, Excretion,* &c" (L 6:118).[25] Moreover, some "bodies alive" are distinguished from others by their capacity to use language and to think rationally.

Scattered throughout Hobbes's writings, then, is evidence of his sense that there are different kinds of bodies and that humans among them are likewise distinctive: we humans are each "*a living Body*" (L 46:691), a "*Body alive*" (L 44:638); we are animate bodies (DCO 25:406–7), we are sentient bodies (DCO 25:391–93), we are "thinking-bodies" (DCO 3:34).

Crucially, when Hobbes forwards these claims, he makes a point of clarifying that we are each of these, not with the quality of "living," "sentient," and "thinking" added to otherwise uniform matter, as if there are bodies that at first have no animation but to which animation is added to create "animate bodies," to which in turn is added "rationality" to form "animated rational bodies" (DCO 2:24). Rather, according to Hobbes, we are each of these as the kind of body simply that is living or that has the capacity for sentience or thinking (DCO 2:23–25).[26]

As this discussion begins to illustrate, any description of Hobbes's account of the subject as "mechanistic" is complicated by his claims that matter takes a variety of forms. In particular, his contention that human beings are moved by a "vital motion" requires that we think more carefully about how to understand the mechanistic principle of cause and effect that is at the center of his materialism. According to Hobbes, vital motion tends toward its own perpetuation, a tendency evinced in the effort of the living organism to persist, to live on, to survive, to persevere when confronted with the events, necessities, and limits of the material world in which it exists.[27] Accordingly, although the movement or action we observe in animate bodies may be provoked by worldly events, we cannot construe it as the movement of a body passively subject to external causal stimuli. Rather, such movement or action must be seen as the response of a living organism to those stimuli. More particularly, such a response is not simply an unmediated reaction to the current event or even the effect of an accumulation of reactions to similar events. Rather, as we shall see in detail in the chapters ahead, it is a response that is textured by the entire complex history of the organism's experiences and responses (L 6:120). What we see in Hobbes's philosophy, then, is that the mechanistic principles that undergird his materialism are made to account for what occurs when the motions of matter in the external world are brought to bear upon and transformed by the history and patterns of motion internal to animate bodies as these are amended by and work upon the world.

The point I would like to draw out in the present chapter is that, for Hobbes, in this complex interplay of the motions that animate and move human bodies we can find the elements of an account of subjectivity—of the possibility of a subject's self-awareness or self-knowledge. The key to this self-awareness or self-knowledge lies in the relationship between the memories and the vital responses that constitute the process of sense perception.

Rethinking Self-Consciousness

According to Hobbes, every single thought or idea we have has sense perception at its root. Any idea we have—even one for which there is at the moment of thinking no object before us—is a residue of previous sense perception, a lasting impression of a past sensory experience. As Hobbes asserts grandly in the opening paragraphs of *Leviathan*, "The Originall of [all thoughts], is that which we call Sense; (For there is no conception in a mans mind, which hath not at first, totally, or by parts, been begotten upon the organs of Sense.) The rest are derived from that originall" (L 1:85). What this means, of course, is that if we want an account of the self-awareness or self-knowledge of the subject conceived as a thinking-body, we will have to explore Hobbes's account of sense. If we do just this, we find that because the process of sense perception is made possible by both the memory and the vital response of the perceiver, the very activity of sensing itself produces a form of self-awareness. The self-awareness that emerges through and indeed is a condition of sensory perception is the nonlinguistic self-awareness of a sentient, animate body.

Hobbes's most succinct definition of sense comes in *De Corpore*, where he states that "Sense *is a phantasm, made by the reaction and endeavour outwards in the organ of sense, caused by an endeavour inwards from the object, remaining for some time more or less*" (DCO 25:391). In other words, sense is a particular kind of reaction in a sentient body whose sensory organs have been provoked by stimuli (393). The "cause of Sense," Hobbes says, "is the Externall Body, or Object, which presseth the organ proper to each Sense, either immediatly, as in the Tast and Touch; or mediately, as in Seeing, Hearing, and Smelling" (L 1:85). The characteristics, qualities, or what he calls "accidents" of objects take the form of motions that impress our sense organs and are communicated or translated through our other bodily organs to our heart and brain—which react—and then back out again (DCO 25:391). The very traversal or "propagation" of these motions through the thinking-body, combined with the thinking-body's reaction, are together what constitute each thought, phantasm, or "apparence" (391).

According to Hobbes, we must conceive of this entire sensory process—and the resultant "phantasm" or percept—as motions in matter. He insists that "[s]ense, . . . in the sentient, can be nothing else but motion in some of the internal parts of the sentient; and the parts so moved are parts of the organs of sense" (DCO 25:390). So when the "accidents" of the objects before us work "on the Eyes, Eares, and other parts of mans body," their impression introduces and provokes motion or movement in the perceiving subject (L 1:85). Conceived as motion, phantasms and sensory percepts must also be understood as "some change or mutation in the sentient" (DCO 25:389). It is important to foreground this description of sensory percepts as "change . . . in the sentient," for it means that we cannot think of our percepts as the continual resonance of a singular kind of motion wrought of the continual stimulation of a particular sense organ. Hobbes argues to the contrary that in order to notice or register the motions that are our percepts, there must be changes or variation in those motions—a range of perceptual objects. As he puts it, "Sense . . . must necessarily have in it a perpetual variety of phantasms, that they may be discerned one from another . . . it being almost all one for a man to be always sensible of one and the same thing, and not to be sensible at all of any thing" (DCO 25:394).

In claiming that sense perception requires that there be "a perpetual variety of phantasms," Hobbes suggests that in the very process of sensing itself we make comparisons among the different forms of stimulation we receive. For when we experience the changes in the motions in our bodies effected by the different objects whose motions impress upon us, our very perception of change—It was like that, and now is like this—implies that we discern a difference between a present sensation and phantasm and an earlier sensation and phantasm, even if that earlier one was just a split second ago. In turn, this discernment of a difference between current and prior sensations implies memory. In fact, Hobbes makes this point explicitly.

As if anticipating how strange is his claim that the process of sense perception entails that we discern differences among sensory stimuli, Hobbes asks, "But you will say, by what sense shall we take notice of sense?" (DCO 25:389). And he responds to his question with the claim that we take notice of sense "by sense itself, namely, by the memory which for some time remains in us of things sensible, though they themselves pass away" (389). In positing in this way an equivalence between "sense itself" and "the memory which . . . remains," Hobbes proposes that memory is not a distinct capacity we have in addition to the capacity for sense perception but is instead integral to the very process of sense perception. He says as much when he explains that "sense . . . hath necessarily some memory adhering to it, by which former and later phantasms may be compared together, and distinguished from one another" (393). For Hobbes, then, memory is a constitutive element of the process of sense perception.

At this point it may sound as if we have a philosophical account of the motions precipitated in a sentient body by a series of stimuli but nothing yet resembling a subject—a being with a sense of self, an "I" who undergoes and is aware of it all. However, in his account of both the animate body's sensory perceptions and its appetitive reactions to sensation, Hobbes makes a distinction that furnishes us (or, rather, the animate body) with a form of subjectivity. This is a distinction between the series of activities that constitute a perceptual event undergone by a thinking-body and the experience of those activities or that event for the animate body in question.

When Hobbes says that "[s]ense, . . . in the sentient, can be nothing else but motion in some of the internal parts of the organs of the sentient" (DCO 25:390), he draws our attention to his claim that we do not perceive objects as they are. In his view, we perceive only our own impressions of their qualities—the motions that they effect in our bodies.[28] As he says quite forcefully in *Leviathan,* the qualities or properties we perceive in objects are nothing "but so many several motions of the matter, by which it presseth our organs diversly. Neither in us that are pressed, are they anything else, but divers motions; (for motion, produceth nothing but motion)" (L 1:86). But importantly, even as he insists that a proper understanding of perception includes the insight that what we perceive, when we perceive, are no more than the motions in our bodies, Hobbes also points out that our experience of that perceptual event is such that the qualities appear to be in the perceptual object itself. The percept is nothing but motions, he says, "[b]ut their apparence to us is Fancy" (86). Bernard Gert has suggested that this observation by Hobbes points to an inconsistency in his argument.[29] But what is really going on is that Hobbes is acknowledging that although, technically speaking, a percept is nothing but motions, we experience those perceptual motions in such a way that the qualities we perceive appear to inhere in the objects without us: "the reall, and very object seem[s] invested with the fancy it begets in us" (86).[30]

Hobbes recapitulates this distinction between the event of perception and our experience of perception in his account of appetite and aversion. As he tells it, the motions that "presseth the organ proper to each Sense" are translated "by the mediation of Nerves, and other strings, and membranes of the body" to the brain and heart where they "causeth . . . a resistance, or counter-pressure, or endeavour of the heart, to deliver it self" (L 1:85). That is, in their traversal of the animate body, perceptual stimuli necessarily aid or abet the body's vital motion. Hobbes explains that with this enhancement or disruption of the body's equilibrium, "the reall effect there is nothing but Motion, or Endeavour; which consisteth in Appetite, or Aversion, to, or from the object moving" (L 6:121). Yet although the "reall effect" of the stimulation "is nothing but Motion" of the animate body toward or away from the stimulating object, "the apparence, or sense of that motion, is that wee either call Delight, or Trouble Of Mind" (121). In other words, while the movement or endeavor of appetite and aversion manifests the effect of the stimulating motions upon vital motion, the experience or "apparence" of those effects for the animate body is its pleasure or displeasure at the presence of a particular object (122).

With this distinction between the "reall" effects and their "apparence," Hobbes captures his insight that the stimuli and the reaction are of consequence to the organism, which is to say that they matter because they affect the organism's vital motion—the energy, the vital processes, the equilibrium—in some way. The organism does not simply undergo stimulation but *feels* or *experiences* stimuli (the pleasure, the pain), does not persist or falter indifferently but *feels* or *experiences* a reaction (the desire, the aversion). The feeling that is so crucial here is a kind of participatory identification: The perceptual event does not merely happen to an organism. Rather that particular organism perceives and responds.

This as yet only vaguely implied sense of an "I" or a "me" that is in play here becomes more sharply defined when we recall Hobbes's claim about the centrality of memory to sense perception. Since memory is an essential aspect of sense perception, the animate body's prior apprehension of and response to various stimuli form a part of the very process of perceiving itself. So the motions provoked by a stimulating object are recognized for having been encountered before as well as for their prior effect upon the subject. Or to put the point in the experiential language that Hobbes's distinction affords, not only does the animate body feel this or that way when it meets the object; it also remembers feeling this or that way when it met this kind of object previously. The animate body remembers the feeling of the prior stimulation and the prior response; this memory of feeling is the memory of how the body's vital motion—its energy, its vital processes, its equilibrium—was affected by prior encounters with the object.

Hobbes's argument here about memory and perception is fascinating, for he suggests that the animate body senses and remembers not just a prior stimulation and response but its very experience of that stimulation and response—the feeling of being stimulated and of responding in that way. In fact, I would argue that, for Hobbes, such an experience of remembering an experience is a kind of turning upon the self that constitutes a form of self-awareness. Hobbes claims that "he that perceives that he hath perceived, remembers" (DCO 25:389), and what is remembered in this case is the experience of being a sentient, animate body. This turning is not a figuratively vertical turn, as in the Cartesian thinking subject's transcendent experience of presiding over its own operations. Rather it is a horizontal turn, a figurative backwards glance by which the subject considers what is past or what has taken place. Accordingly, for Hobbes, self-awareness or self-knowledge takes the form of memory.

Understandably, the assertion that this remembered experience constitutes a form of self-knowledge may raise some skeptical eyebrows: this memory's seemingly mute immanence in the flesh may be an argument against its admission to the status of self-knowledge or self-reflection. Or to pose the possible objection differently, self-knowledge or self-reflection must be something more than this bodily memory of bodily experience. I have two answers for such a reticence.

First, when Hobbes contends that "every part of the Universe, is Body" (L 46:689), he forecloses any argument that we should take ourselves to be anything other than body or matter. What this means is that we cannot hold out the possibility that self-knowledge or self-consciousness might be something other than a bodily experience. In a sentient, animate body, it will have to take the form of a bodily awareness, and in Hobbes's argument, such a bodily awareness is memory.

The second response runs like this. It seems to me that the impetus behind such reticence comes from the sense that language is and must be a condition of thought and thus of subjectivity, from the sense, that is, that only we linguistically endowed humans can think and be self-aware. Interestingly, though, Hobbes does not believe that language is the provenance of thought and (accordingly) he does not restrict thinking to humans.

When Hobbes introduces us to the issue of language in *Leviathan,* he argues that the "generall use of Speech, is to transferre our Mentall Discourse, into Verbal; or the Trayne of our Thoughts, into a Trayne of Words"

(L 4:101). What is important to note here is that, according to Hobbes, we do not use language to mark or signal individual thoughts, as if we could not recall or communicate a thought otherwise. Rather, we use language to mark or signal a succession or "Trayne" of thoughts, "our Mentall Discourse." So when he says that names "serve for *Markes,* or *Notes* of remembrance," what are to be remembered or registered are "the Consequences of our Thoughts" which "slip out of our memory" and so "put us to a new labour" (101). In other words, we can think a series of thoughts and come to particular conclusions all without words, but we need language if we want to remember a conclusion without going through the whole thought process all over again. Hobbes says much the same thing when, in a discussion about error, he presumes that we can reason about possible causes or consequences of particular events without the use of language—that we can "reckon[ ] without the use of words, which may be done in particular things, (as when upon the sight of any one thing, wee conjecture what was likely to have preceded, or is likely to follow upon it)" (L 5:112). To have an evaluative perception, to remember that perception and project it forward in anticipation of the consequences, is a kind of thinking that does not require language. This is, of course, why Hobbes says that as sentient, animate bodies, animals ("beasts") and humans alike are able to anticipate the good or bad consequences of encounters or actions, consider what best to do, and undertake deliberate action in the world (L 6:122–28).

Of course, this is not to say that Hobbes denies the existence of a specific form of self-awareness that depends upon language. As he says, there is an "Understanding which is peculiar to man," that is, the understanding of "his conceptions and thoughts, by the sequell and contexture of the names of things into Affirmations" and such (L 2:93–94). But his acknowledgment that language enables us to get a textured knowledge of our thoughts does not detract from his contention that without language, sentient animate bodies do have self-knowledge or self-awareness in the form of memory.

Language and Self-Knowledge

The question presses: what is the self-knowledge or self-awareness that comes with language? Or to pose it differently, if we humans are distinctive in our capacity for language, as Hobbes claims, do we also have a distinctive form of self-knowledge or self-awareness?

To answer this question, we need first to recall that, for Hobbes, percepts, memories, imaginations, and thoughts are all essentially the same thing, which is to say that they are all motions in the bodily organs. The motions that constitute phantasms (as a general class) can be distinguished from one another by temporal factors: motions caused in the present moment are what we call sense perceptions (L 1:86), whereas those motions that remain when the stimulating object is gone and time has passed are what we call memory and imagination. Yet despite the different temporality of each of these types of phantasms, they are "but one thing, which for divers considerations hath divers names" (L 2:89). This means that what we commonly call thoughts, ideas, or concepts are not phenomena distinct from sensory percepts; they do not constitute a special class of phantasms that are somehow rarefied and have some superior kind of content. Rather, they are collections of variously clear perceptual motions that are retained in the organs of the thinking-body. When we add language to this mix, the character of our thoughts themselves does not change. They remain motions in the animate sentient body. What does change, however, is the relationship of our ideas to one another.

According to Hobbes, when we engage in a process of purposive or directed thinking, our thoughts can be related to one another in two possible ways. The first possible relation between thoughts is that established through particular or specific experiences—which is how we often think, in random musings and instrumental reasoning alike. The second possible relation between thoughts is that established through "ratiocination," which Hobbes describes as a different way of remembering or recalling our phantasms, a different way of "Calling to mind" or "*Re-conning*" them (L 3:96). In ratiocination, we remap our thoughts so that the shifts between them trace the parameters set by the logic of systems of names and definitions. We elaborate the relationships between the names we define, we "add" them together to create propositions, we combine these to create syllogisms, and we arrange the latter to develop arguments (L 5:110). We describe a proposition as "true" when the names connected in the proposition are connected correctly and their definitions comprehend or correspond appropriately with one another (L 4:105). In other words, in ratiocination, we "reckon[ ] . . . the Consequences of generall names agreed upon, for the *marking* and *signifying* of our thoughts" (L 5:111).

The great advantage of ratiocination is that it enables us to engage in complex and abstract thought processes, to gain a finer and richer understanding of our own thoughts. But importantly, the sophistication and nuance made possible by ratiocination do not make the actual activity of thinking or the thoughts themselves more refined—as if of a higher order. The actual activity of thinking in ratiocination is still motions in matter. To understand why, we need to recall Hobbes's contention that in order to aid our recall of our phantasms, we invent mnemonic devices, using visual, vocal, or aural marks to prompt our notice of our thoughts and memories. To provoke other people's notice of one of their phantasms that may be similar to one we notice, we may use similar visual, vocal, or aural stimuli as signs.[31] Names or words are just such marks or signs; they are visual, vocal, and aural stimuli that we use as marks or signs to recall or provoke notice of the phantasms with which they become associated (L 4:109). When we have learned language and the relations between names instituted through language, the motions in the bodily organs set in play by the enunciation of a series of words in speech or by the production of visual signs in writing will draw to our notice a particular series of thoughts.

One of the reasons that language is so important is that it gives a measure of order to what are otherwise often rather messy strings of associations between our thoughts. As I explain in detail in the next chapter, Hobbes contends that, generally speaking, we do not actively direct our thoughts. In *Human Nature,* he gives a neat, pithy articulation of what is a much longer and more elaborate argument in *Leviathan,* claiming in the former that when we think, "one conception followeth not another, according to our election, . . . but as it chanceth us to hear or see such things as shall bring them to our mind."[32] We cannot choose which thoughts shall follow one upon the other. It is because we cannot choose which thoughts to remember that language is useful: language gives the kind of order to our thoughts that we cannot give in the moment that we think them. So if we are thinking philosophically—using words silently in our head, writing a text, engaging in abstract conversation—then (ideally) the trajectory of our thoughts follows the unfolding of linguistic logic.[33] We do not think a thought and use a name to mark it as we go. To the contrary, we give ourselves over to language—we submit to it—and it enables us to recall our thoughts in an organized manner.

Hobbes's argument that language, in a sense, thinks our thoughts for us—or brings them to our notice—is important, for it suggests that our relationship to our philosophical thoughts also takes the form of memory. Indeed this is exactly what Hobbes claims in his Second Objection to Descartes's *Meditations*. Sorting critically through the arguments that Descartes develops in the Second Meditation in order to reach the claim "I am a thinking thing," Hobbes objects to Descartes's account of how the thinking "I" comes to recognize that it is thinking. Rejecting Descartes's contention that he has an immediate awareness of his thoughts in the very moment that he thinks them, Hobbes argues instead: "I do not infer that I am thinking by means of another thought. For although someone may think that he *was* thinking (for this thought is simply an act of remembering), it is quite impossible for him to think that he *is* thinking, or to know that he is knowing" (CSM II:122–23). For Hobbes, the self-reflection of the thinking subject cannot be conceived as a cognition that takes place in the same temporal moment as the act of thinking. As George MacDonald Ross has also observed, Hobbes denies "the possibility of immediate self-knowledge through introspection: we can remember past thoughts, but our present thinking cannot have itself as an object."[34]

According to Hobbes's arguments, then, what may feel like our awareness of thinking is in fact an awareness of something that has already happened. To be aware of oneself perceiving or thinking is actually to remember perceptions or thoughts—or to remember oneself as having perceived or thought. To say this is not to imply that there is a significant or noticeable time lag between thinking and the recognition cum memory that one has thought. It is simply to say that the activity of thinking that takes place in any given instant can be known to us only as remembered. So, in contending that "someone may think that he *was* thinking" and that "this thought is simply an act of remembering," Hobbes proposes that an animate body's self-perception as a *thinking* being also takes the form of memory.

Conclusion

Hobbes developed his materialism—his accounts of subjectivity, ethics, and politics—before the Cartesian subject became the standard figure for subjectivity, before the tropes for its activities became so familiar as to seem a matter of fact. If we can bring ourselves to acknowledge the non-Cartesian character of his work, Hobbes's very familiar philosophy will read strangely. In that strangeness, it will force us to call into question concepts that we no longer know we take for granted.

According to Hobbes, subjects conceived as wholly material beings can be self-aware or can possess self-knowledge. Whether we are talking about animate creatures more generally or about the very special subset of animate creatures who are able to think linguistically and rationally, the form that self-awareness or self-knowledge takes is memory. For Hobbes, then, the turning upon the self by which we come to know ourselves is a backwards glance at what has transpired, an always already historical look at the thoughts and desires that have arisen before our notice. In short, what we call the introspection of the thinking subject is and can only be retrospection.

Hobbes's claim that self-knowledge or self-consciousness takes the form of memory has profound consequences, for it changes what we might call the temporality of the subject—the relationship of the self to the self in and through time. In turn, this change in the temporality of the subject effects a transformation in our conception of what it is to act—or at least, what it is to act deliberately.

In the Cartesian framework with which we are so familiar, the immediacy of the self-consciousness wrought through introspection enables the subject not only to grasp but also to control the emergence and trajectory of thoughts. The self-reflective turn involved in introspection positions the subject figuratively above itself in the very moments of its thinking. Thus positioned, the subject presides over its own internal activities, a veritable sovereign determining the content and direction of its own thoughts and deploying the strength of reason to constrain and conduct the passions.

Hobbes's account of self-consciousness as a form of memory does two things to this figure of the subject. First, it interrupts the temporal horizon of the subject's self-knowledge, which is to say that it disrupts our conception of the immediacy of the subject's relationship to its thoughts and desires. Within Hobbes's schema, the turning upon the self that enables us to know ourselves is not a vertical movement in the present moment but rather a horizontal one, a turn that positions us only to observe what has happened. This position of retrospective observer is one in which it is simply not possible actively to call up or determine our thoughts and passions: Hobbes claims with respect to thinking that "one conception followeth not another, according to our election" (HN 5:34); he claims with respect to desires that "no man can determine his own will, . . . nor . . . any other appetite."[35] But although we cannot determine our thoughts and passions "according to our election," we can through retrospection come to understand what causes particular thoughts and desires to arise. And as we shall see in Chapters 4 and 5, we can also, through the projection of this understanding into the future, anticipate and try to shape the conditions of their future emergence.

In addition to pointing to the need to take a longer view of the activities involved in thinking and desiring, Hobbes's account of self-consciousness as a form of memory also requires that we take a broader view of those activities. Hobbes's contention that our thoughts, memories, and desires are produced through our engagement with the contexts of our action over time blurs the boundaries of the self. That is, his specification that our perceptual encounters are the ongoing basis of our thoughts, passions, and sense of self requires that we conceive of the self not as a unified entity bound in and by the skin but rather as a discrete but nonetheless porous body among other bodies. In other words, Hobbes requires that any account of the self include the social and material conditions in which that self lives and acts. In fact, as I elaborate in more detail in the pages that follow, the shift in temporal orientation entailed by Hobbes's account of self-consciousness as memory combines with the shift in focus toward the individual's relationship with the material and social contexts of its existence to displace the individual as the singular unit of analysis. According to his argument, no individual can be construed as the single source or origin of his or her own thoughts and desires. As a consequence, no individual can be construed as the sole origin or cause of an action. Instead, Hobbes claims that we must consider among the causes of action the state or condition of the very matter of the organism itself, the material histories and social arrangements that coalesce to present the occasion of a particular opportunity at a particular moment, the lifetime of experiences and memories that shape whether someone notices such an opportunity and how she responds to the consequences she foresees, and the complex of histories of opportunities and experiences that shape how others will perceive or receive her initiative. In defining self-consciousness as a form of memory, then, Hobbes places at the foreground of his political theory a much more complex account of the relation between self, context, and community than heretofore we have imagined.

2

Hobbes and the Caprice of Reason

In the opening pages of *Leviathan,* Hobbes depicts thinking as "motions of . . . matter" (L 1:85–86). By describing both thoughts and the process of thinking as motions in matter, he stirs up a host of theoretical issues. For in that very description, he not only dismisses Descartes's contention that matter is essentially unthinking. He also advances the argument that bodies think. And to say that bodies think—nay, that they reason—is to join together some of the conceptual categories whose distinction has been central to the ways we have thought about political subjectivity. Political theorists generally construe reason as the agency within us that grants us our agency as actors: reason is the instrument of our self-control, the faculty that enables us to rise above the turbulence of the moment to make self-conscious and deliberate decisions. Significantly, we can attribute such a role to reason only because we make a theoretical exception of it. That is, we can portray reason as a pivotal characteristic of ethical and political subjects because we except it from the flesh, from the quivering sensitivities and wrenching upheavals to which bodies are inevitably subject.[1] If we go along with Hobbes and conceive of thinking as a corporeal activity, as *nothing other than* a corporeal activity, we undo the exception of reason, we incarnate reason, and in doing so we throw into question, and perhaps jeopardize, the important ethical and political tasks to which it has conventionally been assigned.

For philosophers and political theorists, it has long seemed that the body is a hindrance to reason. For several millennia, the body has been conceived as liable to issue in forces and energies that disrupt the smooth workings of reasoned thought. From within such a perspective, the measure of one's intellectual and moral maturity is conceived as the extent to which one can harness the body's passions and appetites for the edification of the intellect.[2] In more recent centuries, it has been particular bodies rather than bodies in general that have been seen as inimical to reason. Facial features, skin complexion, hair texture, skull shape, skeletal posture, anatomical sex, pelvic aperture, hormonal balance, genetic coding—each has been construed as a natural measure of someone's ability to reason in ways appropriate to ethical and political life.[3] To be designated a person with a dubious body type was to be perceived as having one's inner world subject to the influence of casual encounters, intimate relationships, and the effects of aleatory changes in the flesh and in the material world; the physical characteristics of one's body destined it to serve as vehicle or passage for social, cultural, and environmental forces, marking one as passive in mind, inconstant in thinking, and unreliable in reasoning. Of course, in recent decades scholars have revealed that such suppositions have been both the basis for and product of economic opportunism, imperial ambitions, colonialist adventures, and the consolidation of social and political power. Yet despite the now broad consensus that body type cannot be taken as a qualification or disqualification for the ascription of rationality, and despite a related suspicion of philosophies that oppose mind to body or reason to the passions, the uneasiness long characteristic of our accounts of the relationship between body and reason persists. However, whereas the source of the uneasiness has heretofore been conceived as the potential for the body to upset reason, contemporary science and philosophy suggest instead that our idea of reason may be a hindrance to our understanding of the body, that is to say, that our very conception of reason may stand in the way of our appreciation of embodied subjectivity.

The reason that reason is—and must be—subject to renewed critical scrutiny is beautifully illustrated in Tom Sorell's recent and vexed effort in *Hobbes* to represent Hobbes's account of thinking within the terms of his materialism. When I describe Sorell's reading of Hobbes as "vexed," I do not mean to suggest that he has some kind of animus against Hobbes that causes him to misread his work. Far from it: Sorell's is a generous and in many respects descriptively accurate reconstruction of Hobbes's materialist philosophy. Rather, the vexed character of Sorell's interpretation lies in his finding himself confronted in Hobbes's materialism by a seeming limit of philosophical intelligibility, or rather, by something that breaches those limits and thereby disappears into the realm of the unintelligible. As we shall see below, what stumps Sorell is his fear that Hobbes's materialist account of perception and thinking provides that we can think only what is presented by sensory stimuli, that our mental processes are wholly subject to the vagaries of the sensorial context. He fears that a materialist account of the subject entails utter mental passivity on the part of thinking subjects, an inertial relationship to the world, ourselves, and our thoughts.[4] In other words, haunting Sorell's reading of Hobbes is an unarticulated but strongly held presumption that to accept a materialist account of the subject is to deny that we are the active agents of our own mental activity and thereby to accept the impossibility of thought and reason.

One of the first indications that Sorell finds himself easing along a precipice that opens into gaping philosophical nonsense is his articulated concern that Hobbes's claim that thinking is motions in matter allows for the possibility that stones can think. If thoughts are nothing more than motions in matter, he argues, then we cannot dismiss the possibility that the motions that resound through a stone when it is struck are thoughts.[5] This "embarrassing result" of Hobbes's materialism makes it difficult to discern "the boundary between the animate and the inanimate, and between bodies with minds and bodies without" (75). On the face of it, this is a very silly objection, one that should not merit much attention. Given advances in philosophy of mind, cognitive science, and neuroscience over the past forty years, it seems ridiculous for Sorell to respond to Hobbes's materialism by invoking the absurdity of thinking stones. However, there is something instructive in Sorell's insistence upon the possibility of stone confusion even as he notes Hobbes's own insistence that his materialism does not warrant such a collapsing of distinctions (74–75).[6] Sorell's invocation of thinking stones—his suggestion that within Hobbes's materialism thinking stones and thinking persons might be somewhat indistinguishable—reveals an anxiety about the implications of Hobbes's materialism for our conception of what thinking is. Indeed, adding to the appearance that he is as confounded as he is troubled by Hobbes's materialism, Sorell goes from worriedly conjuring thinking stones against Hobbes's prescient objections to experiencing a lapse of memory, grumbling that "the thought that . . . mental processes might be irreducible . . . seems never to occur to [Hobbes]" (75).[7] One objects: of course Hobbes had considered this thought, for he rejected it vehemently in his disagreements with Descartes. What is it that so unsettles Sorell that he makes claims that are so clearly at odds with the written record? If we read Sorell further, we find that what unbalances him in Hobbes's philosophy is perhaps not the possibility of thinking stones but rather their obverse, stone-like thinkers, thinkers whose thoughts are akin to the motions that resound through stones, which is to say, thinkers whose thoughts really cannot be considered as thoughts at all.

In the course of elaborating Hobbes's arguments about sensation, imagination, and memory, Sorell remarks that, for Hobbes, "thinking comes down to a procession of phantasms or images" (85). Sorell identifies two problems with such a processional account of thinking. The first is that "it makes the medium of thinking and the organization of thinking too simple a by-product of sense. It is plausible to hold that we think in or with *concepts* of things" (85). The emphasis on the term "concepts" is Sorell's own. With it, he seems to imply that the units with which we think might be more than sensory by-products, something other than mere motions in matter. Indeed, pushing against the confines of the flesh, he complains that Hobbes "tends to regard too many concepts as straightforward by-products of our sense-experience" (86). He allows that Hobbes's account of the sensory basis of our ideas does enable us to account for strings of sensory percepts: this leaf is green, that flower smells sweet. However, since memory is the only operator in Hobbes's account of thinking in addition to immediate sense perception, motions in matter cannot account for other, more refined forms of "qualitative comparison and discernment" (84). Put quite simply, the concept of motions in matter provides an account of thinking that "proves too slight" to explain the range of thinking operations of which we are capable—operations that "may depend on non-sensory capacities, like the capacity to reason and speak a language" (84–85). In fact, Hobbes's "oversimplification" with respect to both the stuff of thinking and our manipulation of it means not only that his theory "lacks the resources for a substantial account of the various operations—memory is the only one—that cognition involves" but also—and consequently—that he cannot explain "the extent of our native capacity for cognition and the sources of linguistic ability" (87). As a consequence, Sorell contends, Hobbes's subjects do not really "qualify as full-fledged thinkers" (85).

For Sorell, the issue here is twofold. In his view, to claim as Hobbes does that thoughts are derived from sense perception is to restrict possible thoughts to immediate sensory percepts or to memories of sensory percepts aroused by a current sense perception. This gives us a thin, bland account of what we are able to think about, which is to say that it prevents us from being able to account for the kinds of creative, imaginative, and abstract thinking that come from our capacity for language use and reason. Relatedly, Sorell argues that since Hobbes's materialism seems to restrict the range of our thoughts to sensory perceptions and memories of sensory perceptions, he provides us with no tool or mechanism with which to organize them beyond rudimentary comparison. In other words, he contends that because Hobbes does not grant us the ability or resources to develop and use abstract conceptual categories, conceptual thought—or reason—is nigh impossible.

The second problem Sorell identifies with Hobbes's apparently "processional" account of thinking comes to light when he elaborates his judgment that Hobbes's thinking-bodies lack the qualifications to be considered "full-fledged thinkers." In fact, broaching this issue takes Sorell so close to the figurative edge of philosophical sense that he finds himself compelled to turn away and retreat to safer and more familiar ground. In a series of complaints, Sorell claims that if we follow Hobbes's materialism, "the relation between agents and actions . . . tends to be reduced to a relation between events that take place *in* an agent, and their effects" (95). That is to say, in Hobbes's account of the activities that go on inside the thinking subject, "[t]he idea of an agent's being the source of his actions is incompletely recovered" (95). Hobbes construes the subject as "the *site*" and "the medium" of thinking and willing but does not characterize the subject as "the controller" of such activities (95). Hobbes's materialism, then, compels us to say the following kinds of things: my body engages in these internal motions or movements, but I am not participating. Or, if like Stanley Cavell, we acknowledge that we are not merely the possessors or inhabitants of our flesh but rather *are* our flesh: I am the site and the medium for thinking and willing, but I am not making them happen.[8] This portrayal of the thinking subject as neither agent nor controller of thinking confounds Sorell to such an extent that he breaks off his analysis with a figurative dismissive shrug, stating that the subject that Hobbes gives us is "not much like the deliberator we are apt to conceive pre-theoretically" (95). That is, the apparent unintelligibility of Hobbes's argument stops Sorell in his theoretical tracks and throws him back to a purportedly commonsense "pre-theoretical" understanding of what it is to be a thinker.

The qualifications that serve as the implicit measure in Sorell's rejection of Hobbes's materialist account of thinking form a template for "the deliberator we are apt to conceive pre-theoretically." According to Sorell's argument, common sense says that we are thinking agents, that we are the agents of our own thoughts. Whereas sensory percepts happen to us by virtue of our sensual encounters with the material world, we have other kinds of ideas that we can organize and manipulate in ways that are not determined by experience. Which is to say that in addition to the stimulatory possibilities presented by the sensually perceptible material world, there is something else in us that positions us as both the source and the director of many aspects of our thinking processes. Reason construed as a nonsensory cognitive capacity is the key to this thoughtful agency, for reason enables us to transcend the internal movements and reactions of the body, to initiate and control a train of thinking that is unrelated to or not derived from the body's sensuous activity. Indeed, it is this rational capacity to manipulate non-sensory concepts that enables us to escape the given, the flesh, the world, and to direct ourselves and our actions according to principles other than material cause and effect. For Sorell, then, since the concepts that are the currency of our evident capacity to reason do not derive from sensuous perceptual activity, the motions in matter that Hobbes portrays as thinking actually cannot be said to capture every aspect of our thinking. Or to put Sorell's point differently, since we are agents by virtue of our capacity to reason, real thinking—*conceptual* thinking—must be more than motions in matter. According to Sorell's pretheoretical common sense, then, the thinking subject's rational self-mastery is a predicate of an intelligible theory of thinking. That is to say, the "must" in the "must be more" should be understood as stating a necessary condition of an account of thinking: we must conceive of thinking as more than motions in matter if our sense of ourselves as the directors of our own thoughts is to stand.

As the argument implicit in Sorell's complaints about Hobbes suggests, working against Sorell's genuine effort to grant as much plausibility as possible to Hobbes's materialism is an unarticulated presumption that we have an internal self distinct from, even if related to, our embodiedness, a self whose distinctiveness lies in its very distinction from the body, in its capacity for non-sensory—or conceptual—thought. This self is not a mere medium or site for the activity of thinking. Rather, this self is the agent and controller of thinking, a being whose capacity to act in contradistinction to sensuous bodily activity is the basis for the autonomy of reason. What interests me here, however, is not that the Cartesian subject appears to haunt Sorell's—and possibly our—commonsense understanding of thinking and reasoning. Rather, it is the real difficulty we have in imagining thinking without the tropes of Cartesian dualism.

According to Sorell, thinking and reasoning are activities undertaken by *thinkers,* activities that can be said to be undertaken only by agents who actively control and manage the flow and organization of thoughts. Coming upon the realization that Hobbes's materialist denial of the extracorporeality of thinking and reasoning calls into question the presumption that a thinker is the active agent of his or her thoughts, Sorell spins away from Hobbes's proposals as if they might have a Medusa-like power to transfix or freeze our minds should we dare to take a look. To clarify, the profound disquiet prompted by Hobbes's materialism is not a concern about how to stave off a behaviorist diminution of the role of reason in our lives. Nor is it a fear about sliding down a slippery slope toward the exuberance of passionate irrationality. Rather, it is a fear about falling abruptly into an abyss of arationality, into a philosophical dystopia where reason itself is inconceivable.

Sorell is right that Hobbes's materialist account of thinking is unintelligible from within the terms of our commonplace, pretheoretical self-understanding. But in his fearful recursion to the familiar, Sorell fails to appreciate that Hobbes is not merely ignoring our common sense of ourselves as thinkers but rather is posing a challenge. In his claim that "man" is an "animated rational body" (DCO 2:24), Hobbes proposes that we are animal bodies that have the capacity to think and reason. As he insists that we are wholly embodied subjects, he also presumes and elaborates upon our rationality. Such a strange juxtaposition of claims should provoke not a theoretical recoil but instead our curiosity: what is reasoning in a subject in whom there is no extracorporeal faculty that acts as thought's agent? Indeed, it is important to point out that the query underlying Sorell's analysis—Can a body reason?—is not an empirical one, as if the one posing the question doubted the possibility that humans, embodied as we are, can actually reason. Rather, the question stands in for and is an abbreviation of a broader theoretical question: How are we to imagine what the activity of reasoning is, what the process of reasoning entails, what the force of reason looks like, in a subject who is wholly embodied? Or to put it shortly, how are we to figure the embodiment of reason?[9]

A number of developments in philosophy, biology, and neuroscience have prompted scholars to begin to explore such questions. For example, drawing on research elaborating the intelligence and complex social forms characteristic of a variety of animals, Alasdair MacIntyre has sought to chasten theories of human exceptionalism that rest upon the illusory presumption that rationality enables us to escape or ignore the exigencies of our animality. He observes rather critically that, in many ethical and political theories, the rationality, autonomy, and independence of ethical and political actors are predicated on a denial of their animal embodiment. However, in attributing human superiority over animals to the human capacity to reason, many philosophers have "underestimated the importance of the fact that our bodies are animal bodies, and they have failed to recognize adequately that in this present life it is true of us that we do not merely have, but are our bodies."[10] Reminding us that we are each inescapably a dependent, rational animal, MacIntyre argues that only if we acknowledge the vulnerability and dependence that are a constitutive feature of what it is to be an animal species will we develop full and appropriate accounts of ethical and political life. In his view, the independence and autonomy that we so value in our thinking about ethics and politics are achievements, products of a myriad of relationships, cultural practices, and practical lessons of everyday living. In other words, the experience of rational autonomy is an effect of or rests upon the fact of heteronomy—or of interdependence.

MacIntyre's claim that "we do not merely have, but are our bodies" suggests not simply that we are inseparable from our bodies but also that the thoughts, feelings, and consciousness that constitute our felt sense of self are likewise "our bodies." This possibility is increasingly coming to be seen as the empirical case in contemporary neuroscience and cognitive psychology. As Rose McDermott points out, practitioners of the social sciences, political theory, and philosophy have tended to conceive of emotions as subjective manifestations of bodily states and reactions and to conceive of reasoning as an operation executed by a mind that, though located somewhere in the physical brain, is relatively insulated from and independent of whatever changes, stresses, and excitations the body happens to undergo. Consequently, they have "generally assumed . . . that rational processing takes place independently of emotional processing and that the latter only inter-feres with the proper functioning of the former."[11] However, neuroscientists and psychologists have recently begun to reconsider the crucial importance of emotions for our ability to reason, judge, and make decisions, finding that "emotion is intertwined with cognition in a way that requires the processes to be analyzed interdependently" (699).[12] Significantly, the claim here is not that emotion is a factor that must be considered when thinking about ratio-nality. Rather, it is that "emotion is, inescapably, an essential component of rationality" (699). Indeed, McDermott notes that in some situations, our emotions make "decisions" for us that are rational even as they do not involve parts of the brain that are typically associated with cognitive ratio-nal processing (694). In other words, our physical bodies undertake what we might think of as unthought, emotional activities and produce "ratio-nal" outcomes. If such findings seem to make an utter confusion of what reason is, they suggest that we have misconceived what reasoning entails and accordingly have misunderstood the centrality to reasoning of the emotions, appetites, and physical transformations that are a fact of our embodiment.

William Connolly has taken up the findings of this neuroscientific research to call into question the notion that the ethical and political judg-ments we make are the fruit of reason conceived as an activity essentially distinct from emotions, affects, and physiological responses. Connolly argues that our brains are structured in such a way that the trajectory of our ethical thinking and political judgment and our ability to apprehend and adhere to principles in action are shaped by unthought memories and culturally informed patterns of emotional response that come to inhabit the flesh.[13] Our perceptions, thoughts, and judgments have visceral and affective dimensions that are historical in the sense of belonging to the individual's lifetime of experience. As a consequence of that history made flesh, the content, tenor, and direction of our perceptions, thoughts, and judgments are beyond our immediate control: we may want to believe in the principle of pluralism, for example, and yet not be able to do so in a way that is reflected in our actions. Connolly argues that if we acknowl-edge—as we must—the effect of the history and memory of each person's culturally infused, neurochemically active body on the process of making judgments, then we can start to develop ethical practices through which we can work upon and transform the patterns of affect and visceral response that shape how open and generous we can be toward ideas, identities, and political arrangements that differ from those that we hold to be true and good. In other words, to recognize that reason is neither unencumbered nor the vehicle of self-directed and autonomous thinking is to transform one's relationship to oneself and consequently to transform the way we understand our relationship to others.

As these scholars indicate, to embody reason is to have to set aside our belief in its autonomy. But what is distinctive about reasoning in comparison with other forms of thinking if its distinction does not lie in its autonomy? What does reasoning become when we acknowledge that it is a heteronomous thinking process? Contemporary science shows that as living, thinking animals, human bodies perceive, think, decide, and act in such a way as to enhance the equilibrium and the future possible equilibria of the organism itself. That is, the body's internal activities and reactions "are aimed, in one way or another, directly or indirectly, at regulating the life process and promoting survival."[14] As we have seen, the neurological mapping of emotions and thought processes in the body gives us warrant to suspend our disbelief that matter can think and to entertain the possibility that to conceive of subjects as thinking-bodies is not to condemn them to being stonelike thinkers: we evidently do think and reason. Yet we find ourselves in the theoretically awkward position of being too empirically bound if we must talk about embodied thinking and reasoning in terms of the multiple flashes of neural activity and the complex relays of chemistry and energy as the different higher and lower brain regions communicate with one another. In other words, we do not yet have a way to figure the several and interrelated energies, tasks, and movements of thinking and feeling in human organisms. However, if we arm ourselves with neurological fact against Sorell's fear, we can extend our curiosity toward Hobbes's materialism to find that he gives us the conceptual language and schema not only to imagine what thinking and reasoning are in a wholly embodied subject but also to explore the ethical and political implications of being a thinking-body.

The Thinking of the Thinking-Body

How are we to understand what Hobbes means when he claims that thinking is motions in matter? What does the process of thinking look like if percepts, thoughts, and memories are "but divers motions" in the organs of the body (L 1:86)? As has begun to come clear, when Hobbes makes such claims, he not only compels us to reconsider our common-sense notion that matter is essentially unthinking but also calls on us to reimagine the activity of thinking itself.

For our purposes, Hobbes makes several claims about thinking that we must consider before we can explore the processes of thinking more extensively. The first is that sensory percepts are not distinct from thoughts. That is, there are no "non-sensory concepts," as Sorell would have us hold. For Hobbes, perception, imagination, and memory—thoughts, concepts, and ideas—are all essentially the same thing, to wit, motions in the bodily organs. And as the argument in Chapter 1 proposes, our awareness of them is our experience and memory of those motions.

In Hobbes's account of sense perception, the "qualities" or "accidents" by which we perceive objects are a form of motion in those objects that presses on our sense organs and is "propagated through all the media to the innermost part of the organ" (DCO 25:391). That is to say, the motions that constitute the "accidents" of an object are translated or communicated "in some of the internal parts of the sentient," and both the motions themselves and the reaction these motions prompt in an animate, sentient body constitute what we call a phantasm, a representation, a fancy, or an "apparence" (DCO 25:390–91).[15] According to Hobbes, the motions in the bodily organs that constitute such phantasms or fancies can be distinguished from one another by temporal factors. Motions caused in the present moment are what we call perceptions whereas those that remain when the stimulating object is gone and time has passed are memory and imagination. Explaining this point in *Leviathan,* he remarks that sense "is nothing els but originall fancy, caused . . . by the pressure, that is, by the motion, of externall things upon our Eyes, Eares, and other organs thereunto ordained" (L 1:86), imagination "is nothing but *decaying sense,*" and "*Imagination* and *Memory,* are but one thing, which for divers considerations hath divers names" (L 2:88–89).[16]

Importantly, the seeming distinctions Hobbes makes here are not really substantive ones. He explains that "[t]he decay of Sense in men waking, is not the decay of the motion made in sense; but an obscuring of it, in such manner, as the light of the Sun obscureth the light of the Starres" (L 2:88). That is, even though imagination and memory may appear as a decaying of the motions first prompted by a stimulating object, their relative lack of clarity or vibrance is really a result of being partly drowned out by the manifold other stimulations to which we are subject as we move through the world.[17] In other words, the motions in the bodily organs that constitute a phantasm or percept are the very same motions that constitute imagination and memory. What this means is that what we commonly call thoughts, ideas, and concepts are not phenomena distinct from sensory percepts or phantasms; they do not constitute a special class of phantasms that have some sort of ethereal content qua meaning. Rather, they are variously clear collections of perceptual motions that are retained in the organs of the thinking-body.

A second claim that is crucial to our understanding of Hobbes's account of thinking is his contention that there is no "mind's eye," or a common organ of the senses that can be said to synthesize all the sensory stimulation into a coherent single "idea." Such a common organ of sense is central to Descartes's account of thinking. In Descartes's view, the common organ of sense is the pineal gland. This small organ in the brain functions as the intermediary between the physiological states of stimulation constitutive of sensory perception and the insights of the incorporeal mind. Descartes explains in *The Passions of the Soul* that the soul "has its principal seat" in the pineal gland. This "small gland located in the middle of the brain" is the place "where the two images coming through the two eyes, or the two impressions coming from a single object through the double organs of any other sense, can come together in a single image or impression before reaching the soul."[18] In other words, the combining of sensory information into an image and the consequent assumption of that image into a thought process take place in a singular location: the pineal gland— or to step back one or two paces, the brain or the head.

For Hobbes, to the contrary, there is no central organ in which our sensory percepts are synthesized, transformed, and transmitted to the mind as mental ideas. As we saw above, in his account, perception, imagination, and memory are motions that traverse the stimulated sense organs, the contiguous organs that translate the motions inward (and then outward), and both the heart and the brain. In other words, they traverse significant portions of the entire thinking-body. This suggests that perception and thinking are activities that involve the whole of the thinking-body. And indeed, in explaining that variation in the stimuli we receive is crucial to our being able to discern the objects before us, Hobbes explicitly rejects Descartes's claim that we have a central thought-processing organ through or with which our percepts and memories are processed, compared, and recalled. He claims instead that "this observation of differences [in the accidents we perceive] is not perception made by a common organ of sense, distinct from sense or perception properly so called, but is memory of the differences of particular phantasms remaining for some time" (DCO 25:399). That is to say, the very organs that are stimulated in sense perception have "memories" in the form of retained motions; such memories function both to compare stimuli in the process of receiving them and to distinguish between the percepts raised by different objects as perception takes place. Since such memories are concentrations of motions in the bodily organs throughout the thinking-body, we can say that the comparisons between different perceptual stimuli and the organization of a given set of stimuli into a coherent percept, phantasm, or thought involve the entire thinking-body. In other words, for Hobbes, there is no one particular venue that serves as the theater in which thinking takes place. Rather, the entire body is involved in the process of perceiving and thinking.

Given Hobbes's contention that all manner of thoughts are motions in matter and that those motions involve the entire body and not just a specific region of it, we can begin to elaborate what thinking itself is, that is, we can trace the form taken by the transitions between thoughts that together constitute the activity of thinking. When Hobbes depicts thinking as motions resonating between contiguous organs throughout the entire thinking-body, he provides us with the means to understand how one phantasm or idea might be related to another phantasm or idea. His account of thinking as motions translated by contiguous bodily organs suggests that the patterns of motions that constitute thinking are metonymic in structure. Now, we generally understand metonymy to be a literary trope or a figure of speech in which the name of one thing is used to stand in for something else to which it is spatially related or, to put it more simply, in which the name of a part of a thing is used to stand in for the whole. For example, one might say that one is "counting noses" when one counts people because there is a commonly understood spatial relationship between noses and the people who have them.[19] But as we explore Hobbes's argument, two significant amendments should be made to this general understanding of metonymy. Both of these amendments give us the conceptual tools and the latitude to appreciate how Hobbes develops an account of the process of thinking in keeping with his claim that "[t]here can be no cause of motion, except in a body contiguous and moved" (DCO 9:124).

First, the spatial domain of the metonymic relation is not limited to the relationship between the part and the whole. In psychoanalysis, linguistics, and film theory, the spatial domain of the metonymic relation is quite expansive and is understood to include the context in which an object is located. As Kaja Silverman points out, in this broader sense, metonymy "exploits relationships of contiguity between . . . a thing and its attributes, its environment and its adjuncts."[20] According to this broader understanding of the metonymic relation, one might picture a graveyard in order to refer to the church nearby, or one might describe a podium in order to characterize the speaker who is using it. This amendment will be useful for explaining Hobbes's account of how the relationship between perceptual objects in the world affects the patterning of our thoughts. As we shall see, Hobbes argues that the spatial contiguity of the objects of our sense perception effects a contiguity in our percepts that makes shifts between our thoughts possible.

Second, and related, in addition to giving us an account of the relationship between verbal or written images, metonymy can give us an account of the relationship between thoughts conceived as neural activity. As Antonio Barcelona claims, metonymy is not a trope whose use is limited to the realm of literature or verbal expression. To the contrary, in cognitive linguistics, metonymy is also understood as a "mental mechanism," or an active relationship between ideational contents evident in brain activity, a relationship whose effectivity may not be evident in our speech but may nonetheless affect our behavior.[21] This amendment to our understanding of metonymy will help us explain how the predominance of the motions that constitute one phantasm might be displaced by the predominance of the motions that constitute another. As we shall see, Hobbes argues that the very manner in which phantasms are constituted make it possible for our awareness of them to shift from one idea to another. In fact, if we analyze Hobbes's account of thinking with these broader understandings of metonymy at hand, we can see that the very metonymic shifts that make thinking possible also undermine our mastery of or control over our own thought processes.

The Metonymic Structure of Thinking

At the beginning of his discussion of "Mentall Discourse," or the "Trayne of Imaginations," Hobbes makes a claim that is so profound in its significance that to ignore it would be to miss the one principle that makes his entire account of thinking make sense. Recalling us to the embodiedness of the thinking subject, reiterating his claim that our thoughts are "Motions within us" that initially were precipitated by sense perception, Hobbes contends that "we have no Transition from one Imagination to another, whereof we never had the like before in our Senses" (L 3:94). That is, *every possible transition from one thought to another is conditioned by a similar transition in sense perception at some earlier juncture.* If there were no such prior conjunction of two particular sensory percepts (apple and house, for example), then it simply would not be possible to have those two ideas follow immediately one upon the other in sequence. What Hobbes suggests here is that the sequencing of the sensory perceptions that constitute thoughts shapes the patterns of possible relations between thoughts.

According to Hobbes's analysis, the reason that possible sequences of ideas can only be patterned upon prior sequences of sensory percepts is quite simple. The motions that the accidents of one object precipitate in us are followed by the motions precipitated by the accidents of the next object we perceive. Significantly, this succession of sensory perceptual motions is retained as a feature of the motions themselves. No percept, phantasm, or idea is wholly discrete. Rather, each percept is partially constituted by the motions that constitute the percepts that preceded and followed it in perception. As a consequence, when the motions that constitute one phantasm come to dominance—as in recollection—the motions that earlier succeeded them in sense perception also follow "by coherence of the matter moved" (L 3:94). In other words, their temporal or sequential contiguity in the process of sensory perception is recapitulated in memory and imagination.

As Hobbes's explanation suggests, any particular sequencing of sensory percepts and thoughts is dependent upon the spatial relationships between the objects that stimulate the sense organs. To make the point simply at first, as we draw our eyes across a scene, objects that are close to one another will make an impression upon our visual sense organs in the order that we encounter them. The phantasms created in that sweeping visual encounter will retain as one of their characteristics their relationship to one another. Since the motions that constitute one phantasm are also, in part, the motions of the antecedent and subsequent phantasms, each phantasm can provoke our notice of the motions constitutive of those phantasms that, in part, compose it. This shift in our notice of our thoughts, this shift from one thought to another, is essentially a metonymic shift.

Importantly, the sequencing of sensory percepts that provides the conditions for metonymic shifts from one thought to another is not limited to the visual register. The sensory perceptions that are sequentially ordered can include a mix of all the sensory possibilities: sight, sound, smell, touch, taste. But no matter how complex the variety of possible perceptual objects, the temporal and spatial contiguity of objects necessarily effects the sequential contiguity of sensory percepts, which in turn necessarily effects the co-constitution of phantasms that enables a metonymic shift from one idea to another.

At first run-through, Hobbes's proposal that the sequencing of our thoughts depends upon prior sequences of sensory percepts may seem to give us an unduly restrictive account of thinking. We can ask one of Sorell's questions: can Hobbes account for the evident richness and complexity of our imaginations? That is, can he account for anything more than a mere reproduction of a given perceptual palette? The short answer is yes. For over time, different sequencing of percepts in sense perception will multiply the number of metonymic shifts possible with each idea. As Hobbes explains,

whilst we turn our eyes and other organs successively to many objects, the motion which was made by every one of them remaining, the phantasms are renewed as often as any one of those motions comes to be predominant above the rest; and they become predominant in the same order in which at any time formerly they were generated by sense. So that when by length of time very many phantasms have been generated within us by sense, then almost any thought may arise from any other thought (DCO 25:398).

What Hobbes tells us here is that a sensory perception of a tree, for example, may be followed one time by a perception of a bird singing, another time by a perception of the scent of a flower, and yet another time by the feeling of twigs crackling underfoot. The phantasm of a tree, then, is constituted of motions that include the motions constitutive of the phantasms of birdsong, flower scent, and snapping twigs. The multiple instances of co-constitution that come to characterize the phantasm of a tree provide the conditions for a metonymic shift from tree to birdsong, from tree to flower scent, or from tree to snapping twigs. Expand the time frame and extend the variety in the perceptual environment and we will find that "almost any thought may arise from any other thought."

For Hobbes, the partial constitution of each phantasm by multiple others means that "in the Imagining of any thing, there is no certainty what we shall Imagine next" (L 3:94). But our lack of certainty about which thought will follow from another is not to be construed as an indeterminacy or randomness in our thinking. Hobbes argues that although the relationship between one idea and another may appear to be random in mental discourse that is "*Unguided, without Designe,* and inconstant" (95), in fact the relationship between them "is not altogether so casuall as it seems to be. Not every Thought to every Thought succeeds indifferently" (94).[22] Even though we cannot know ahead of time what the pattern of metonymic shifts will be in our nonpurposive thinking, we can be certain that each thought "shall be something that succeeded the same before, at one time or another" (94). In other words, a random thought process actually has a determinate structure.

Hobbes gives a wonderful example of the determinate structure of seemingly random trains of thought in *Human Nature.* There he notes that we may have an apparently nonsensical train of thoughts that runs thus: St. Andrew, St. Peter, stone, foundation, church, people, tumult. Restating his claim that the relationship between ideas is caused by "their first coherence, or consequence at that time when they were produced by sense," he points out that the movements between these thoughts are not as random as they seem (HN 4:31). The move from one thought to another is a metonymic shift that is structured by the sequential contiguity of prior sensory percepts. We move from St. Andrew to St. Peter "because their names are read together" (31). We move from St. Peter to stone "for the same cause," and "from stone to foundation, because we see them together" (31). Each of the ideas in this train of thoughts is partially constituted by the ones immediately before and after because of the original sequencing of sensory percepts. Each particular sequence among the percepts is caused by the contiguity of the stimulating objects—the names and words in a story, the features of a landscape, the elements of a social scene.

It is important to highlight something that is probably obvious. The sequential relationship between percepts that both conditions and precipitates the metonymic shift from one idea (St. Andrew) to another (St. Peter) does not extend beyond that particular set. In other words, the metonymic relation between "St. Andrew" and "St. Peter" is distinct from the metonymic relation between "St. Peter" and "stone." This is because in sense perception, "to one and the same thing perceived, sometimes one thing, sometimes another succeedeth" (L 3:94). That is, sometimes "St. Peter" is said aloud or read in the same story as "St. Andrew;" sometimes "St. Peter" is said aloud or read in a different story along with "stone." Accordingly, the phantasm "St. Peter" can be in a metonymic relationship with either of the phantasms "St. Andrew" or "stone." But even though "St. Peter" is in both sequences, the phantasm "St. Andrew" is not metonymically related to the phantasm "stone." In fact, it is because the metonymic relations between thoughts are limited by the sequential contiguity of percepts that shifts between thoughts can be creative or innovative rather than simply reproductive. This circumscription or delimitation of the metonymic relation means that we can mix or "compound" thoughts derived from our experience to develop thoughts of things that have not been "presented to the sense" as whole objects but are rather "a Fiction of the mind" (L 2:89).[23]

Now, in the example from *Human Nature* cited above, Hobbes explains how we can make sense of a seemingly random and nonsensical train of thoughts. By highlighting the effect of the sequential contiguity of sensory percepts on the very form of phantasms themselves, he enables us to understand why we might have a series of individual thoughts that, superficially, do not seem to be related to one another. But the insights that he gives us into the structure of thinking are not limited to series of thoughts of which we are aware. In another example, he also suggests that the metonymic shifts that constitute thinking can take place without our awareness.

In *Leviathan,* Hobbes draws on his account of the determinate structure of nonpurposive thinking to explain the sometimes sudden appearance of non sequiturs, of single thoughts or questions that appear to arise from nowhere. In particular, he ventures to account for the reason that someone might be so impertinent as to ask after the value of a Roman coin in the midst of the English civil war. Gesturing to the historical context and tracing the metonymic shifts possibly precipitated by that context, Hobbes claims that

the Cohaerance to me was manifest enough. For the Thought of the warre, introduced the Thought of the delivering up the King to his Enemies; The Thought of that, brought in the Thought of the delivering up of Christ; and that again the Thought of the 30 pence, which was the price of that treason: and thence easily followed that malicious question; and all this in a moment of time; for Thought is quick. (L 3:95)

The shifts between thoughts here are metonymic in structure, much as are those in the St. Andrew / St. Peter example. The movement from the thought of the civil war to the thought of the deliverance of the king to his enemies entails a shift from a whole of an event or story to a part of an event or story. The shift from the thought of the betrayal of the king to the betrayal of Christ is facilitated by popular representations comparing the two moments. Similarly, the movement from the thought of the delivering up of Christ to the thought of the thirty pence that were paid for that betrayal is a shift facilitated by the proximity of the two ideas in the same story. And so on.

There are a number of interesting things about Hobbes's reconstruction of the train of thoughts that preceded the untimely question. The first is that, rather than simply elucidating the connections between a number of different phantasms—as in the St. Andrew / St. Peter example—Hobbes supplies us with the phantasms that, in his reconstructive exercise, he supposes arose between the phantasms "civill warre" and "Roman Penny." That is, he does not claim that the impertinent offender engaged in a more or less belabored effort to move from contemplating the contemporary war to pondering the value of a particular coin in ancient Rome. Rather, he suggests that there were two recognizable phantasms—"civill warre," derived from the political context, and "Roman Penny," a seeming non sequitur. It is his reconstruction that supplies the intervening phantasms that make sense of the sequence. In other words, he suggests that some phantasms in the sequence arose and passed unbeknownst to the thinker. This possibility that there are moments in our trains of thought of which we are unaware is bolstered by Hobbes's claim that all these metonymic shifts took place "in a moment of time; for Thought is quick." In his telling, the chain of associations that started with the civil war and eventuated in the query took place almost instantaneously—took place faster than the ability of the thinker to experience the memory of each thought. Since our experience of such memories constitutes our awareness of our thoughts, we could surmise that the reason some of the intervening phantasms needed to be supplied by Hobbes in his reconstruction is that some moments in the train of thinking occurred beyond the register of the thinker's conscious notice. The implication here is that our thinking processes are not wholly transparent to us. In fact, all these points considered together suggest that the thinker did not think the thoughts but rather that the thoughts happened to the thinker. Indeed, reflecting upon a similar discussion in *Human Nature,* Hobbes makes just such a claim, noting that when we think, "one conception followeth not another, according to our election, . . . but as it chanceth us to hear or see such things as shall bring them to our mind" (HN 5:34). To put the point differently, the metonymic shifts that constitute the very possibility of thinking entail that we are not in control of or master over our own thinking processes.

Instrumental Reasoning

According to the analysis above, the metonymic shifts that enable Hobbes to make sense of apparently random trains of thought are basic to thinking itself. That is to say, the movement from one thought to another that is characteristic of thinking is possible only because of the partial co-constitution of phantasms wrought by the processes of sense perception. But in recognizing this, we are presented with a pressing problem. If each phantasm is partially constituted by the many other phantasms that at various points were sequentially contiguous sensory percepts, if each phantasm might shift our notice equally well to any one of those other phantasms, how do we corral the many phantasms that might rush to our notice? How is it that people are not always and necessarily "snatched from their purpose, by every thing that comes in their thought, into so many, and so long digressions, and Parentheses, that they utterly lose themselves" (L 8:136)? Is it possible to constrain the metonymic shifts that make thinking possible so that we can think purposively? If the process of thinking is structured in the way Hobbes argues—if it happens to us—are we capable of instrumental reasoning?

Interestingly, Hobbes suggests that desire makes directed thinking or reasoning possible. That is to say, desire regulates the metonymic shifts that constitute the process of thinking, giving "Steddinesse, and Direction" to our thoughts (L 8:136) and making the course of thinking "more constant" (L 3:95).[24] How does desire do it? As I elaborate further below, each phantasm is inflected with a feeling tone, which is to say that each is partially constituted by the motions that are the reaction of the thinking-body to the initial sensory stimulation. This affective or passionate dimension of each of our phantasms makes it possible for our desires to direct or regulate the progress of our thinking.

To understand how this works, let us revisit for a moment the basic elements of Hobbes's account of thinking. According to Hobbes, when we perceive an object, the motions that constitute the object's accidents effect motions in the organs of sense, motions that are translated by the intermediate organs of the thinking-body to the brain and heart and back again. These motions cause "a resistance, or counter-pressure, or endeavour of the heart, to deliver it self" (L 1:85). In other words, the motions in the body, precipitated by the motions of the accidents, aid or aggravate the body's vital motion and provoke the thinking-body's reaction—a reaction that is experienced as appetite or aversion, or the movement toward or away from the stimulating object (L 6:119). Importantly, as a consequence of this reaction, the motions in the body that constitute percepts must be conceived not only as signaling the accidents of the objects beheld but also as reverberating with the positive or negative reaction of the thinking-body (L 1:85). That is to say, each percept, each phantasm, thought, or memory, is invested with a value commensurate with its positive or negative effect on the vital motion of the thinking-body. Indeed, it seems that in Hobbes's account, there is no clear distinction to be made between an idea we have of an object and our passionate evaluation of that object: the motions constitutive of a phantasm necessarily include those that constitute the thinking-body's appetitive response.

One of the important implications of the fact that percepts, thoughts, and memories have an affective as well as an accidental dimension is that percepts, thoughts, and memories may be related to one another through *either* dimension. To put the point in Hobbes's terms, "as appetites and aversions are generated by phantasms, so reciprocally phantasms are generated by appetites and aversions" (DCO 25:401).[25] So when we recall a phantasm, we also unavoidably and at the same time experience a feeling tone, for the motions in the bodily organs that constitute the recalled phantasm (continue their) work upon the thinking-body's vital motion and give that phantasm an affective value. Likewise, when we experience a particular emotion or passion, we also unavoidably and at the same time recall a phantasm of an object, occasion, or person that has as one of its dimensions that particular feeling tone.

The partial constitution of each phantasm by an appetitive response or feeling tone is what makes purposive thinking possible. As we will see in Hobbes's discussion of reasoning, below, when our notice settles on the feeling tone associated with a particular thought, that feeling, desire, or appetite has a significant influence on the direction taken by the metonymic shifts that constitute the process of thinking: the particular feeling, desire, or appetite holds our notice of the phantasm of which it is a part and constrains our notice of the various phantasms that are metonymically related to a particular phantasm. Indeed, the relationship between reasoning and desire is not one in which reason must rein in and control the passions nor one in which the passions master reason for the purposes of their satisfaction. Rather, and strangely to our habits of theoretical understanding, desire is what makes reasoning possible in the first place.[26]

When he describes the process of instrumental reasoning, Hobbes explains that "[f]rom Desire, ariseth the Thought of some means we have seen produce the like of that which we ayme at; and from the thought of that, the thought of means to that mean; and so continually, till we come to some beginning within our own power" (L 3:95–96). At first, this account may portray instrumental reasoning as a rather straightforward process. A desire for a particular absent object draws our notice of the phantasm of that desired object. As with any phantasm, the phantasm of the desired object will be partially constituted by the phantasm of the object or activity that, in past experience, was next before the having of the once attained and now desired object. In turn, the second, or derivative, phantasm will be partially constituted by—or contiguous with—the phantasm of the object or activity that, in prior experience, was next before that, and so forth. However, this process of recalling the means to a desired end is not as linear or direct as it initially appears.

The metonymic relation that enables a shift from one idea to another is a function of the prior sequential contiguity of percepts. And importantly, the metonymic relation—or the metonymic shift that is possible between phantasms—is restricted to those phantasms that partially constitute one another and that consequently are contiguous with one another. As we saw in the St. Andrew/St. Peter example, "St. Andrew" is in a metonymic relationship with "St. Peter" but is not in a metonymic relationship with "stone." What this means in the context of instrumental reasoning is that the phantasm of the desired but currently absent object is not in a metonymic relationship with the immediately available means to attain the object. The phantasm of the desired object is partially constituted by and constitutive of the phantasm of *some* means to attain the object, but not necessarily those means before us. The metonymic shifts that might possibly be made from the phantasm of the desired object do not extend beyond the phantasms that partially constitute the phantasm of the desired object. As a consequence, the phantasm of the immediately and not so immediately available means to a given end are not retrieved simply as a matter of course. There are multiple intervening phantasms "till we come to some beginning within our own power." In other words, there are multiple metonymic shifts to be undertaken . . . and consequently many opportunities for digression.

Such digressions might occur for the following reason. If each phantasm has as part of its constitutive features the motions that constitute the many other phantasms that at some point were sequentially contiguous sensory percepts, then any number of those other phantasms may come to our notice. In other words, because each thought is partially constituted by the motions of other phantasms, a phantasm drawn to our notice through its metonymic relation to the phantasm of the desired object may not be directly relevant to our desire. In fact, there is no certainty that the phantasms that do draw our notice will be at all related to our plans. More importantly, since these metonymic shifts take place too quickly for us to control, we cannot restrict ahead of time which metonymic chains of association are provoked by the phantasm of the desired object. The phantasm of the desired object will be the beginning of a series of metonymic shifts that will sprout manifold different phantasms that may or may not be relevant to our plans vis-à-vis the desired object. If we are to recall the means to a particular end, then, we must sort through the multitude of phantasms raised by the desired object. It is in this process of sorting that desire becomes significant.

Hobbes describes the process of sorting between the various phantasms raised by the phantasm of a desired object as a kind of directed roving or roaming, comparing it to situations in which "a man seeks what he hath lost; and from that place, and time, wherein hee misses it, his mind runs back, from place to place, and time to time, to find where, and when he had it; . . . [and] from thence, his thoughts run over the same places and times, to find what action, or other occasion might make him lose it" (L 3:96). This seeking is akin to the ranging of a spaniel over a field "till he find a sent," akin to the running of a man "over the Alphabet, to start a rime," or akin to the manner in which "one would sweep a room, to find a jewell" (97). What is important in Hobbes's characterization here is his suggestion that as the strings of recalled phantasms draw our attention, we measure each against our desire, assessing each for its pertinence. Much as we try out different words or sounds when trying to compose a rhyme, so our notice moves from phantasm to phantasm, plumbing the relevance of each to the desire. Hobbes explains that "because the End, by the greatnesse of the impression, comes often to mind, in case our thoughts begin to wander, they are quickly again reduced into the way" (96). In other words, the desire that is a constitutive element of the phantasm of the desired object prompts the thought of the desired object to come to our notice again and again. Such a repeated foregrounding of the phantasm of the desired object gives a focus to the patterns of metonymy, orienting and reorienting our shifting thoughts. So, even though our thoughts may scatter willy-nilly because of the metonymic relationships between our phantasms, our desire functions to recall us. And significantly, it recalls us not so much as an end point toward which we drive in a linear fashion, as if impelled, but rather as a beacon against which we measure our direction.[27]

Of course, over time and with repeated success, the contiguity between the various end-appropriate phantasms will be more readily apparent, and the other metonymically related but nonetheless manifestly irrelevant phantasms more readily distinguished. Or perhaps it is better to say that with experience, the phantasms are reconstituted such that the sequence of means to particular desired end becomes a facet of the phantasms themselves. In such cases, we find ourselves able quickly and effortlessly to discern what we need to do to gratify some among our desires. This increased ease in discerning the means to the ends we seek is practical reason, or what Hobbes calls "*Foresight,* and *Prudence,* or *Providence;* and sometimes *Wisdome*" (L 3:97).

If we can reflect for a moment before we move on, the argument developed above suggests that for Hobbes, a particular habit of desire—and habitual success in gratifying such a desire—makes a specific line of reasoning possible, easy, and fast. That is, as desire is a condition of thinking itself, so a pattern of experiencing and satisfying a desire facilitates practical reason. Conceivably, then, a disruption of such a habit, that is, a disturbance or perturbation of the desire or passions that guide reasoned thought, could result in the impairment of practical reason or in a different line of reasoning altogether. In other words, because desire is a condition of possibility for reasoning, reason itself can be capricious. The possibility of such caprice should not lead us to abandon reasoning—as if reasoning is only a useful or worthy form of thinking if we can guarantee a priori the consistency of its outcomes. Rather, the dependence of the movements of reasoning upon desire alerts us to the possibility that the valences of the passions shape what an individual is capable of conceiving as rational. The point here is not the rather banal one that different desires make different decisions rational in the sense of being end-appropriate. The point is that the very processes of reasoning—the steps in the calculus itself— shift as different desires or passions come to the fore. Consequently, to think about practical or instrumental reasoning is to have to think about the habits, practices, material opportunities, and social interactions that shape the passions. As we shall see in Chapters 4 and 5 in particular, this dependence of practical reasoning upon desire entails that, in their ethical and political activity, individuals consider how material contexts and social relations shape and transform which passions—and which kinds of thought processes—predominate.

For now, however, we can leaven any disconcertion about the caprice of reason by turning to reconsider the role of language in thinking. As we saw in Chapter 1, Hobbes contends that we use language to mark or signal the insights and conclusion of our trains of thought and so to save us from having to repeat the belabored seeking-sorting process in the future. In fact, Hobbes suggests that, in addition to desire, language is a crucial factor in our being able to contain the metonymic chains of association that constitute the process of thinking: just as our thoughts can be reconstituted and repatterned through experience, so they can be reconstituted and repatterned through the assiduous and carefully logical use of language, which is to say, through ratiocination.

Ratiocination

In Hobbes's philosophy, in addition to prudential or instrumental reasoning is another kind of purposive thinking: mathematical or abstract reasoning, or what Hobbes calls ratiocination. As Hobbes describes it, ratiocination is a different way of remembering or recalling our phantasms, a different way of "Calling to mind" or "*Re-conning*" them (L 3:96).

Ratiocination foregrounds the relationship between the names with which we mark or signal our phantasms. It is, Hobbes says, a "*Reckoning . . .* of the Consequences of generall names agreed upon, for the *marking* and *signifying* of our thoughts" (L 5:III). In this form of reasoning, then, we do not rely upon a desire to orient and constrain the metonymic shifts between phantasms that have been determined by the sequencing of percepts attained through experience. Instead, we should understand ratiocination as a remapping of phantasms in relation to one another, a remapping in which the shifts between our thoughts trace the parameters set by the logic of systems of names and definitions. In fact, the best way to conceive of ratiocination is as a palimpsest or an overlay: it is a form of thinking in which we try to ignore the experientially based metonymic chains of association that erupt with each phantasm at the same time that our thoughts trace the metonymic chains of association instituted through linguistic definition. Such an achievement does not come easily or naturally to us. As Hobbes explains, the kind of reasoned thinking that characterizes ratiocination "is not as Sense, and Memory, borne with us; nor gotten by Experience onely; as Prudence is; but attayned by Industry; first in apt imposing of Names; and secondly by getting a good and orderly Method in proceeding" (L 5:115).

Let us reflect for a moment on the elements of ratiocination. For Hobbes, the peculiar resonance of motions occasioned in sense perception is retained in the thinking-body as phantasms. To prompt our recall of our phantasms, we invent mnemonic devices, using visual, vocal, or aural marks. To provoke other people's notice of thoughts and memories that may be similar to the ones holding our attention, we use similar visual, vocal, or aural stimuli as signs.[28] Names or words are just such marks or signs, which is to say that names are visual, vocal, and aural stimuli that we use as marks or signs to recall or provoke notice of the phantasms with which they are associated (L 4:109).[29] Interestingly, according to the argument elaborated here, the stimulation or the bodily motions set in play by such marks and signs become a feature of the phantasms themselves. For a subject who is in and of language, then, phantasms are partially constituted by the motions that constitute the marks and signs designated to recall them. Indeed, it is when the bodily motions precipitated by marks or signs come to partially constitute their respective phantasms that marks and signs can provoke our notice of the motions that together constitute the phantasms.

What ratiocination requires is that we (at least partially) reconstitute our phantasms so that the metonymic shifts between our phantasms trace the logically designated relationships between the vocal signs for those phantasms. That is to say, our phantasms are linguistically amended so that the sequencing proper to the logic of signs becomes a feature of the phantasms themselves. When we learn to count, for example, the repeated recitation of vocal signs of phantasms of quantities of objects ("one," "two," "three") institutes a sequential contiguity of the percepts aroused by the enunciation of those signs. In other words, the sound percept "one" is partially constituted by the sound percept "two," with the effect that over time the sequence will trip off one's tongue almost automatically. Further, the recitation of vocal signs reorganizes the sequencing of the phantasms of quantities. And through repetition, such recitation reconstitutes the phantasms in the sequence such that the phantasm that is partially constituted by the vocal sign "one" becomes partially constituted by the phantasm that itself is partly constituted by the vocal sign "two," and so on. So when we have learned to count, not only do the vocal signs follow one another easily or automatically, but the shifts between the relevant phantasms of quantities of objects also take place quickly and without too much danger of digression.[30] To take a different example, ratiocination requires that we establish and learn an alternative set of associations between our phantasms so that we can trace the relationship between universal names and particular names. In Hobbes's account, general or "Universall" names are those that are "imposed on many things, for their similitude in some quality, or other accident" (L 4:103). They designate a class of things whose coherence as a "class" is a function of a particular feature that they share. So "the Name *Body*" is imposed on anything that is material. And because this name can be used to designate a huge array of things, it is "of larger signification than the word *Man,* and comprehendeth it," or includes it within its scope (102–3). In other words, since "man" is a name for a particular form of matter, the name is included within or comprehended by the general name "body." What we do when we engage in ratiocination is order our thoughts according to just such relationships between names: having originally learned the structure of the relationships entailed by definitions, we try to discern whether the form taken by the relationship between the visual signs "body" and "man" is identity or nonidentity, equivalence, comprehension, or subsumption.[31]

As we elaborate the relationships between the names we define, we "add" them together to create propositions, we combine these to create syllogisms, and we arrange the latter to develop arguments.[32] We describe a proposition as "true" when the names connected in the proposition are connected correctly and their definitions comprehend or correspond appropriately with one another.[33] This is what Hobbes means, then, when he describes ratiocination as "conceiving of the consequence of the names of all the parts, to the name of the whole; or from the names of the whole and one part, to the name of the other part" (L 5:110).

As suggested at the opening of this discussion, what is particularly interesting about ratiocination is that it represents an effort to override the metonymic shifts made possible through experience. Of course, the shifts between ideas in the process of ratiocination are still metonymic in structure. However, the metonymic relation at stake is an artificial one that we must forge between phantasms according to the relationships between the marks or signs we use to provoke our notice of them. If we think very carefully in ratiocination, our thoughts will pattern themselves according to the philosophical logic of language.

However, we do not rely only upon the fact that learning language and the techniques of ratiocination reconstitutes our phantasms in such a way that they follow one another logically. Hobbes claims that, as in prudential reasoning, desire constrains our notice of the manifold possible chains of associations raised by the phantasms recalled through the use of marks and signs. But when we engage in ratiocination, the desire that guides us does not have as its object a specific trinket, pleasure, or conclusion (as in prudential reasoning). Rather, what orients and gives focus to our thinking in ratiocination is a desire to comprehend an entire system of relations and conclusions (L 5:112), a desire for knowledge or a love of science, a desire, Hobbes says, to contribute to "the Benefit of man-kind" (116).

Yet the artificiality of the metonymic relations between ideas that are established through language does not insulate our abstract reasoning from the possibility of disruption or digression. Because phantasms are multiply constituted, because desire can shape the direction of our thoughts, and because language itself is liable to metonymic and metaphoric slippage, we may sometimes unknowingly drift off the course of ratiocination and arrive at a conclusion that we believe to be true but is not. Since "*truth* consisteth in the right ordering of names in our affirmations," we can increase the likelihood of reaching "precise *truth*" if we "remember what every name [we use] stands for; and . . . place it accordingly" (L 4:105). But even such care gives us no guarantee that our thoughts have proceeded according to the strictures of linguistic logic. As Hobbes famously notes, the inconstancy and diversity of the evaluative dimension of our phantasms undermines the reliability of the names we use to provoke our own and others' notice of our ideas.[34] He explains that "seeing all names are imposed to signifie our conceptions; . . . when we conceive the same things differently, we can hardly avoyd different naming of them" (109). As a consequence, we must "take heed of words; which besides the signification of what we imagine of their nature, have a signification also of the nature, disposition, and interest of the speaker" (109). The inconstancy of signification and consequently the instability of ratiocination are obvious problems in discussions of politics, for the words we use—such as "wisdom," "fear," "justice," "cruelty," and "gravity"—are quite predictably inflected by the variety of our dispositions and evaluations. In fact, Hobbes says that since we cannot ever be sure that our individual appetites and aversions do not disruptively guide our political thoughts, the polyvalent names we use in politics "can never be the true grounds of any ratiocination" (109–10). But the potential for digression from a linguistically logical train of thinking in ratiocination is not restricted to controversial or obviously interest-laden topics. Hobbes points out that in even the most rarefied subject of ratiocination, mathematics, as well as in other subjects, "the ablest, most attentive, and most practised men, may deceive themselves, and inferre false Conclusions" (L 5:111). He contends that those who deny this possibility and insist upon the rectitude of their own individual thought processes would "have every of their passions, as it comes to bear sway in them, to be taken for right Reason" (112).[35]

Significantly, Hobbes does not believe that to acknowledge that ratiocination is inevitably and constitutively unstable is to acknowledge the impossibility of philosophy. He believes that if we impose names aptly and proceed from names to assertions with "a good and orderly Method," we can reason quite effectively. Indeed, he suggests that if we avoid misnaming or making improper connections, "it is not easie to fall into any absurdity, unless it be by the length of an account," in which case one "may perhaps forget what went before" (L 5:115). The most important thing is to be cognizant of the possibility of error and to acquiesce when another discovers an error in one's own thinking. As Hobbes observes, "all men by nature reason alike, and well, when they have good principles. For who is so stupid, as both to mistake in Geometry, and also to persist in it, when another detects his error to him?" (115).

Conclusion

In claiming that thinking is "motions in matter," Hobbes does not reduce a fabulously complex phenomenon to something akin to the vibrations of a stone that is struck. Quite to the contrary, his commitment to a thoroughgoing materialist conception of the subject equips him to specify the incredible richness and complexity of the activity of thinking in a human subject who lives in this world with and among other humans. As we have seen, in his account each thought in a thinking-body is composed of a complex coalescence of the following kinds of motion:

The motions precipitated directly by a perceptual object's accidents
The motions that constitute the response of the thinking-body to those perceptual motions
The accidental and appetitive motions of phantasms that are metonymically related because of the prior sequential contiguity of percepts
The motions that constitute the relevant visual, aural, and oral marks and signs intentionally associated with the phantasm
The motions that constitute visual, aural, and oral marks and signs that are, in a sense, topically irrelevant to the phantasm but metonymically related to the relevant marks and signs

As this list suggests, phantasms are neither discrete modules of informational content nor singular bounded entities. Rather, they are constituted by a vast and complicated array of motions and memories that bear the perceptual and affective history of the thinking-body.

According to Hobbes's argument, it is because phantasms are so complex in their structure that thought processes happen and that we are able to think. That is, it is because phantasms are constituted by a multitude of perceptions, memories, affects, and (often) linguistic signs that our notice of one thought can occasion our notice of another. In other words, the shifts between thoughts that characterize flights of fancy, instrumental reasoning, and ratiocination alike are made possible by the very manner in which thoughts are constituted. Further, and importantly, since each thinking-body constantly undergoes new perceptual and linguistic experiences, the constitution of thoughts themselves is continually augmented and modified. Variations in the material and social environment, modulations and mutations in the body, and ever-shifting patterns of language use and other forms of symbolization together modify the metonymic possibilities and qualify the desires that guide our trains of thought. As a consequence of this dynamic constitution, the number and combination of shifts between ideas necessarily change over time and in different contexts.

It may seem that Hobbes's argument entails that we conceive of thinking as an activity that is wholly determined by the vagaries of the stimulating context. In claiming that our thoughts in thinking follow one another only "as it chanceth us to hear or see such things as shall bring them to our mind" (HN 5:34), Hobbes appears to delimit the possibilities for our thinking to what is available as an experiential trigger. To be sure, Hobbes's account of the development of prudence suggests that the habits of daily living give a kind of ordered regularity to each individual's practical everyday thinking while the exigencies provide for the nuance and flexibility that the stability of regularity allows. Likewise, the fact that we are language users means that our linguistically marked thoughts are patterned in ways that reflect the logical and metonymic possibilities of the language(s) we know and the other forms of representation we encounter. According to Hobbes's argument, then, both experience and language break down the distinction between the inner and outer world of the subject, making thinking into a socially or culturally inflected process that reflects the material conditions of the context in which thinking takes place. One might well wonder whether Hobbes condemns those living in the same locale to thinking exactly alike. Or to pose the concern differently, how does Hobbes provide for the fact that most of the time we do not all think exactly in the same way, even if we are confronted with identical situations?

There are two concerns here. One centers on the circumscription and indeed suffocation of imaginative and creative possibilities if we do not elicit our thoughts ourselves but if, rather, they can be precipitated only by chance perceptual encounters with features of the environment.

The other related concern centers on the worrying prospect that given a collective social and political situation, Hobbesian subjects will think en bloc, which is to say that every person's thoughts will be equally saturated by the material and ideological conditions that characterize the context.

The first concern can be allayed by recalling our discussion of the metonymic shifts that structure and make possible thinking. As we saw above, for Hobbes, although there is a determinate structure to even random trains of thought, the extent of determination is not in the whole string of thoughts together but rather is restricted to the metonymic shift between one phantasm and another. Each shift is determined, yet no one phantasm determines the entire pattern of shifts. Indeed, since any phantasm produced in perception is partially constituted by the motions constitutive of any number of other phantasms, the visual, aural, or tactile perception that raises one phantasm may occasion our notice of any metonymically related phantasm—whether it is topically relevant or not. And each of these possible thoughts might set off any of an infinite variety of trains of thought. For example, I may sit down at my desk and observe, as I do every day, the multi-colored birdhouse feeder hanging outside the window: that perceptual trigger may equally well jog a thought about the next step in the argument I was developing yesterday as I sat at my desk, a thought of my mother-in-law's impending visit (she so loves birds), a thought about the effect of the global economy on local farmers (we don't buy birdseed at major food stores), or a thought about the laundry that is waiting to be put away (my kid looks particularly cute in his red sweater). In other words, while the manner in which phantasms or thoughts are constituted means that thought processes are triggered by (changes in) perception, the complexity of that constitution combined with the delimitation of the determination of the metonymic shifts between thoughts means that the possible and actual combinations or chains of our thoughts are vast in number. Since "almost any thought may arise from any other thought," the possibility of creative or productive thought rests less on the presence or absence of a particular perceptual stimulus in the environment and more on the way in which an individual's perceptual and affective history inflects the passions that propel the forms of thinking known as fancy, wit, and judgment (L 8:134–35).

The second concern can be addressed with similar arguments. Hobbes accounts for the evident diversity in what we think, how we think it, and

with what affective value through his sensitivity to the irreducible unique-
ness of every thinking-body. According to Hobbes, no individual is identical
with another. Indeed, since our bodies are constantly changing—growing,
aging, sloughing, imbibing, digesting, excreting, and so forth—we would be
hard pressed to specify a stretch of time during which we are identical even
to ourselves (L 6:120). The singularity of Hobbesian individuals, or what
Richard Flathman calls their "unicity," means that the patterns of reception
and response to perceptual stimuli and the amendment and consolidation
of these patterns through the acquisition of language(s) are specific to the
particular and constantly evolving life history of each individual.[36] That is,
although we are all human organisms, the ineluctable specificity of each
individual organism's first encounters with the material and social world,
the manner in which those encounters are digested and remembered, and
the ways in which those enfleshed memories both shape and are shaped by
later encounters means that no one person's thoughts and feelings upon
experiencing a shared event can be exactly the same as those of another. To
be sure, were a stimulus to be constant enough, or its affective value great
enough, individuals might end up having similar ideas about it and reach
similar decisions about how to act with respect to it. Indeed, it is just such a
possibility that makes Hobbes nervous about crowds and also prompts him
to emphasize the importance of the supremacy of the sovereign power.[37]
The point, however, is that with Hobbes's materialist account of thinking, similar patterns of thinking and acting—broadly shared behaviorist
responses to environmental stimuli—are possible in the extreme but not
inevitable simply by virtue of the nature of thinking.

At the same time that we push to recognize that Hobbes allows for
creativity and individuality in the ways in which context, culture, and language are taken up by and manifested in the thinking of a thinking-body,
it is important to emphasize that, in his argument, thinking is emphatically
not an activity that occurs in a mind closed off from the body and material world. In his view, the thinking subject is a porous subject, one whose
thoughts are derived from its ongoing engagement with others and with the
world and whose thinking processes are provoked and modified by the passions and desires that arise through that engagement. Indeed, as this chapter has shown, for Hobbes, even the form of thinking known as reasoning
is neither sign nor measure of the subject's autonomy or self-sovereignty, for
the shifts between thoughts in reasoning are dependent upon the strength

and direction of the passions as well as upon the conventions and irregularities of language.

In fact, the tremendous importance of desire for purposive, rational thinking entails that we consider the constituent elements of the passions when we think about ethics and politics. If habits of desire produce certain patterns of rational thinking—and so, through the very process, preclude others—then it becomes vital to understand not only the conditions for particular passions and the specific patterns of thinking provoked by them. We must also understand the conditions for and the effects of their disruption. To make the point in more concrete terms, if the direction taken by our thoughts is shaped by the affects and responses elicited by regular and occasional social encounters as well as by the enduring and evolving features of the context in which we move, then the social and material conditions that effect those passionate responses assume ethical and political significance. In other words, we must examine what causes the passions and dispositions that shape individuals' ethical and political thinking. To pose the issue as a question: What is it that determines the desires that determine the course of practical reason? When we acknowledge the heteronomy of reason, we are compelled to move beyond the individual as a discrete unit to consider the dynamic relationships both among individuals and between individuals and their environment. The point here is not that every single thought an individual has is determined directly by his or her response to other people's actions and to the broader material conditions of existence. Rather, the point is that to the extent that social relations and material contexts shape an individual's passions, to that extent do they shape the tendencies in that individual's thinking. So, if we are to avoid a situation in which we have escaped the bogey of mechanistic behaviorism in thinking only to find ourselves trapped again by the passions that guide thinking and reasoning, we must explore Hobbes's materialist theory of the passions. And as we shall see in the next chapter, to work carefully through Hobbes's account of the determination of the passions is to have to rethink our conception of determinism itself.

3

The Time of Determination

Movement, Will, and Action

One of the defining principles of Hobbes's materialist philosophy is the claim that the movement of any body can be seen only as an effect of the translation of motion from another body that itself is in motion.[1] In other words, any movement or action in an object can come only "from the *action* of some other immediate *agent* without itself."[2] Put differently, this principle maintains that no object is spontaneously self-moving or, as Hobbes articulates it, that "nothing taketh beginning from *itself*" (LN, 274). This claim is not simply a description of the parameters of the movement of inanimate objects. It also covers the movement of thinking-bodies—or people—as well. In including people under the rubric of this principle, Hobbes suggests that human actions are initiated by forces beyond the subject and antecedent to the subject's felt decision to act. That is, he calls into question the notion that a subject is the origin of his or her own action. To put the point differently, when Hobbes contends that "nothing taketh beginning from *itself*"—or as he puts it in *Leviathan,* "nothing can change it selfe"—he claims that we cannot conceive of people as self-determining, self-directing, or self-sovereign agents (L 2:87).

In fact, Hobbes explicitly repudiates the idea that each individual has an autonomous or free will that is the faculty responsible for making choices. Just as he rejects Descartes's claim that the mind is an immaterial entity whose characteristic activities are different in kind from the movements of matter, so he rejects the notion that the will is an immaterial agency that is free and self-determining in its activities. In his scathing dismissal of such arguments, Hobbes declares that "if a man should talk to me of . . . *Immateriall Substances;* or of *A free Subject; A free-Will;* or any *Free,* but free from being hindred by opposition, I should not say he were in an Errour; but that his words were without meaning; that is to say, Absurd" (L 5:113). It is to counter such "absurdities" that Hobbes presses his argument that people are thinking-bodies—material organisms, bodies, matter. In his view, just as we must characterize thinking as motion in bodily organs (L 1:85–86), so we must conceive of willing as movements in matter. More than this, we must conceptualize the movements constitutive of willing in terms of the material causes that effect them. According to Hobbes, then, we must conceive of the will not simply in materialist terms. We must also think of the will and of action as determined.

Hobbes's arguments about the determination of the will present serious challenges to political theorists and philosophers whose visions of ethics and politics rest upon an understanding of the self as a free and (relatively) self-sovereign agent of action. Indeed, as G. A. J. Rogers notes, Hobbes's philosophy had many vociferous detractors among his contemporaries.[3] Among the "anti-Hobbists," the most persistent in vehemently opposing Hobbes's deterministic materialism was John Bramhall, the bishop of Londonderry. Bramhall was alarmed at Hobbes's arguments against the incorporeality of the soul and the possibility of freedom of the will, and he railed against the political and religious scandal he saw in both. And of course, Bramhall's complaints did not go unanswered: as Quentin Skinner notes, the dispute between Hobbes and Bramhall became something of a pamphlet war, with statements, attacks, and defenses issuing back and forth between them for over a decade.[4] Richard Tuck remarks that this long and bitter controversy between Hobbes and Bramhall is a particularly "illuminating discussion" because of what it provokes Hobbes to say in defense of some of the theological arguments he presents in *Leviathan.*[5] However, I find the exchanges instructive for a different reason. For in the arguments through which he elaborates his rejection of the determinism entailed by Hobbes's materialism, Bramhall brings into relief aspects of Hobbes's arguments that otherwise might go unnoticed. These arguments not only remove from Hobbes's philosophy the danger of a crude behaviorism but also provide a counterpoint to assumptions about deterministic materialism that, even today, remain unarticulated but nevertheless operative when theorists raise concerns about the political implications of a materialist account of the subject.[6]

What interests me most in Bramhall's attack on Hobbes's philosophy are those arguments that center on the political consequences of Hobbes's materialist determinism. To state his complaint shortly, Bramhall is concerned that Hobbes's materialist philosophy would eventuate in the "overthrow [of] all Societies and Commonwealths in the world."[7] Bramhall's argument runs roughly thus: Hobbes's materialist philosophy entails "the necessity of all things" (2). Indeed, Bramhall contends, "if his opinion be true all actions, all transgressions are determined antecedently inevitably to be done by a naturall and necessary flux of extrinsecall causes. Yea, even the will of man, and the reason it self is thus determined" (97). According to Hobbes, Bramhall claims, every action we undertake is inevitable before the undertaking; every turn of the will and every insight of reason is determined antecedent to its event. However, he laments, if this is the case, then there is nothing that we, as individuals, can do to alter the course of affairs. That is, within the terms of Hobbes's materialism, "[w]e cannot hope to alter the course of things by our labours" (92). This argument for our helplessness in the face of necessity would make a farce of justice: any inducement to the people to observe the law—any consultation, advice, or deliberation—would be in vain, and the laws themselves would require that we punish people for what they could not help but do (91). In other words, the laws would both prescribe and proscribe actions over which we have no control. But according to Bramhall, Hobbes's philosophy would not only render ineffectual and unjust the laws that structure and make possible society. Because of his claim about the prior determination of all events, all study of sciences and any advancement in the inventions by which we aim to transform the world and improve our fortunes would be futile. "[L]et the necessary causes do their work," Bramhall says mockingly. "[W]e have no remedy but patience, and shrug up the shoulders" (92). Given these frightful entailments of Hobbes's materialist philosophy, Bramhall contends, we must "[e]ither allow liberty, or destroy all Societies" (92).

What is striking in Bramhall's attack on Hobbes is his evident sense that the determinism that accompanies Hobbes's materialism is "a naturall and necessary flux of *extrinsecall* causes" (Bramhall, 97; italics added). As

Samuel Mintz points out, Bramhall conceives of the causal forces at play as external to the subject and as having an immediate (which is to say, unmediated) effect on the subject's behavior.[8] This conception of causal necessity as movement outside the subject, with a trajectory going from the outside to the inside, makes for a dire philosophical picture when Hobbes denies the incorporeality of the soul. For as we shall see, Bramhall, like Descartes, believes that the incorporeality of the will is both the mark and the condition of the subject's autonomy and freedom. In other words, for Bramhall, the incorporeality of the will functions as a bulwark against and enables the subject to act in contradistinction to the determinations of the causal forces of the material world.

If we explore Bramhall's arguments against Hobbes's materialism, then, we see that they rest on the supposition that if we deny the incorporeality of the thinking self—if we extract that soul from our philosophical picture—all that remains is a lump of a body utterly subject to the determinations of its context. Incapable of acting independently of the context of its existence, devoid of internal initiative or direction, this body effectively has been gutted of all that makes a subject a subject. It neither engages nor resists the events that occur around it; it neither intervenes in nor redirects the causal forces at play. Rather, this body is a passive medium that merely reiterates and translates the forces that impinge upon it. So Bramhall rejects Hobbes's materialism because he believes that Hobbes's insistence on the materiality of the soul makes it impossible to suppose that there is anything taking place on the inside of the subject that might make it something more than a vehicle for the causal forces in the world in which it lives. In his view, it is this inertia of the material subject in the face of external forces that courts political disaster.[9]

The Necessity of Autonomy: The Cartesian Will

The bulk of the exchanges between Hobbes and Bramhall are hot-tempered and somewhat rude, with Bramhall accusing Hobbes of heresy and each accusing the other of illogic and stupidity. Throughout their arguments with one another, a central point of contention is the nature of the soul: is it a corporeal or incorporeal substance? Insisting both on the incorporeality of the soul and on the political importance of the freedom of the will, Bramhall forwards arguments that are grounded (perhaps unwittingly) in Cartesian assumptions: he conceives of the mind as incorporeal, thinking and willing as the proper activity of the mind, the body as substantively distinct from mind, and the body as essentially incapable of the kinds of activities characteristic of the mind. In fact, if we read Bramhall's arguments against the backdrop of Descartes's philosophical account of willing, we can appreciate more fully what is at stake in Bramhall's political contestation of Hobbes's materialism. In what follows, then, I lay out Descartes's account of willing and then proceed to explore how the assumptions that Bramhall shares with Descartes shape his response to Hobbes's materialist philosophy.

According to Descartes, the will is the active or volitional force of the mind or the rational soul. As he explains in *The Passions of the Soul,* "the activity of the soul consists entirely in the fact that simply by willing something it brings it about that the little gland to which it is closely joined moves in the manner required to produce the effect corresponding to this volition" (343).[10] The "little gland" is, of course, the pineal gland, the organ that enables such an intimate proximity between body and soul that the soul can direct or effect the body's actions. It has not been entirely clear to his readers how the interaction between the incorporeal mind and the material body could possibly occur.[11] However, Descartes argues that when the mind makes a judgment or decision, the intentional force of that judgment acts upon the pineal gland, organizing and corralling the body's energies so as to compel the body to realize the judgment in action.[12] As the force of the mind that moves the "little gland," then, the will is the faculty that enables the mind to act—upon the body, upon the world, and upon itself.

Importantly, since the will is an aspect of the mind, it shares in the mind's incorporeality. Indeed, it is as a consequence of its incorporeality that the will is free of the determinations of the material world. Just as the workings of the mind qua cogito are qualitatively different from and unaffected by the workings of matter, so the workings of the will occur on a nonmaterial plane. In fact, as the volitional force of the incorporeal mind, the will receives its direction from the mind rather than from the physical world. As Descartes explains, the volitions that constitute the will "are absolutely within its [the soul's] power and can be changed only indirectly by the body" (PS, 343). The mind is the sole direct determinant of the will's direction. Or to put the point differently: as an aspect of the mind that is directed by the mind of which it is a part, or better, as the mind in its active, forceful mode, the will is wholly self-determining. Referencing this absolute power of the soul over its own volitional force, Descartes claims that the will is "by its nature so free that it can never be constrained" (343). In fact, he contends that the freedom that inheres in the will is so basic that it presents itself to the intellect as clearly and certainly as does the incorporeality of the mind. As he articulates it, the idea that we have "freedom in our will . . . is . . . among the first and most common notions that are innate in us" (PP, 205–6).[13]

As is suggested in Descartes's contention that the volitional force of the soul is only *indirectly* changed by the body, the claim that the will is free and self-determining is not a claim that the subject's actions are never affected by the body, its impulses, and its reactions to the stimuli of the world. Descartes explains that when the body receives stimulation from the external world via sensory perception, the physical excitations work so as to exert pressure upon the pineal gland. This pressure upon the pineal gland arouses passions such as desire or fear, which may affect the will or "dispose the soul to want the things for which they prepare the body" (PS, 343). If these passions toward particular objects or actions are slight, the soul can ignore them—as one might do with a slight noise or a mild itch. In such a case, the volitional force of the soul—or the will—is not moved by the bodily stimulation. However, if the excitations of the body are so great as to make the felt passions strong, the triumph of the soul over the body is not so readily assured: the will can resist but not without quite some struggle. Descartes explains that this conflict between soul and body takes the form of an "opposition between the movements which the body . . . and the soul . . . tend to produce at the same time in the gland" (346). Indeed, in such a case, "[t]he most the will can do . . . is not to yield to [the stimulation's] effects and to inhibit many of the movements to which it disposes the body" (345). That is, the will must work defensively upon the pineal gland, pushing it this way rather than that in order to prevent the body's limbs and appendages from acting in accordance with the reflexes and impulses provoked by the body's engagement with the world.

The will, then, is akin to a sentry leaning against the pineal gland to provide a counterpressure to the irrational impulses issuing from the body (PS, 346). The will arbitrates the effects of the world upon the subject's actions. In fact, without the will to mediate and manage the susceptible body and its capricious excitations, the body might quite literally be overwhelmed by the stimulation provided by the world, carried along willy-nilly by forces beyond its control. Since "everything that can be observed in us to oppose our reason" should be attributed to "the body alone" (346), we can portray the will as the internal initiative or force that compels the body to be the instrument of the rational mind's intention: it is through the agency of the will that the mind's rational intention overpowers the impulses of the body.

Although Descartes's depiction of the battle over the pineal gland is rather cartoonish from our perspective—and one to which we might find ourselves hard-pressed to subscribe—his arguments about the work of the will undoubtedly ring familiar. In his view, the will is the force of the rational mind that holds in check the impulses, reflexes, and appetites of the body. This is of signal importance for our purposes, for in enabling the mind to interrupt and redirect the bodily actions provoked by worldly stimuli, the will makes possible the subject's self-mastery (PS, 347–48). Any body with a rational incorporeal soul has the potential to be master over him- or herself.[14] Descartes notes that "[e]ven those who have the weakest souls could acquire absolute mastery over all their passions if we employed sufficient ingenuity in training and guiding them" (348).

For those whose will is strong, then, for those who have mastery over their bodily passions, the mind is the sole origin of any given volitional activity. Or to put the point differently, the self-mastery made possible by the will makes each voluntary action a realization or active expression of the mind's intention. As the manifestation of the mind's judgment and decision, each voluntary act necessarily bears the signature of the soul who initiated it. Since both the decision that precipitates the mind's activity as willing and the aim toward which that activity is directed are specified by the mind—and only the mind—the very event of a voluntary act refers to the rational soul whose self-determining activity was its origin. As events original to the acting subject, such actions add an effect to the world that otherwise might not have come to pass. They also have a proprietary character that provides the basis for identifying and assigning responsibility for them. It is the very possibility of such "additive," or creative, actions and of accountability for them that is at stake in Bramhall's rejection of Hobbes's materialism.

The Necessity of Autonomy: Bramhall's Reprise

In *A Defence of True Liberty*, Bramhall presents a collection of strident arguments attacking Hobbes's philosophy and the principles of necessary causation it forwards. In elaborating his objections to Hobbes's arguments, Bramhall recapitulates in a political idiom many of Descartes's arguments about the incorporeality of the soul, the freedom of the will, and the possibility of self-mastery. Above all, Bramhall wants to hold fast to the idea that the will is free. What counts as freedom here is "an universal immunity from all inevitability and determination" (Bramhall, 17). Which is to say that the will is free when its movement and direction come from neither antecedent worldly forces nor the imperatives of the physical body but rather derive from the spontaneous internal directives of reason. As Bramhall puts it, the true liberty of the subject "consists in the elective power of the rational will" (9). In his view, it is only if we admit such liberty that we can continue to imagine progress in learning and stability and justice in politics.

At the forefront of Bramhall's worries about Hobbes's philosophy is its apparent denial to reason of its role in determining the direction of the will. For Bramhall, when Hobbes maintains that the principle that "nothing taketh beginning from *itself*" applies equally to human action as to the movement of objects, he seems to suggest that the deliberation that is to inform the will and action is superfluous. If the actions we undertake are determined by the patterns of causal forces in the world *before* we act, is there anything that reason could discern or convey to the will that would change the course of action? For Bramhall, the answer to this question is no, for "what deliberation can there be of that which is inevitably determined by causes, without our selves, before we do deliberate?" (Bramhall, 3). In other words, any insight or judgment produced by reason will have no bearing on what the subject does. Bramhall claims that to argue thus not only makes the "concurrence and consent" of the subject a mere ornament but also empties the notion of choice of all meaning. As he puts it, "if it be inevitably imposed upon me by extrinsecall causes, it is both folly for me to deliberate, and impossible for me to choose, whether I shall undergo it or not" (9–10).

In response to this implication of Hobbes's argument, Bramhall notes, "If his will do not come upon him according to his will, then he is not a free, nor yet so much as a voluntary agent. . . . If the will have no power over it self, the agent is no more free than a staff in a mans hand" (13). If the force that directs the will is but another fruit of the material forces external to the subject, then there is nothing within the subject that enables him to act against the direction and compulsion of them—there is nothing for the subject to add to the string of causal forces determining his action. In other words, with Hobbes's philosophy we can construe each subject's actions only as a continuation of preexisting vectors of movement in the material world beyond.

Bramhall finds this vision of the subject quite horrifying. As he points out in his appalled response to Hobbes's argument, there is a terrible problem in arguing that our actions are but a product of causal forces in the material world. The problem, he explains, is that "he who holds an absolute necessity of all things, hath quitted [his] dominion over himself, and (which is worse) hath quitted it to the second extrinsecal causes, in which he makes all his actions to be determined" (Bramhall, 3). By including both reason and willing among those things that are determined by material factors external to the subject and beyond the subject's control, Hobbes forecloses by giving up the possibility of "self-dominion" or self-mastery. For Bramhall, to consent to such a foreclosure is tantamount to surrendering the subject to the blind force of worldly cause and effect.

As is probably evident in the language he uses to dispute Hobbes, the crux of Bramhall's argument is his objection to the notion that a person is nothing but a medium through which the mechanistic "extrinsecall" forces of the world pass (Bramhall, 17). In his view, such a conception of the subject is descriptively incomplete: if people hold different beliefs and behave differently in similar circumstances, then something must be going on inside them that makes for the difference. Pointing by way of example to his disagreement with Hobbes, he declares that the root of the difference in their opinions "must be in our selves, either in our intellectuals, because the one sees clearer then the other, or in our affections, which betray our understandings, and produce an implicite adhaerence in the one more than in the other. Howsoever it be, the difference is in our selves. The outward causes alone do not chain me to the one resolution, nor him to the other resolution" (4). According to Bramhall, what makes him and Hobbes differ—what makes it possible for them to differ—is an intellectual insight or emotional inclination that is underdetermined by

the aggregate of external forces acting upon them. Such judgments or decisions are produced by internal activity that is independent of the "exte-
riour causes without our selves" (5). That is, they are rendered necessary
by reason's own determination, by the mind's self-determining activity of
rational deliberation. Bramhall insists, then, that there must be an autonomous "concurring" element within both him and Hobbes that contributes decisively to the differences in their insights and actions (9–10, 16).
It is this internal element or activity that makes Bramhall's arguments distinctively his and Hobbes's distinctively Hobbes's.

In both his claim that Hobbes's philosophy assigns determinative force
to "extrinsecall causes" alone and his insistence that there has to be something taking place on the inside of the subject that is not caused by external forces, Bramhall reveals something important about his understanding
of Hobbes's materialism: he finds it impossible to imagine a wholly material subject having any "internal" activity that is not a direct and immediate result of external stimuli. According to Bramhall's argument, when
Hobbes claims that the subject is wholly material, when he stipulates that
there is no "incorporeal" element within, he leaves us with a disturbing
body—a body that is disturbing because it is devoid of precisely all those
capacities that separate and distinguish it from the rest of the material
world. Without the incorporeal soul, the Hobbesian body-subject is internally resourceless, figuratively naked—it has nothing to insulate it from
the pressures of the world as they work upon the flesh. This body-subject
lacks that moment of internal indeterminacy that might enable it to arbi-
trate the reach and effect of the causal forces in the material world. Internally inert, it is without the means or energies to resist and intervene in the
patterns of worldly events.[15] For Bramhall, it seems, there is no inside on
the inside of the Hobbesian subject—or at least no inside that could make
a difference. Accordingly, when the forces coursing through the material
world titillate and tickle the body-subject, the body becomes one with the
stimulation, moving in concert with the causal imperatives it takes in.

For Bramhall, Hobbes's materialism is not only descriptively incomplete in its depiction of the complete determination of the subject's thoughts
and activities by external causes. In its denial of the self-dominion made
possible by the freedom of the will, his materialism is also normatively
dangerous. Indeed, Bramhall offers his critique of Hobbes's materialist
philosophy in defense of the arts and of society itself. In several specula-

tive comments, Bramhall invokes fantasies of injustice that signal not only the philosophical impossibility of his acceding to the terms of Hobbes's materialism but also a corollary moral necessity for his belief in autonomy. Reading these fantasies, we can see that Bramhall's very inability to imagine that there might be something going on inside this subject causes him surreptitiously to reinstate the incorporeal soul—to give Hobbes's lump of body some semblance of recognizable subjectivity. That is, because Bramhall cannot imagine a "self" in the body that Hobbes gives us, because he cannot personify this body, he implicitly restores the incorporeal soul, acknowledging its apparent absence while presuming that, all along, it is there. So even though the incorporeal subject ostensibly has been metaphysically banished, for Bramhall it is not really gone. Rather, its existence is simply being denied. Thus denied, the incorporeal subject haunts Bramhall's analysis, reappearing in spectral form as anxiety about the injustices made possible by Hobbes's materialism.

Bramhall recognizes that when Hobbes depicts the will as subject to the determinations of material cause and effect, he forecloses any argument that the self is the single locus of initiative and the origin of activity. The very notion of a single locus or origin of activity becomes suspect, for the so-called "origin" of action dissipates into several or many causes. With this dissipation, each individual is positioned as a mere vector of motion, a mere moment in a chain of reactive movements between bodies. Accordingly, any question of the individual's own contribution to an event is moot from the very start. But, worries Bramhall, if an individual is not conceived as the single, identifiable locus for the causal force that precipitates a particular act, then that individual cannot be identified as the responsible agent for anything that follows from his or her actions; more than this, the individual has no control over what occurs. As Bramhall entertains the possibility of just such situations, the incorporeal subject reappears both in the vexing prospect of a malicious manipulator of Hobbes's argument and in the distressing anticipation of a hapless victim of misplaced condemnation.

In the first case, Bramhall imagines a wily antihero somehow reinstalled in and occupying the body-shell that he sees as Hobbes's materialist subject. This antihero is a soul who has control over the body and its actions but is malicious in its self-mastery. With a disingenuous invocation of the principle of necessity, this specter disowns its self-control in order to avoid retribution. In the fearful scene that Bramhall imagines, when such malefactors are called to acknowledge their wrongdoing, "[h]ow easily might they answer according to T.H. his doctrine, Alas blame not us, Our wills are not in our own power or disposition" (Bramhall, 14). The danger, as Bramhall sees it, is that in claiming that our actions are the product of antecedent, material causes, Hobbes makes it impossible to hold people responsible and accountable for their actions. All they need do in their defense is to point to the "extrinsecall causes" that Hobbes argues determine all actions and events. In other words, by undermining the presumption of the autonomous will that is central to the assignment of blame and the just dispensing of punishment, Hobbes sets us on a course to the complete disregard for law.

In addition to making the laws effectively pointless, Hobbes's materialism would also make of them an instrument of injustice. That is, in addition to preventing us from accusing people who manipulate philosophy for the sake of wrong, it might prevent us from acquitting others of actions over which they had no control. Apparently anticipating just such a difficulty, Bramhall declares, "No man sins in doing those things which he could not shun, or forbearing those things which never were in his power" (15–16). In this second case, it seems that material reality conforms to Hobbes's materialism yet neither the "inner self" nor the legal realm have yet done so. In the scenario that is implied by his call for clemency, Bramhall conjures a poor incorporeal soul who is in fact there inside the body, but whose presence is ignored and irrelevant. There in ostensible fact, while not there in effect, this miserable wretch cannot communicate with, direct, or control the body as it encounters external causes. This soul is captive in the vehicle of the body, a desperate prisoner helpless to change what the body is compelled by the world to do. Aggravating this terrifying situation, the laws purport to assign blame for what is done. Yet, in this fantasy, any action or inaction that gives offense cannot be said to have its origin in the intention or will of the soul trapped within. In fact, Bramhall suggests, since there was no real "agent" of the action, to assign blame would be to commit a gross injustice.

In these imagined scenes of injustice, Bramhall portrays the incorporeal soul as either forsaking us (the manipulator) or having been forsaken (the captive). The implication of these portrayals is that we betray ourselves and society at large if we adopt the materialist philosophy he sees offered by Hobbes. The point Bramhall urges upon us throughout is that in order to save society as we know it, and in order to do justice to ourselves, we must reject Hobbes's materialism and avow the incorporeality and freedom of the soul.[16]

There are a couple of insights I want to draw out of this discussion before we move on to explore those among Hobbes's arguments that serve as a rejoinder to Bramhall's critique. First, in his elaboration of the social and political troubles augured by Hobbes's materialism, one of Bramhall's primary concerns is to defend the notion of agency conceived as the capacity of a subject to act according to the dictates of an autonomous decision. But as his discussion of justice suggests, what is at stake in the language of free choice is not the ontological possibility of free choice per se but the possibility of a subject acting in contradistinction to the causal imperatives of the context of action. To be more specific, Bramhall seeks to preserve the possibility of identifying an actor's distinctive contribution to a series of events, the possibility, that is, of tying an actor fairly unequivocally to his or her act such that he or she might be held accountable for it. In other words, the language of choice is a rubric for questions about proprietorship of actions and about responsibility.

Second, and related, there is something quite instructive in Bramhall's inability to imagine the Hobbesian subject as anything more than a shell or a remainder—that which is left after the incorporeal thinking self has been removed. In figuring the Hobbesian body-subject as an empty receptacle through which "extrinsecall causes" reverberate, Bramhall depicts the Hobbesian body-subject's actions as a direct and unmediated translation of worldly forces. His portrayal of the directness and immediacy of this transformation of material causes into the subject's actions is striking not simply for its suggestion that the material body-subject is merely a passage for the forces that move through it. More particularly, Bramhall's conception of the immediacy of the transition from cause to act is striking for its suggestion that the transition happens somewhat instantaneously. This incredibly brief temporal horizon for the determination of the subject's actions is significant, for with it Bramhall implies that a wholly material subject can be conceived only as internally inert because matter has a compromised relationship to time. That is to say, Bramhall's conception of the material subject's internal inertia is related to a conception of matter as atemporal. The point here is not that the material subject has no subjective experience of time: Bramhall does not really touch on this. Rather, the point is that for Bramhall the material body-subject, in its very materiality, appears not to bear the marks of its existence through time.

According to Bramhall's analysis, although the material body-subject is an object in a history of serial encounters with various causal forces and other objects in the world, it does not absorb and retain the effects of that history. Conceivably, if it were to retain that history, the direction and strength of the forces that emerged "out" of the subject would be at least somewhat different from those that traveled "in." And that history retained in the flesh would refract subsequent forces working upon the matter of the subject so that, over time, the direction and force of the subject's actions would be quite distinct from the projective proddings of ambient causal forces. To make the same point negatively, it is only if the matter of the body is not modified by the forces that work through it that we can claim that there is no alteration of the transient force: in such a case, the body-subject is a mere transit point for extrasubjective causes. Such appears to be Bramhall's argument. According to him, the body absent an incorporeal soul does not contribute to or change the trajectory of movement in the world. Rather, the material body-subject is simply a lumpish node for the transfer of causal forces. So, for Bramhall, what renders the material body effectively inert in the face of the causal forces at play in the material world is its suspension in a "perpetual now." In other words, the body-subject's particular motion is indistinguishable from the causal forces coursing through both it and its surroundings because of the atemporality of the matter of which it is composed. Significantly, then, it is not simply the case that, in its materiality, the Hobbesian body-subject is effectively empty. This very emptiness is premised upon the ahistoricity of matter, upon the assumption that matter lacks any temporal depth.

Hobbes: The Many Face(t)s of Determinism

There is much in Hobbes's philosophy to suggest that Bramhall is correct in contending that his materialism entails such a thoroughgoing determinism that deliberate, self-consciously undertaken action becomes difficult to conceive. Hobbes himself claims that every event or action is the effect of a hugely complex range of causal factors. He says, "*That* which

I say *necessitateth and determinateth every action . . . is the sum of all things, which being now existent, conduce and concur to the production of that action hereafter, whereof if any one thing now were wanting, the effect could not be produced"* (LN, 246). In other words, together, everything that exists has a determining effect on any given action. Our actions are determined not by just one or two causal factors but rather by "the sum of all things," an incredibly broad swath of causal factors. In a fairly whimsical comment, Hobbes even grants that astrological factors may have some (impossible to calculate) causal weight (246).[17] With the aggregate contemporary force of the entire universe behind us, it is difficult to imagine how we might take actions to which we ourselves make a distinctive contribution.

Hobbes's understanding of what "the sum of all things" is turns out to be quite complicated. Not only does he envision causation to be so complex as to defy taxonomic prediction and direction, but the temporality he attributes to the subject conceived as a thinking-body also answers Bramhall's concerns about the possibility of subject-specific actions. In fact, Hobbes's account of the temporal complexity of imagination and desire makes his materialist determinism both less overwhelming and less prone to produce hopelessness and injustice than Bramhall fears. Quite to the contrary, as we shall see in the succeeding chapters, it provides the basis for Hobbes's astute insights about ethics and politics.

Let us begin by examining further the broad determinism described just above. Hobbes claims that the immense range of causal factors that contribute to determining an action are not connected in a unilinear fashion, as if one thing leads to the next, which leads to the next. The "sum of all things" is not "one simple *chain* or concatenation, but an innumerable number of chains, joined together . . . and consequently the whole cause of an event, doth not always depend on one single chain, but on many together" (LN, 246–47). For example, the rolling of double ones when someone throws dice is determined or necessitated by incalculable factors such as the weight of the dice, "the posture of the parts of the *hand,* the measure of *force* applied by the caster, the posture of the parts of the *table,* and the like" (276–77). The way we hold and throw the dice, the way the table is made—and we may even add the kind of bounce produced by a particular kind of wood, by the cut of the wood, by the effect of humidity on the wood—have a determining effect upon which faces of the dice appear. Every one of these factors is a part of a distinct set of causal chains—habits of bodily movement, patterns of physical energy, practices of forestry and carpentry, routes of trade, climate conditions, social customs—and each is brought to bear upon the others at the particular moment of the toss. In fact, Hobbes suggests that since the causal forces at play on the occasion of throwing the dice are so very complex, whatever faces appear seem to us to be quite a matter of chance.

Hobbes's qualification here suggests a number of things. First, the extreme breadth of the range of causal factors means that it is effectively impossible to trace all the factors that contribute to a particular outcome. There are simply too many to identify. In other words, determinism does not entail perfect hindsight. Second, and related, the vast range of causal determinants makes it impossible to foretell with certainty what events the future might bring. In other words, determinism does not entail easy prediction. And third, since countless and untraceable factors have an unpredictable but nonetheless determinative effect upon every event, we cannot unfailingly regulate or influence ahead of time what event will occur or transpire. That is, Hobbes's determinism is so complex as to not be determinable: the specter of a crude political behaviorism can settle back down. Yet Hobbes's elaboration of the nonlinear complexity of causation does not in itself dispose of his arguments with Bramhall about freedom of the will. More particularly, it fails to address Bramhall's politically fraught claim that people do not merely reproduce or relay extrasubjective causal imperatives but rather add something distinctively "theirs" to the world when they act. It is when we press Hobbes's argument to deal with this concern that the temporality of the subject emerges as a crucial issue.

As noted at the beginning of this chapter, Hobbes rejects the idea that the will constitutes an exception to the rules of material causality. Arguing against the notion that the will is incorporeal and hence intrinsically free, Hobbes claims that the actions that people undertake are subject to the same causal forces as acts that issue from other material things. Indeed, in his view, the liberty of the will that Bramhall defends is an illusion born of our inability to perceive or trace all the causes that contribute to the event of an action. He explains that when "we see not, or mark not the force that moves us, we then think there is none, and that it is not *causes* but *liberty* that produceth the action" (LN, 265). However, our oblivion of all the forces that compel us to do this rather than that does not make the argument that the doing was the result of free will. For Hobbes, our inability to ascertain or predict all the causes that coalesce to produce an action does not detract from the fact that every action has a necessary cause.

In Hobbes's view, the will is caused by forces other than itself. He denies that anyone "can determine his own will."[18] To the contrary, he contends that "every volition or act of the will . . . had a *sufficient*, and therefore a *necessary* cause, and consequently every *voluntary* action was *necessitated*" (LN, 260). According to Hobbes, then, there is no motion or movement within us—and no action we can undertake—whose beginning is outside of or beyond the imperatives of material causation. We are, inescapably, creatures of necessity. Or as Hobbes insists, "*free from necessitation*, I say, no man can be" (262).

Yet the ethical and political thinking that constitutes the bulk of *Leviathan* surely indicates that Hobbes does not worry that the determinism entailed by his materialism obviates the need for laws and deracinates justice. Nor does he appear to be troubled by the thought that his acknowledgment of necessity renders futile any attempt to intervene in or change the course of worldly events, to learn or develop new technologies for transforming the world and ourselves. In his view, thinking-bodies can innovate and choose. However, just as creativity in thinking is an effect of determinate metonymic shifts, so he points out that in choosing "not only the *effect*, but also the *election*, of that particular effect [is] *necessary*" (LN, 247). In other words, we can choose, but the particular choice we make at any specific juncture is itself determined. If we do not presume from the outset that Hobbes is simply being perversely paradoxical—if not philosophically incoherent—in forwarding such an argument, then we must assume that we have heretofore misunderstood how the deterministic principles of his materialism are elaborated in his account of human willing and action.

As we have seen, Bramhall's critical rejection of Hobbes's work derives in part from his having confounded a materialist determinism and an inertial account of activity. However, when Hobbes argues that the internal activities of willing and choosing are determined or "necessitated," he does not mean that the causes contributing to that necessity work simply from the outside inward, as if forces external to the subject work in a direct and unmediated fashion upon the internal movements of the thinking-body. Hobbes's subject is not a passive target for and recipient of stimuli that compel it, moment by moment, to perform the causal mandates of the external material world. To the contrary, he attributes a temporal complexity to the determination of the imagination and the passions that attenuates the direct "from the outside to the inside" determination of action supposed and feared by Bramhall. Indeed, it is because Hobbes argues that the body is modified by and bears its own history that his materialist determinism neither implies nor entails the inertia of the subject.

As we have seen in previous chapters, the wholly material subjects Hobbes imagines are animated by a vital motion that is specific to each particular organism. The force of this vital motion produces bodily movement in response or reaction to the causal stimuli that assail the body. Clearly, then, what is at issue is not *whether* the body reacts but rather the *quality* of that reaction. Attending to the liveliness that vital motion gives to the body, we might suppose that Hobbes's subject reacts to stimuli in strict accordance with vital motion's imperative to preserve itself: an immediate response. However, Hobbes gives us no reason to delimit the body's possible responses to stimuli to those derived from the restabilization of the equilibrium of the organism at the very instance of stimulation. For as we saw in Chapter 1, in his account, the possibility of sense perception itself requires that the sensate being should have memory, which is to say that the response has a longer temporal horizon than the present moment. Granting that the sentient living organism has a modicum of memory, we might suppose that it could develop a habitual response to repeated stimuli: a learned response, a Pavlovian effect. But as Chapters 1 and 2 show, memory in the thinking-body is a far more complex phenomenon than a mere imprinting and accumulation of sensory impressions. For Hobbes, memory is constituted of a collection of sensory experiences and affective states whose relations to one another do not follow a linear, forward-moving temporal logic. Rather, the ideas and affects that constitute perception and memory are related to one another through a combination of anticipatory, recursive, and temporally "horizontal" metonymic shifts. It seems, then, that we must consider the temporal complexity of perception, memory, and experience when we consider the quality or character of the thinking-body's determined responses to causal stimuli.

As we shall see in more detail in the remainder of this chapter, Hobbes depicts the thinking-body's memory as a tangle of residual stimulation that undergoes constant modification by experience at the same time that it both affects the embodied subject's perceptions in the present and gives it a specific disposition toward the future.[19] Which causal stimuli are received and noticed by the thinking-body and how the thinking-body responds to them depends upon that specific body's history of thinking patterns and passions—a very particular history derived from and continually transformed by experience. The thinking-body's dual and interrelated histories of thinking and feeling are provoked and brought to bear as the subject moves through and engages the situations and possibilities it encounters in the world. In Hobbes's argument, then, the actions undertaken by a thinking-body are indeed determined, but not solely by those stimuli currently "external" to the subject. They are also determined by the imaginative and affective patterns of memory brought into play by a particular instance of a possibility, by the effect of those memories upon the subject's current perceptions and upon his or her anticipations of what the future might hold. A determined response, to be sure. However, the causal determinism at work in this response is one that is peculiar to the singular internal history of a specific organism on the occasion of a particular stimulus at a specific historical juncture. If we were to make the point oversimply, we could say that when someone acts, a complex internal determinism engages and is engaged by a complex external determinism. However, such a formulation would reinstitute and reinforce a strict boundary between the internal and external that is hard to maintain in Hobbes's materialist philosophy. Perhaps a better way to pose the issue is to say that the distinctiveness of someone's actions rests upon a disjuncture in the temporality of the manifold causes that determine those actions.[20]

The Temporality of the Imagination

One of the most striking features of Hobbes's account of action is the imagination's displacement of the will as the signal capacity that enables us to choose. That is, although he insists that many interrelated causes in the material world bring us to the occasion of acting, he claims that "the Imagination is the first *internall* beginning of all Voluntary Motion" (L 6:118; emphasis added). So even though the interior realm of the subject is not the single origin of a voluntary act, it does make some contribution to the causal chains that determine an act. Indeed, as "the first internal beginning" to the determination of action, the movements of the imagination give to someone's action its singularity or distinctiveness.

In *Leviathan,* Hobbes points out that animate forms of matter (i.e., thinking-bodies and animals) have "two sorts of *Motions* peculiar to them" (L 6:118). One of these is "Vitall Motion," which as we have seen is the motion that constitutes the very liveliness of the organism. The other is what he calls "*Animall motion*" or "Voluntary *motion;* as to *go,* to *speak,* to *move* any of our limbes, in such manner as is first fancied in our minds" (118). In claiming that we can go, speak, or move "in such manner as is first fancied in our minds," Hobbes suggests that some of our actions follow not from the direct compulsion of immediate "extrinsecall causes," as Bramhall fears, but rather from our thoughts or "fancies." Indeed, Hobbes remarks that it is because "*going, speaking,* and the like Voluntary motions, depend always upon a precedent thought of *whither, which way,* and *what*" that we must specify the causal initiative of the imagination (118). Of course, Bramhall was concerned that Hobbes's determinism entails the claim that the imagination's responses to "whither, which way, and what" are themselves determined directly by the worldly forces at work at the moment of thinking—and that consequently the imagination could only superficially and somewhat misleadingly be described as the "internall beginning" to action. However, Hobbes argues that although our thoughts and fancies are indeed determined, that determination—the determination of the imagination—occurs in a different temporal frame than the determinations that constitute the current contextual moment.

According to Hobbes's argument, the imagination is a decisive capacity for voluntary action not because it enables us to suspend ourselves above or to insulate ourselves from the causal forces immediately at work upon the body but rather because the thoughts and "fancies" that constitute it are noncontemporaneous with the immediate causal stimuli. As Hobbes explains, the very existence of memory means that when we consider an opportunity before us, we "thinketh of some like action past, and the events thereof one after another; supposing like events will follow like actions" (L 3:97). As we have seen in earlier chapters, this moment of comparison is both a feature of sensory perception and a function of the metonymic structure of thinking. Hobbes goes on to argue that, extrapolating from that memory, we make "a *Praesumtion* of the *Future,* contracted from the *Experience* of time *Past*" (98). In other words, drawing on the similarities we register between the current situation and past experience, we anticipate the possible future consequences of acting this way or that way in response to a particular provocation or opportunity. Significantly, then, a stimulus does not simply cause a phantasm to arise. Rather, it provokes memories and experiences that, in combination with the phantasm of the stimulating object, we project forward imaginatively through time. Our imaginative anticipation of the quality of that future prompts further memories that in turn evoke a slightly different future. In other words, through the work of imagination, the present evokes several pasts and several possible futures. Indeed, it is the affective or passionate force generated by both those past memories and future memories that determines what we do upon the occasion of a current circumstantial stimulus.

However, this brief description of the temporality of the imagination does not yet account fully enough for the temporal disjunction in determinism that gives the all-important distinction to any given subject's actions. As we saw in Chapter 2, according to Hobbes, the train of memories evoked by and partially constitutive of a current sensory percept and the trajectory of the imaginative anticipation of the future are both determined. That is, the pattern of memories and the projection of those memories forward in anticipation are subject to the determinate metonymic shifts by which any train of thoughts moves. Whereas these metonymic shifts are made possible by the sequencing of different series of events and encounters in the past—by prevailing patterns of contiguity in the ideas or memories that initially were derived from those experiences—the shifts themselves are propelled by habit, by language, and also, perhaps most importantly, by the passions. Indeed, the significant role of the passions in moving the imagination means that in order to appreciate the temporality of the imagination, we must also understand the temporality of the passions.

The Temporality of the Passions

As we have seen, against Bramhall's contention that the will is free and that its freedom is the condition of our being able to make choices, Hobbes argues that the will is corporeal and subject to necessity. Indeed, in a remark whose very articulation questions Bramhall's presumption that a subject might be self-sovereign over his or her own actions, Hobbes denounces the idea that the will has anything to do with self-mastery. He observes that underlying the bishop's criticism of his materialist philosophy is the mistaken belief that "*to will* is to have dominion over his own

actions, and actually to determine his own will" (QCL, 34). Countering
such a mistake, Hobbes declares to the contrary that "no man can determine his own will, for the will is appetite; nor can a man more determine
his will than any other appetite, that is, more than he can determine when
he shall be hungry and when not" (34). With this declaration that "will is
appetite," Hobbes makes a claim that ruptures the very basis of the Cartesian subject's self-mastery.

For Hobbes, an appetite is an impulse or movement of the body
either toward something that gives pleasure or away from something that
causes displeasure (L 6:119). In contending that "will is appetite," then,
Hobbes renders the will a part of a physiological imperative, a particular
mode or instantiation of the body's self-sustaining activity of vital motion.
Significantly, Hobbes's claim that the will is appetite is not the claim that
it is one appetite among others, as if it were a *"Rationall* Appetite" that
might exist alongside and work with or against a feeling of hunger, a dislike of a book, or a desire for recognition. To suppose that the will is "a
Rationall Appetite, is not good," he explains, because then "could there
be no Voluntary Act against Reason" (127). Rather than being a particular kind of appetite itself, the will is a form taken by appetite—by any
appetite in those moments when appetite is realized in action. As Hobbes
states in *Leviathan,* the will is "the last Appetite, or Aversion, immediately
adhaering to the action, or to the omission thereof" (127). The will is the
impetus of a passion as it propels us to act. It is the very movement of an
appetite or an aversion into action. Willing is not a distinct antecedent to
action; it is not sequentially and temporally separate from action. Rather,
Hobbes sees it as *a part of* action. For him, willing is incipient activity. It
is the liminal moment and movement in the transition between appetite
and action.

By figuring the will as a modality of our appetites and aversions,
Hobbes forecloses the possibility that it might be the agency that man-
ages those appetites and aversions. That is, in depicting willing as the
bodily movement of a passion as it is realized in action, he strips the will
of its character as a counterforce to the material causes that work upon
the embodied subject. Gone is the notion of a self-transparent faculty of
the mind whose motive source is purely intellectual and whose force constrains the passions of the body and holds the seductions of the world in
abeyance. Indeed, in his view, we cannot "use" the will as if it were a tool

in order to manage our passions, control the concupiscence of our bodies, or marshal our physical strength. The will is not an agency that enables us figuratively to suspend ourselves above the emotional fray. Nor does its working initiate a suspenseful pause in activity that provides the subject with an opportunity either to measure the strength of its resolution or to wait for the best moment to act. Since the will is no more than the force of a desire as it begins to be realized in action, it cannot be construed as the condition of possibility for the subject's self-mastery or as the measure of the subject's autonomy.

Importantly, however, as in the case of his arguments about the imagination, Hobbes's claim that the activity of willing is determined rather than free does not mean that the will is determined directly and immediately by those material causes in the world that work upon the subject's body. Hobbes defines willing as *"the last Appetite in Deliberating"* (L 6:128), the last appetite, that is, in a series of appetites that arise at the imagined prospect of the consequences of an action. In a sense, then, the will is determined by the particular trains of anticipatory imagination instigated by a particular stimulus. But since those very trains of anticipatory imagination are directed by the force of the passions, we must also conceive of the determination of the will in terms of the appetites and aversions that partially constitute phantasms or ideas and that facilitate shifts between them. According to Hobbes's argument, just as the determination of the imagination has a temporal complexity, so the determination of the appetites and aversions that arise in the course of deliberation has a complex history.

As we have seen in previous chapters, Hobbes argues that when a thinking-body encounters objects in the world, the effect of each perceptual object upon the equilibrium of the thinking-body's vital motion becomes a constituent element of the memory of what that object is. A positive effect on vital motion compels the organism to draw closer, an impetus felt as appetite or desire; a negative effect on vital motion repulses the organism, a movement felt as aversion (L 6:119). Appetite and aversion, then, are the felt experience of the imperceptible movement or "endeavour" in a thinking-body toward or away from a stimulating object "before [these movements] appear in walking, speaking, striking, and other visible actions" (119). Indeed, if a specific instance of appetite or aversion were to unfold uninterrupted, it would eventuate in the gross movement of the body that Hobbes calls voluntary action. According to Hobbes, these "small beginnings of Motion" in the body "toward" or "fromward" (119) become an element of the motions that are constitutive of each perceptual phantasm and they remain in the body as memory (L 2:88–89). As the phantasms of which they are a part become more complex through the effects of experience, memory, and anticipation, appetite and aversion evolve into more or less complex passions. The passions, then, are tendencies or dispositions of the body that are evoked when the thinking-body's notice is drawn to a given phantasm: to recall a particular memory is to experience a modified version of the draw or the repulsion felt by the body upon the encounter with the stimulating object.

One of the most significant of Hobbes's claims about the passions is that although some very basic and general appetites "are born with men," such as the desire to eat, to excrete, or to urinate, "[t]he rest, which are Appetites of particular things, proceed from Experience, and triall of their effects upon themselves, or other men" (L 6:119–20). That is, some of the body's motions of "approaching" and "retiring" (119) arise as a consequence of its rote physiological workings—the biological manifestations of the vital motion that constitutes and perpetuates the life of each particular organism. However, many if not most of our other appetites and aversions are felt not as a consequence of bare physiological imperatives but rather as the result of the body's ongoing encounter with the world. In this context, Hobbes's claim that "nothing taketh beginning from *itself*, but from the *action* of some other immediate *agent* without itself" means that the thinking-body is not the origin, source, or cause of its own desires (LN, 274). Rather, what a thinking-body desires or fears is determined by his or her particular experience of stimulation and response, by the acquaintance, amendment, and refinement that come with trial and error. Indeed, Hobbes notes that even "when first a man hath an *appetite* or *will* to something, to which immediately before he had no appetite nor will, the *cause* of his [appetite or] *will* is . . . *something* else not in his own disposing" (274). But this claim that our desires and aversions neither emerge spontaneously nor are under our control is not the claim (as Bramhall feared) that our desires are caused simply by the work of the "immediate agent without itself." Although most of an individual's possible desires are determined from "without" at some point in an individual's history, no currently felt desire is determined directly and solely by the causal stimuli currently working upon the thinking-body. To the contrary, as we shall see below, for any particular felt desire, there is both a current provocation and a history—a history of appetitive and aversive experiences.

Hobbes's most complex single statement of the origins or causes of our desires comes in *De Homine*. There he claims that "men's inclinations toward certain things, arise from a six-fold source: namely from the constitution of the body, from experience, from habit, from the goods of fortune, from the opinion one hath of oneself, and from authorities."[21] What is most interesting about this description of the source of our "inclinations" is that it is "a six-fold source." That is to say, there are not six different sources that may, separately or individually, shape what we desire. Rather, there are six factors that together combine to constitute a desire. In other words, each appetite or aversion has a multidimensional past and as complicated a causal history as any event that occurs in the material world. In fact, if we examine some of Hobbes's observations and comments about each of these six factors, we can begin to get a sense of the array of causes that transform the thinking-body as it gains experience so that, upon a particular occasion, he or she desires one or another particular thing. In other words, we can come to appreciate the temporal depth and complexity of the determination of desire.

In citing the constitution of the body as one among the six factors that contribute to the formation of our desire, Hobbes draws our attention to a couple of things. First, he points us to consider the singularity of our bodies—the temperament, the maladies, the physiological deficiencies and excesses that are peculiar to a specific thinking-body and that give that thinking-body a propensity to respond to stimuli in a particular way, to retain particular memories, and consequently to seek out one kind of satisfaction rather than another. The particularity of the living matter that composes a specific thinking-body makes any desire-formative series of experiences peculiar to that specific thinking-body. In other words, the singularity of the constitution of the body gives rise to a singularity in the experiences that constitute desires and related passions.

In addition to foregrounding the ways in which the singular physiology of each person entails a fundamental singularity of experience, Hobbes's reference to the constitution of the body compels us to consider the singular history of each body—the continuously changing state of the living, thinking organism as it exists through time. According to Hobbes, the living body is in a state of constant flux; life itself is motion or move-ment in and through the bodily organs (L 6:118). Such a continual state of motion in the body affects the constitution of thoughts and desires. As Hobbes notes in a discussion about memory, "the continuall change of mans body, destroyes in time the parts which in sense were moved" (L 2:88–89). The continuous modification of the body that is simply part of the living process distorts the motions that are retained in the organs and flesh as memory. According to the logic of his argument, such distor-tion can disrupt prevailing patterns in the metonymic shifts that constitute the process of imagining. The effects of such a disruption include diffi-culty in recalling a memory over time: phantasms that might have come to the fore in the past are displaced by others. If we take into consideration the comparisons that are a part of the very process of sense perception, the effects of such a disruption might also include a slight misrecognition of a perceptual object: as memory becomes fuzzy over time so that similarities and dissimilarities become either accentuated or more pronounced, we might see a particular thing as less like that and more like this. Similarly, Hobbes explains that "because the constitution of a mans Body, is in con-tinuall mutation; it is impossible that all the same things should alwayes cause in him the same Appetites, and Aversions" (L 6:120). The incessant internal activity of the body, the perpetual adjustment of the body's vital motion by perceptual stimuli and memories, and the continual degenera-tion and regeneration of the flesh through time make the felt experience of a remembered passion different from the felt experience of the initial pas-sion—or, through the metonymic play of (disintegrating) memory, give to the felt experience of a current passion some but not all of the affec-tive texture of a remembered passion. The constitution of the body is an important factor in the determination of desire, then, not simply because it shapes how the thinking-body responds to stimuli but also because its state of constant transformation shapes how the thinking-body both bears and recalls the memories of experiences that are so central to the percep-tion of and response to currently available opportunities or objects.

Experience adds another complex dimension to the determination of desire. In Chapter 2 we saw that, for Hobbes, experience shapes our think-ing patterns and our ability to make judgments. Importantly, it also func-tions as a register of our exposure to stimuli that might become objects of our desire or aversion. Hobbes describes experience as "[m]uch memory, or memory of many things" (L 2:89). Or, when he is more specific, he depicts it as "Memory of the consequences of like actions formerly observed" (L 25:306). Memories of this kind are important to the formation of desire not simply because they remind us whether something we encountered in the past is to be avoided or pursued if encountered again but also because they are the basis of what Hobbes calls "Naturall Witte" (L 8:134). As he explains it, an accumulation of memories of the desirable and undesirable consequences of past events facilitates "*Celerity of Imagining,* (that is, swift succession of one thought to another)" and helps give our imagination a "*steddy direction* to some approved end" (134–35). As we saw in the discussion of prudential or instrumental thinking in Chapter 2, according to Hobbes, when we experience pleasure and seek out more of the same, or when we feel aversion and seek to avoid its source again, patterns of association in the process of thinking are established such that the movement of imagination from event to consequences or from desired effect to causes takes place increasingly directly and without excessive distraction. As we gain more experience, such particular patterns are repeated and become relatively predominant in the movement of imagination. One consequence of the emergence of such patterns is that we sharpen our observation of the similarity or dissimilarity of a present opportunity to a past opportunity: we are able to discern increasingly quickly and directly whether or not an object will likely give pleasure and satisfaction and what needs to be done in order to obtain or avoid it. When Hobbes claims, then, that "Appetites of particular things, proceed from Experience, and triall of their effects upon themselves, or other men," he points not simply to the exposure of individuals to more possible objects of desire as time passes but also to the modifications of the thinking-body through experience that effect a refinement in judgment and a growing attunement to what provokes and satisfies desire (L 6:120).

Furthermore, according to Hobbes, with the refined capacity for judgment that comes from experience, thinking-bodies err less frequently in their conjectures about the consequences of their actions. In fact, if we consider that "Prudence is a *Praesumtion* of the *Future,* contracted from the *Experience* of time *Past*" (L 3:98), then it makes sense to suppose, as Hobbes does, that "much Experience" would make one more prudent (L 5:117). The effect of such prudence upon the formation of desire is quite significant: Hobbes says that as someone becomes more prudent through greater experience, "his expectations the seldomer faile him" (L 3:97). According to Hobbes's account of the passions, when someone is often confirmed in his expectations of the good or ill to follow from an action, he may not only be hopeful about attaining what he wants (L 6:123) but may also develop the kind of "well grounded *Confidence*" that "begetteth Attempt" or prompts him to act (where another, whose confidence is grounded less in experience and more on "the flattery of others; or onely supposed by himself," may not venture to act) (125). In other words, over time, one's experiences can lead one to develop a recurrent expectation about one's ability to shape the future, an expectation that produces a particular orientation toward a current stimulus or situation—either a can-do attitude that fosters a propensity to act or, if one's experiences have been generally disappointing, a sense of hopelessness that constrains one's efforts.

Habit is another of the factors Hobbes specifies as an element of the sixfold source of our "inclinations toward certain things." As a precipitate of experience, a habit also has fairly complicated etiology and effects. A habit not only points to patterns of behavior made possible or impossible by the availability or scarcity of particular objects over time—a reference to the determinative effects of the context in which we desire, the "goods of fortune," and the material and social fruits and effects of our continued success or failure. A habit also refers us to the effects of frequent or long-standing repetition upon the movements of thought and desire in the thinking-body. In his discussion of madness, Hobbes points out that "the vehemence, or long continuance of [a] Passion" can result in "the hurt, and indisposition of the Organs" (L 8:139–40). So, for example, "excessive desire of Revenge, when it becomes habituall, hurteth the organs, and becomes Rage" (140). And rage, in Hobbes's description, is an exorbitant expression of passions uninhibited by any consideration of the consequences of action (140–42). If we can take the extremes of habit as giving us an indication of what goes on in less extraordinary instances of habit, we may surmise that repeated patterns in the motions that constitute thinking and feeling can transform the body and its organs—damage them, even—making what might otherwise have been a pattern of discernment derived from memory and experience a characteristic of one's physical constitution. With habit, then, the movement from perceptual notice to the particular responsive activity is not mediated by anticipation, consideration, or judgment but instead is reflexive and immediate. That is to say, whereas the memories derived from experience provide the basis for finding similarities among objects and thereby expanding possible objects of desire, the inscription of movements in the body that both develops and is the product of habit precludes our perceptual notice of other possibilities, delimiting the horizon of possible objects of desire to those that fit the repetition. To put the point differently, while experience fosters in a thinking-body a disposition toward the future, habits bind it to its past.

Another aspect of the "six-fold source" of our "inclinations toward certain things" is what Hobbes calls "the goods of fortune." In his view, the goods of fortune can be seen as "the secret working of God, which men call Good Luck" (L 10:150) or the "favour" or disfavor of God that is manifested in success or failure (155). They are helps and hindrances to our actions over whose occurrence we have no control or whose possible occurrence we cannot predict. They can take the form of particular skills, talents, or characteristics such as "Strength, Forme, Prudence, Arts, Eloquence, Liberality, Nobility" (150). They can also be events, situations, or opportunities that unexpectedly contribute to the cause of our success or failure (150). Hobbes notes, of course, that the common attribution of good fortune to divine grace does not mean that there is in fact a true preference on God's part, for "the causes of good and evill fortune for the most part are invisible" (L 12:169). Indeed, it is our ignorance of such causes, combined with our curiosity about them, that constitutes part of "the Naturall seed of *Religion*" or the basis of our religiosity (168–72). Despite the superstition that surrounds our perception of them, the goods of fortune can be said to be among the sources of our desires, for a couple of related reasons. First, they are the seeming cause of our exposure to certain possible objects of desire. Indeed, since exposure to and experience with objects constitute the very condition of desire—that without which we would have no desire—the fortune, luck, or untraceable chains of causation that coincide to produce an opportunity to encounter a particular object must be included as a causal determinant in the formation of our desires. Second, our lucky (or unlucky) possession of specific characteristics and skills has an important effect upon whether we are able to satisfy our desires over time. Luck or fortune, then, contributes to the determination of the opportunities, capacities, experiences, and memories that in turn determine our immediate as well as our more considered responses to perceptual objects and possibilities for action.

As we saw above, the development of prudence through experience can lead to self-confidence or a high "opinion of oneself." In his observation that, generally speaking, "Vertue . . . is somewhat that is valued for eminence; and consisteth in comparison" (L 8:134), Hobbes suggests that we gain a sense of ourselves not simply through the travails of our own experience but also through comparing ourselves with others. Indeed, it is because we compare ourselves with one another that the effects of the joy that arises "from imagination of a mans own power and ability" (L 6:125) are larger than those provided by the hope and confidence that "proceed from the conscience of Power" (L 10:155). According to his analysis of reputation, when someone becomes hopeful and confident as a result of experience, her own opinion of her power—and indeed, the success that is the basis of that opinion—may generate other people's confidence in her. As Hobbes puts it, "Good successe is Power; because it maketh reputation of Wisdome, or good fortune; . . . Reputation of Prudence . . . is Power" (151). Such a reputation wins friends, adherents, or servants—people eager to assist in and gain from the prudence or success (150–51). To have such friends, followers, or servants is itself a form of power in that "they are strengths united" and provide "assistance, and service" (150–51). Because such an increase in power might inspire one to attempt to do something one has not done before, it can open up new horizons of possibility for both appetite and aversion. Never-before-encountered opportunities and objects may titillate or terrify the subject, setting the stage for novel experiences, new passions, and possibly a further revision or enhancement of our sense of self. Put differently, an individual's personal history, along with his or her assessment of it, transforms the social and material context of desire, a transformation that affects expectations, available objects, capacities for action—and consequently desire.

Finally, when Hobbes names "authorities" as among the sixfold source of our desires, he points to each individual's "particular education" (L intro.: 83) by parents, teachers, broadly popular people, and of course, the figure of the sovereign. He contends that "the first instruction of Children, dependeth on the care of their Parents" (L 30:382). As children mature into adults, however, the responsibility for the "*Culture* of their mindes" (L 31:399) shifts from the nursery and schoolhouse to the institution of the laws. As Hobbes proposes in the introduction to *Leviathan*, properly speaking it is the "*Reward* and *Punishment*" promised by the sovereign's laws that prompt "every joynt and member" of the body politic "to performe his duty" (L intro.: 81). That is, laws and the incentives and disincentives that accompany them add an artificial but nonetheless certain set of consequences to actions—the purpose being to influence the passions in such a way that "*the will of men may thereby the better be disposed to obedience*" (L 28:353). Of course, not everyone looks to the laws to "direct and keep" their actions "in such a motion, as not to hurt themselves by their own impetuous desires, rashnesse, or indiscretion" (L 30:388). As Hobbes points out, "like little children, that have no other rule of good and evill manners, but the correction they receive from their Parents, and Masters," some people rely on customary practice for their sense of right and wrong (L 11:165–66). In other words, they make "Custome and Example the rule of [their] actions" (165), letting their motives and desires be shaped by the precedent of cultural habit and practice. Other people may "by the flattery, and by the reputation of an ambitious man" be "drawn away from their obedience to the Lawes" to do something that undermines the sovereign's authority (L 29:374). Indeed, it is to mitigate such possible ill influence upon the formation of subjects' desires that Hobbes suggests that the sovereign undertake to instruct people weekly in the "Essentiall Rights . . . of Sovereignty" and the whys and ways of justice (L 30:379–82). Presumably, such instruction would amplify people's awareness of the legal consequences of their actions, with the effect of modifying their desires in an appropriate manner. Either way, Hobbes is clear that, no matter whether the source is familial, educational, cultural, or political, individuals' desires are influenced in part by deference to the perceived wisdom or power of commanding figures or enduring practices.

As this survey begins to make clear, the elements that combine to constitute the "six-fold source" of our desires or appetites inform one another: the particulars of our physical constitution affect the initial response to stimulating objects that forms the basis for the memories of pleasure and unpleasure that shape our future responses to stimulating objects; our physical constitution makes us susceptible or insusceptible to the habits that modify the body and affect the course of experience; the goods and ills of fortune—which can include bodily attributes as well as extrasubjective opportunities and obstacles—contribute to the experiences of success and failure that shape our sense of self; fortune (chance), custom, and authoritative practice not only influence the availability of objects of possible desire or habituation but also shape the environment in and from which the living body is formed and conditioned. To combine the insights further: the state of the body (its condition, its habits, its enfleshed experiences) affects how the configuration of material opportunity, social support, self-esteem, and perceptual stimuli determines which patterns of memory and affect are provoked and recalled at a given moment. The extent to which one is pulled to the past by habit or propelled toward a possible future through anticipation depends upon which among the sixfold elements of a passion predominate in a particular situation. As Hobbes puts the point in a different context, in the formation of a particular desire at a particular moment, there is "an innumerable number of [causal] chains, joined together" (LN, 246–47). The longer we live and the more experiences our longevity affords us, the more complex the mutual transformation of the causal determinants of desire and aversion. Even more importantly, this collection of mutually transforming determinants of desire has a temporal complexity and depth. So, for Hobbes, a specific desire is determined not only by the provocation of a current occasion, opportunity, or object but also by the interplay between the singular experience and life history of each particular thinking-body and the evaluative anticipation of an imagined future made possible by that experience and history. The different elements of the past are not ever simply left behind or accumulated, for as the elements of the individual's history are carried in and through the body, they are modified by the body as they modify the body in turn. So, rather than a forward-moving accumulation and expansion of causal effects, the determination of desire is characterized by a complicated interplay of a set of recursions and projections.

Of course, as is the case with the complex causal chains that determine worldly events, we may not be aware of all the memories that contribute to the course of anticipation; we may be oblivious to many of the elements of the desires that propel the metonymic shifts pushing our notice to a particular imagined future consequence. Nonetheless, Hobbes maintains, "to him that could see the connexion of those causes, the *necessity* of all mens voluntary actions, would appear manifest" (L 21:263). Yet, despite this necessity, the acts that have their beginning in the movements of the imagination neither feel nor appear to be determined. According to Hobbes's argument, the fact that the determination of the imagination is not directly synchronous with the causal mandates of the present moment combines with the untraceable complexity of that determination to make the actions that proceed from the imagination appear as if they break out of the necessities of material causal relations—as if we are "free" in some intrinsic existential sense.

The Determination of the Will

The determination of both imagination and desire through the combination and coincidence of historically deep chains of causality means that we must reconceptualize the process of deliberation formative of the will that precipitates voluntary action. As noted above, for Hobbes, the process of deliberation is one in which we anticipate and react to our anticipation of what may transpire if we pursue a particular course of action. Although it depends upon our imaginative consideration of the possible consequences of our choices, deliberation itself is a passionate process rather than an intellectual one. As we consider the different plausible and probable outcomes of an action—the work of imagination—we go back and forth between wanting to do it and not wanting to do it. According to Hobbes, "the whole summe of Desires, Aversions, Hopes and Fears, continued till the thing be either done, or thought impossible, is that we call Deliberation" (L 6:127). In other words, deliberation is the serial transformation of desires and fears, of intentions and inclinations, as the potential consequences of a possible action are conjured and assessed. The process of deliberation ends when a particular valence of the appetites becomes decisive in the sense that the thinking-body moves to realize it—or to put it more simply, the thinking-body acts.

Hobbes's account of the temporal depth of the determinants of imagination and desire suggests that the activity of deliberation is not necessarily an activity we undertake self-consciously upon the instance of confronting a possibility or choice. That is, deliberation is not temporally delimited by the moments directly preceding a decision and action. In fact, in his dismissal of the possibility that crimes of passion are excusable, Hobbes suggests that the deliberation formative of the will can itself be seen as having an exceedingly long temporal horizon. He explains that on those occasions in which "deliberation is short" and we do not give explicit consideration to the possibilities and potential consequences that confront us, we are still presumed to have deliberated. The reason he gives is that "no *action* of a man can be said to be without *deliberation,* though never so sudden, because it is supposed he had time to *deliberate* all the precedent time in his life, whether he should do that kind of action or not" (LN, 272). In specifying the supposition that someone has "time to deliberate all the precedent time in his life," Hobbes depicts deliberation as a shaping of the passions that takes place over an extended period of time—a lifetime, perhaps—and not solely in those moments immediately before an action. In other words, the judgments and assessments that precipitate our actions are formed through long experience and the enduring effects of that experience upon our perceptions of and engagement with the world.

If there is possibly a lifetime's worth of determinants in the development of desires and fears, then it may well be impossible for us to apprehend, be conscious of, or remember all of the imaginative and passionate causes that combine to make us have this particular desire to do this particular action rather than that other one.[22] We may simply not be able to be aware of each moment in the complex series of imaginations, appetites, and aversions that combine at each particular moment to "*make every man to* will *what he willeth*" (LN, 270). In fact, it is because we are not aware of all the causal determinants of our desires and actions that we feel as if what we will to do emerges spontaneously at the moment.

So when Hobbes contends that "the liberty of *election* does not take away the *necessity* of *electing* this or that *individual* thing" (LN, 245), he means that upon the occasion of an opportunity, a thinking-body chooses subject to the determinations of her own experience. What a thinking-body decides to do is determined not solely by the sum of the causal forces that confront her but also by the complex of causal determinations peculiar to her particular experience and history. Indeed, it is because the determinations of the thinking-body's imagination and desire are noncontemporaneous and nonsynchronous with the determinations of the context of her decision that an action taken by a specific thinking-body can be said to be distinctively hers. Yet, even though Hobbes's conception of the temporal complexity in determinism grants us a sense of the distinctiveness of a particular individual's action, that very complexity also attenuates any simple designation of responsibility for it.

Hobbes's account of the temporal depth of imagination and desire requires a further shift in our understanding of the process of deliberation.

Remarking upon the "six-fold source" of our dispositions for particular things, Hobbes points out that "[w]hen these things change, dispositions change also" (DH 13:63). This claim that changes in the sources of our desires precipitate changes in our desires is seemingly a minor and obvious point. And it is minor—except that the "six-fold source" of our dispositions designates such a broad set of phenomena. If we include in this set—as Hobbes does—parents, teachers, government officials, popularly influential figures, our daily interlocutors, and the ever-changing material conditions of our everyday living, the responsibility for the ongoing permutation and transformation of our desires that constitutes the process of deliberation cannot be said to belong to the individual alone. In a sense, the individual is not the only party to his or her deliberations. If changes in the sources of our desires alter our desires, then deliberation involves those events and figures in the (history of the) context in which the thinking-body deliberates. Hobbes confirms this implication of his argument when, for example, he suggests that the sovereign is partly responsible for legal infractions if punishment is "not great enough to deterre men from the action" and indeed serves as "an invitement to it" (L 27:339). More importantly, as we shall see in the next chapter, Hobbes's suggestion that participation in deliberation is broader than that of the individual deliberator alone is central to his account of ethics. In other words, the ability to specify the distinctiveness of someone's actions does not in itself mitigate the dissipation of responsibility that Bramhall feared would follow from the acceptance of Hobbes's materialism. So before we move to Chapter 4, we must consider anew Bramhall's concern that Hobbes's arguments about deliberation and willing so disperse responsibility for actions as to make justice impossible.

Hobbes claims that the will "is not properly the *whole cause* [of an action], but the last part of it, and yet may be said to produce the effect *necessarily,* in such manner as the last feather may be said to break a horse's back, when there were so many laid on before as there wanted but that one to do it" (LN, 247). In other words, the will that eventuates in action is neither the origin of an action nor the entire cause of an action. Rather, it is something equivalent to the figurative "last feather," the last factor that, when added to all the other factors in the myriad relevant causal chains, brings about the effect or the movement. To claim, as Hobbes does, that an action undertaken by a thinking-body has numerous partial causes, with the will being simply the last cause piled upon all the others, is to suggest that responsibility for the action or the effects of an action belongs not just to the thinking-body who acted but also to the many other persons and factors that were contributory causes. In other words, Hobbes's account of both the long stretch of time within which the processes of deliberation take place and the extremely broad set of causal determinants contributing to the form and direction of deliberation suggests that Bramhall's concern about how justly to pinpoint responsibility has some basis.

Hobbes addresses the problem of how to ascertain responsibility for actions that have so many causes by marking the distinction between the *attribution* of responsibility for an action to someone and the claim that someone's responsibility for an action is an *ontological fact.* That is, recognizing that his theory of deliberation and willing denaturalizes individuals' responsibility for or ownership of their actions, Hobbes depicts the identification of someone as responsible as a social—or ethical and political—activity. "A person," Hobbes says, "is he *whose words or actions are considered, either as his own, or as representing the words or actions of an other man. . . .* When they are considered as his owne, then is he called a *Naturall Person*" (L 16:217). What is often seen as interesting in this definition of a person is Hobbes's account of authorization and representation, of the way that one person's actions can be "owned" or "authored" by another who is held to be the responsible party.[23] For the purposes of this discussion, what I find interesting is his denaturalization of the "Naturall Person." In his definition, a person is someone whose words or actions are considered his own, which is to say that the acts are ascribed a proprietary character such that the named "person" is considered to own and be responsible for them. Hobbes's formulation here—actions are considered, which is to say they are seen in a particular way—suggests that not all actions "belong" to the people from whom they appear to issue.[24] He means this not simply in the sense of representation generally associated with his discussion of persons. As we shall see in the next chapter, he means it also in the sense that an individual might act and yet, for various reasons, not be held responsible for—not be considered as owning—his or her action. For Hobbes, then, "personhood" is an ascribed status. To say that someone is a person is to ascribe to that someone responsibility for his or her actions. Such an ascription narrows the field of vision in the sense that it represents a decision to ignore other causal determinants of an action and to hold someone accountable as the determining cause of an act. But its status as an ascription leaves open the possibility of taking into account those other causal determinants, of considering the bearing of the historical and material conditions of our actions upon our actions themselves. From within this perspective, to see the will as in fact originating in the subject and to see the actions issuing from the will as the sole responsibility of that subject is not simply to naturalize a fiction, to naturalize what is, in fact, merely an ascription. *Pace* Bramhall, it is also to obscure the broad determinants of our actions and to make individuals suffer the justice of acts and events for which a larger community—and a longer history—might in fact be responsible.

4

The Ethics in Determinism

Intersubjectivity, the Collective, and Peace

In her thoughtful analysis of philosophical and popular evaluations of lying, Sissela Bok argues that, generally speaking, we tend to believe that it is wrong to lie, that we are responsible for misfortunes that occur consequent to our deceit, and that mishaps that occur consequent to our telling the truth are horrible and tragic and yet not something for which we are morally culpable.[1] Among other things, this tendency suggests that a Kantian sensibility permeates our ethical and political thinking: Immanuel Kant claims that any deceitful declaration in response to a direct question is morally wrong, for "a lie always harms another."[2]

Curiously, however, Thomas Hobbes suggests that sometimes it is better to lie than not to. For example, he suggests that if we despise or have no respect for another person, we should nevertheless not "*declare Hatred, or Contempt*" by any "*deed, word, countenance, or gesture*" (L 15:211). Likewise, he says that even if we believe ourselves to be far superior to another, we should not declare or act in such a way as to convey this to others, but rather we should each publicly "acknowledge other for his Equall by Nature" (L 15:211). Admittedly, Kant would have us avoid declaring hatred or our sense of our superiority to others, but in doing so, he would have us actually believe in the principle of equality or in the principle that we each have an absolute worth as persons. In his concern for the quality of our regard for one another (for what we truly think about one another), Kant is after our souls, as Richard Flathman might say, whereas Hobbes is concerned only with our behavior.[3] Indeed, Hobbes's call for us merely to *treat* one another as equals and as worthy folk—and possibly lie in the course of doing so—rather than actually *regard* one another as equals and worthy folk is what interests me.[4] For what is curious about Hobbes's encouragement to engage in lying is that the forms of lying he advocates appear to have some sort of ethical or moral value: the mandates mentioned above are some among the laws of nature that he depicts as both a precondition for and an ongoing condition of political life. In other words, for Hobbes, lying is a crucial part of ethical life in a polity—not *all* kinds of lying, it is important to say, but certainly some, including the form of deceitful statements in response to direct address of which Kant so heartily disapproves.[5]

The possibility that Hobbes does not simply not disapprove of lying but indeed advises us to adopt it as an important element in a coherent set of ethical practices compels us to reconsider his ethics. What kind of ethics is it that allows for and even encourages forms of lying? If we conceive of an ethical theory broadly as telling us something about how we should behave toward one another—as implying sociality in the very articulation of the ethical injunction—then what kind of social world does Hobbes imagine, such that a form of lying or deceit is a crucial, indeed, a morally necessary, feature of the political landscape?

As we began to see more clearly in Chapter 3 above, Hobbes effects a theoretical displacement of the individual when he brings into focus the broad and temporally complex determinants of imagination and desire. For Hobbes, the patterns of thinking and feeling that cause our actions are shaped by our ongoing movement in and through specific social, cultural, and political contexts. Indeed, in his view, we cannot properly conceive of individuals having thoughts and passions absent such contexts; it is only through individuals' continual and varied engagement with others and with the material world that thinking and desiring are possible. So one of the implications of the determinism accompanying Hobbes's materialism is that, for any individual, the social is always already there as a condition of selfhood. That is, according to Hobbes's argument, we are necessarily intersubjective creatures. Of course, to point to this intersubjectivity is not the same as to say that we are sociable: Hobbes is clear that often we are not. Rather, his point is that we become who we are—we come to think, to feel, and to know ourselves—only through our encounter and engagement with others. Hobbes's insight here—that individuals are profoundly and ineluctably socially embedded—entails that when we conceive of individuals, we do so in terms of their intersubjective existence, that is, in terms of their relations to others over time.

The foregrounding of individuals' intersubjectivity in Hobbes's materialist determinism has an important bearing on his theory of ethics. In his view, because social interaction contributes in so many ways to the formation of the thoughts and desires that determine action, an encounter between individuals in the present moment must be seen as a contributing factor in the formation of the thinking and passions that will determine actions in the future. In other words, each and every encounter between individuals is a determinant of future actions and interactions. This particular entailment of Hobbes's materialism prompts us to examine how the qualities of the actions and interactions taking place at any moment might affect the quality of the relations and interactions they produce. Indeed, it is just such a concern that underlies Hobbes's identification of "ethical lies." In the theory of ethics that follows from his materialist metaphysics, Hobbes demands that we evaluate actions and behavior in terms of their effects upon and implications for the social relations that constitute the context for action. In other words, for him, the ethical value of a lie is conditioned by the social consequences of that lie.

It is important to point out, however, that Hobbes's ethics is not a utilitarian consequentialism. For, as we shall see, even though his ethics requires that we focus on the consequences of action for a broader collection of persons, it does not require either that we subsume the individual to the collective or that we hold gross utility or happiness as the standard measure for evaluation. For Hobbes, the individual is not an indistinct element of a collective. For although his deterministic account of action displaces the concept of the individual from theoretical priority, it does not thereby render it obsolete. As is suggested in his portrayal of the complex temporality of the determination of imagination and desire, at the same time that Hobbes conceives of individuals as shaped fundamentally by their existence in a social context, he also imagines individuals to be distinct enough from that context to be considered in relation to it. Indeed, it is the quality of that relationship—or, more properly speaking, the quality of the many relationships that together compose the collective—that constitutes the focus of his ethical attention. Hobbes is concerned not that people be happy but rather that their relationships with one another be peaceful. In fact, for him, peace is the primary ethical value.[6] Accordingly, as we shall see in the discussion ahead, his primary concern in his theory of ethics is whether our actions and interactions promote or undermine the possibility of enduring peace.

The Ethics in/of Determinism

Since the ghost of Kant seems to linger when it comes to conventional thinking about lying, it will be useful to outline his arguments against the very possibility of ethical lying before we explore the reasons behind Hobbes's argument that there are lies whose telling is an integral part of ethical practice. The aim here is not to make the point that Kant's and Hobbes's moral visions are different.[7] Nor is it to use Kant's thinking as a foil for demonstrating the superiority of Hobbes's argument. Rather, the aim is to use the juxtaposition of Kant and Hobbes to elucidate aspects of Hobbes's moral philosophy that often are overlooked. So, by reading Hobbes's work alongside a broadly popular and philosophically sophisticated ethical framework, I hope to do two things: first, to bring into relief Hobbes's distinctive understanding of the social world in which ethics can and must come into play and, second, to bring into focus his urgent conviction that we must make the production of peace a priority in just about everything we do.

The metaphysical arguments that underlie Kant's moral philosophy are clearly distinct from those proffered by Hobbes. In fact, in some respects Kant's arguments resemble those articulated by Bramhall as he sought to defeat or deflate Hobbes's materialism. Like Bramhall, Kant claims that if we are to make sense of human beings' ability to behave in ways that do not seem to be predetermined by the mechanics of physical causality, we must presume that some nonphysical faculty is active when we act. That is, since our actions often appear not to be predicated by the causal necessities incidental to the extant empirical conditions for action, we must assume the possibility of free will.[8] Now, as Robert Pippin reminds us, it is important to acknowledge that Kant does not assert such freedom as a matter of fact. Rather, he posits freedom as a condition for making claims about our own action.[9] To be able to comprehend human action, Kant argues, we must assume that our will is autonomous, that our will is such that it can be determined solely by the force of reason. Consonant with this assumption, the will is conceived as a faculty distinct from volition—the latter of which is the sullied arena of appetite, emotion, and strategic motivation. Indeed, it is the presumption that the will is free and determined purely by reason that gives rise to the possibility of a wholly principled moral choice, a choice whose moral character derives from the universal applicability of the principle underlying the choice. In short, Kant's account of a human freedom that transcends empirical necessity is the foundation for his claim that a moral code must make reference to the universality of rational principles.

As is well known, Benjamin Constant replied to the publication of Kant's *Foundations for the Metaphysics of Morals* with the famous—now textbook—question about a murderer. Wouldn't it be acceptable to lie, Constant asks, if someone with a weapon were to enter one's house and demand to be told whether the person he intends to murder is hiding in the house?[10] In responding to Constant, Kant refutes his suggestion that one might lie to prevent harm to another with two arguments. In the first one, he reasons in a manner consistent with his moral philosophy more generally. He appeals to the broad necessity for universal principles and contends that to make "an intentionally untruthful declaration to another man" is wrong because to do so is to undermine the credibility of any principled statement whatsoever and thereby to threaten the integrity and coherence of the system of universal principles that together constitute the moral order (64). In other words, lying sabotages the practice of truth telling that is the basis both of contract making and of the *rechtstaat,* or the organization of political life based on mutual respect for rights (67). Consequently, he reasons, a rational subject could not will a universal law that permitted exceptions to truth telling. From within such a perspective, even philanthropic lying is wrong.

Kant supports his rather standard argument against lying with another that is somewhat bizarre. As if acknowledging that the argument from principle might not be adequate to bind the will of his interlocutors, Kant appeals to self-interest.[11] That is, he remarks upon our lack of control over the events of the empirical world and argues that since we can neither foretell nor determine whether our lie might bring about a good or an evil, we can avoid having "public justice lay a hand on [us]" if we opt always to tell the truth (65). He goes on to explain that if our honesty should result in a harm done to another, we are not blameworthy because "[i]t was merely an accident (*casus*) that the truth of the statement did harm" (66).

Now, one of the striking things about this "avoiding the hand of public justice" argument is that, with it, Kant intimates that acts of lying and truth telling have—formally speaking—different causal ramifications. He figures the telling of a lie as an intervention in an empirical causal series for which we gain responsibility. Events may have taken such and such a course but for our lie and even though the effects of our lie may exceed our intentions, we are morally and legally responsible for all of the effects, anticipated and unanticipated. Lying, then, implicates us in all of the unforeseen consequences of our actions irrespective of our intentions.

Conversely, Kant figures truth telling as a discrete act of principle, as a result of which we only passively or accidentally participate in an empirical causal series for which someone else (i.e., the proverbial murderer) is to be held accountable. According to his argument, when we uphold the principle that we must always make true statements, the act of truth telling is self-contained and has no causal force in the empirical world. When a truthful individual speaks and acts, what she can be understood to be doing is bounded by what she self-consciously intends and wills to do. In other words, honesty limits the responsibility we have for the effects of our actions to the intended effect—namely, that of telling the truth and upholding the truth-telling principle. In this case, then, the causal series initiated by the truth teller's action is distinct from, even if adjacent to, the other causal series of events taking place in the empirical world. So, even though someone else might use the information the truth teller provides for nefarious ends, she is exempted from responsibility because these extended effects of her actions are incidental and accidental. What this means is that someone can participate in or contribute to an event or an activity—a murder, for instance—without being seen as having any morally significant causal relationship to it.

Hobbes's materialism, and more specifically the way his materialism ties together theories of subjectivity and causation, generates a different sense about what might be wrong—or right—about lying. As we saw in the previous chapter, Hobbes's materialism includes an account of action that rests upon the claim that nothing can be self-moving, or that every action is the product of some other action. Because of the philosophical priority Hobbes grants to this claim, he quite simply refuses to acknowledge the possibility of the kind of freedom that Kant claims we must presume for the sake of moral argument. For Hobbes, every act, whether mental, emotional, or physical, is the necessary effect of some antecedent material cause. In his view, the ineluctable determination of our actions must be included in, if not at the center of, any account of our ethical obligations. In fact, it is precisely his understanding of the ways in which the patterns of our thoughts and desires are determined that informs his suggestion that there are some circumstances and occasions when lying is ethically required. I will briefly elucidate some of the reasoning behind this argument before elaborating upon the substance of the laws of nature.

The first thing to note, of course, is Hobbes's insistence upon conceiving of the subject as a thinking-body. Hobbes's repudiation of Descartes's dualism and his corollary rejection of the notion of free will can be seen as a refusal to imagine a realm of philosophical or subjective reality that is split from the empirical. For Hobbes, people are passionate, rational, animate bodies who are ineluctably subject to necessity: the patterns of each individual's desires and imagination are determined through the confluence of the history of that individual's life experience and worldly causes. Accordingly, any exploration of the ethical demands that befall such beings must take into account the empirical—material—conditions of their existence. Or to be more specific, such an intellectual foray requires that we consider the conditions that contribute to the formation of particular patterns of desire and imagination. Indeed, it is here that Hobbes's notion of the thinking-body makes a difference. His argument that desire underlies the movements of reason in thinking-bodies means that he cannot, like Kant, have an account of reason as purified of the passions or sensibility. His account of the subject as a thinking-body precludes the exception of the passions and desires from his ethical inquiry. Quite to the contrary, since the process of reasoning itself has the passions as its enabling condition, the passions must be conceived as central to ethics. And consistent with the terms of this argument, Hobbes identifies the passions as the defining subject of the field of ethics. As he notes in the table of science or philosophy outlined in *Leviathan*, for him, ethics is knowledge of "Consequences from the *Passions* of Men" (L 9:149). The displacement of reason here is quite thoroughgoing and in fact positions reason as a derivative rather than a predicate of ethical thinking—a point that will be borne out in Hobbes's articulation of the laws of nature. What I mean is that to define ethics as the science of the passions that underlie and guide reason is to install ethics as, in a sense, prior to reason. Ethical behavior and its effects will shape what interlocutors actually perceive as reasonable, or what they can conceive as a rational course of action.

Second, Hobbes's contention that ethics concerns the effects or consequences of our passions engenders a very particular conception of the nature of the audience or collection of beings to be referenced in the course of evaluating the ethical value of an act. According to his materialism, a subject's sense of self, and his or her patterns of desire and thinking, are not ever wholly his or her own. They are not autogenetic, autonomic phenomena. Rather, individuals' subjective self-identity, their thoughts, and their desires are constituted and modified by their ongoing encounter and engagement with one another and with the world. So when Hobbes claims that ethics is about the consequences of passions, we must take note of the intersubjective and worldly character of the passions. More than this, we must understand him to be saying that ethics requires us to attend to the effects of our passions upon one another. Obviously, the subjects who are referenced or invoked in the course of such ethical consideration are not the philosophically conjured rational wills who compose Kant's postulated moral community. Quite to the contrary, the constituents of Hobbes's ethical theory are those very passionate, rational thinking-bodies that history and circumstance have thrown together. Further, the ethical relations between such subjects are not abstract and mediated by the intellectual manipulation and consideration of rational principle. Rather, as Hobbes's elaboration of the determination of desires and the imagination stipulates, the relations between Hobbesian subjects are visceral, relentless, and fundamental to their sense of who they are, what they imagine is possible, and what they want.

Third, given the character of this ethical collective, that is, given both the inevitability and the profound significance of social relations, what is ethically important is not the universalizability or the integrity of the rational principle underlying an action. Rather, what is ethically important is the effects of individuals' passions and actions upon the development and trajectory of their own and others' passions and actions. Put slightly differently, what matters ethically for Hobbes is the character or tenor of the relationships between the individuals who together constitute the collective. In fact, as the discussion of the laws of nature will illustrate, the focus of Hobbes's ethical thinking is the effect of the quality of those relationships upon the course of individuals' interactions. If thinking-bodies are driven by a vital motion whose primary aim is to preserve itself—as Hobbes contends—then the quality of relationships and the actions that follow from them must be such as to support that aim. In Hobbes's view, peace is the condition most conducive to the preservation of life (L 15:214–16). As a consequence, the principle that orients his ethical thinking must take as its focus the cultivation of peace. And indeed Hobbes contends that "the first, and Fundamentall Law of Nature," the one from which all others are derived, "is, *to seek Peace, and follow it*" (L 14:190).

Fourth, for Hobbes, since the pursuit of peace is the primary ethical injunction, and since that injunction is structured around attention to the complex ways in which the passions are formed and the ways in which they generate effects, it does not make sense to restrict ahead of time the range of effects that could possibly be considered ethically significant. Hobbes could not subscribe to a view in which rational principles themselves are held hallowed "let the consequences be what they may."[12] From within the terms of his materialism—as, indeed, in Kant's understanding of the mechanisms of force in the natural world—the relationship between act and effect is indissoluble. Each and every action has effects, many of which redound beyond what we can anticipate. As Hobbes puts it, "There is no action of man in this life, that is not the beginning of so long a chayn of Consequences, as no humane Providence, is high enough, to give a man a prospect to the end" (L 31:406). In such "chayns" or series of consequences, "there are linked together both pleasing and unpleasing events," both of which sorts we must recognize as the effects of our actions (406).[13] For Hobbes, however, the impossibility of foreseeing all the possible consequences of an action does not result in the adoption of an ethical perspective in which an action might be imagined as self-contained or circumscribed by the moment of its event. In his philosophy, each action is the product of a conjunction of a complex of causal series, as well as being the cause of other effects elaborated in other causal series. In his ethics, he likewise sees actions in terms of the coincidence and dispersion of causes and effects. For him, then, what falls under the purview of ethical evaluation in an action is the panoply of antecedents and consequences that can be said to belong to an action—an opening up rather than a narrowing of the ethical domain.

Finally, all these points together combine to require a distinct temporal horizon for the pacific principle that structures his ethics. To put the point shortly, Hobbes's materialist emphasis on individuals' intersubjective existence entails that when we consider the ethical value of an act, we take account of the historical depth of the social relations that constitute the determining context for that act. In other words, we must see the relationships that are both the context for and the product of individuals' actions as themselves bound up in and a part of "long chayn[s] of consequences." For Hobbes, then, the temporal frame for thinking about the ethical value of actions is neither the timelessness of the universal principle nor the immediacy of the instance of an act but rather the relationship between the past, the present, and the future. To put the point another way, his understanding of the determination of thoughts and desires gives rise to the ethical injunction to examine what actions in the past have contributed to the character of individuals' relations and actions in the present and what a particular present encounter or act will mean for future actions and relations. In fact, it is this concern for the future effects of actions—for the effects of individuals' actions upon the tenor of their future interactions—that underlies Hobbes's argument that some forms of lying are ethical.

For Hobbes, the very act of lying does not have an ethical value in itself. Rather, since the consequences of our actions are the causal antecedents of other actions and events, the ethical value of telling a truth or telling a lie depends upon the contribution it makes to the series of actions and events of which it is inevitably a part. What is at issue, in particular, is the effect that our telling has on the formation of our relations with one another—and on the formation of our imagination, desires, and actions—in the immediate and not-so-immediate future. In Hobbes's view, we all suffer from the instabilities and flashes of violence that arise when people live in insecurity (L 13:184–86). None of us can live peacefully or well when some or all of us feel threatened. As a consequence, the question that guides his evaluation and justification of the ethical value of actions is whether or not they foster bellicose or pacific orientations and actions in our interlocutors. More pointedly, it is this: does the telling of this lie or this truth generate a relational context in which individuals' interlocutors can give an affirmative answer to the query, "Can I trust you not to kill me?" Intimating that just such a question is at stake in the lying that he advocates, Hobbes suggests that lying is ethical when it enables us to interact without the threat of imminent violence, that is, when it facilitates the development of a quality of interrelationship that enables us to believe in the possibility that we can live together in peace.

The Laws of Nature, Appearances, and Peace

For Hobbes, the primary ethical injunction is "*to seek Peace, and follow it*" (L 14:190). When he elaborates some of the practices that this injunction enjoins in his account of the laws of nature, he gives us important insight into the broader ethical vision of which the laws of nature are a part. According to his analysis, each individual's patterns of thinking and desire are shaped to a great extent by the intentions and aims he or she perceives in other individuals' actions, gestures, and visible attitudes in the course of interaction. The significance of such perceptions in determining people's future patterns of anticipation, judgment, and action means that the effort to "seek peace" requires individuals to be aware of how they are perceived by the others around them. The profound manner in which social interactions shape individuals generates the ethical mandate that individuals attend to their appearances. They must not merely be cognizant of and conceive of themselves as objects of a public gaze, as people whose actions, gestures, and visible attitudes affect the prospects for peace. They must also fashion and amend their appearances so that they are seen by others as well disposed toward peace.

Hobbes's description of the antithesis of peace—war—provides a useful starting point for examining the laws of nature. Here he suggests clearly that the complex temporal dimensions of social causation must be an integral part of individuals' attention to and cultivation of a peace-oriented appearance. In his definition of war, Hobbes contends that

Warre, consisteth not in Battell onely, or the act of fighting; but in a tract of time, wherein the Will to contend by Battell is sufficiently known: and therefore the notion of *Time,* is to be considered in the nature of Warre; as it is in the nature of Weather. For as the nature of Foule weather, lyeth not in a showre or two of rain; but in an inclination thereto of many dayes together: So the nature of War, consisteth not in actuall fighting; but in the known disposition thereto, during all the time there is no assurance to the contrary. All other time is Peace. (L 13:185–86)

In claiming that "the notion of *Time,* is to be considered in the nature of Warre," Hobbes takes account of the time of determination—the temporality of the determination of the imagination and desires that coalesce to produce our actions. Defining war as a matter not of what happens at any particular moment but rather of what happens over a period of time, Hobbes reminds us again that what we conceive to be possible and what we want are shaped over the course of a series of interactions with one another. War, then, consists not in isolated incidents of violence. Rather, it is a context in which the disposition to fight is "sufficiently known" or in which "there is no assurance" over time that fighting or "Battell" is not a part of individuals' future plans. Under this definition, war is a state of hostile insecurity that prepares us for, and thereby in a sense becomes a cause of, physical conflict. That is, war is a period in which the quality or tenor of our interactions with one another is such that we anticipate hostile confrontations and find ourselves oriented accordingly in our desires, imagination, and actions.

Hobbes's contention that war consists in social relations characterized by evident antagonistic intentions over a period of time implies that the injunction to seek peace must also be seen as incorporating an appreciation for the temporality of the determination of our desires and imagination. If war is a "tract of time" in which there is no assurance among individuals that they do not intend to engage in violent conflict, and if peace is "all other time," then we can describe peace as the "tract of time" during which individuals manage to convey to and assure one another that they do not intend to fight one another. Put more positively, it is a period of time in which individuals' relations with one another are characterized by the effort to convey peaceable dispositions now and into the future. And in fact, it is precisely this sense of peace and of what individuals can do to promote peace that runs through Hobbes's account of the laws of nature.

Hobbes lists nineteen laws of nature that "concern the doctrine of Civil Society" and dictate "Peace, for a means of the conservation of men in multitudes" (there being other laws, he says, that forbid "other things tending to the destruction of particular men" but that are "not necessary to be mentioned, nor are pertinent enough to this place") (L 15:214). Of these nineteen, the first half in particular outline the antagonistic and peaceable attitudes and responses that thinking-bodies provoke in one another when they behave and are perceived in a particular way. Importantly, however, the laws of nature are more than a lexicon of gestures for the purposes of enabling individuals to interpret and make judgments about the intentions manifested in one another's actions and demeanor. Since they lay out the "means of the conservation of men in multitudes," they bear the weight of the imperative to seek peace. Consequently, they must be seen as delineating how individuals must contrive to be seen. That is to say, they elaborate the kind of self-presentation individuals should undertake in order to appear to their interlocutors as thinking-bodies who are well disposed toward the cause of peace.

The third law of nature, for example, specifies that people must "*performe their Covenants made*" (L 15:201). In a commonwealth, the performance of this imperative can be ensured by the sovereign power. However, if we consider that for Hobbes the laws of nature are a condition of politics and therefore of the constitution of the sovereign, we must attend to the dimensions of this promise-keeping requirement beyond legal enforcement. Considered as such a condition, the third law of nature bids individuals to imagine themselves as situated in a social setting in which their actions declare their will in ways that affect the prospects of peaceable confederation. By way of explanation, Hobbes invokes the dissenting voice of the Foole who "seriously alleag[es], that every mans conservation, and contentment, being committed to his own care, there could be no reason, why every man might not do what he thought conduced thereunto: and therefore also to make, or not make; keep, or not keep Covenants, was not against Reason, when it conduced to ones benefit" (203). The Foole as Hobbes depicts him here presents the instrumental-rational argument that one might break a covenant if it is in one's interest to do so: if one is responsible for one's preservation, and if one must do whatever one deems necessary to meet that imperative, then one might justifiably and in good conscience deceive, cheat, break promises, or violate the faith of one's compatriots. Among the arguments Hobbes levels against this "specious reasoning" is the contention that even though a Foole might succeed in deceiving his confederates for some while, he simply cannot "foresee, nor reckon upon" the duration of the period that he is able to "live in Society . . . by the errours of other men" (204–5). When the Foole's conniving mendacity is discovered—as Hobbes says inevitably it will be in due course—his actions will declare to all that he "thinks it reason to deceive those that help him." Such a declaration announces to all who witness and hear of it that the Foole "cannot be received into any Society, that unite themselves for Peace and Defence, but by the errour of them that receive him" (205).[14] Hobbes points out that to make such an announcement is foolish because it is to risk being cast into perpetual exile or killed as an enemy of war. If one wishes to avoid such a political or even literal death, one must not only develop an awareness of what one's actions say to others about one's dispositions and intentions but also act with an eye to one's social existence and reputation over time.[15] In other words, for the sake of the very possibility of peaceful coexistence with others, one should "perform covenants made" and thereby cultivate a public self whose affect and actions bespeak the desire to live in peaceful league.

The imperative to act as if one is disposed toward peace takes a slightly different direction in the fourth law of nature. Here Hobbes explains that the mandate to seek peace requires that an individual who "*receiveth Benefit from another of meer Grace, Endeavour that he which giveth it, have no reasonable cause to repent him of his good will*" (L 15:209). That is, it entails that when one is presented with an unwanted gift that is proffered in a gesture of goodwill, one must accept the gift with a display of gratitude rather than reject it with disdain. This enjoinder to ensure that a benefactor not regret a gesture of goodwill has its roots in Hobbes's belief that such a gesture is an indicator of peaceable intentions. As Hobbes also argues in his analysis of the granting of honors by a sovereign, gratitude fosters allegiance, which in its turn has a socially cementing effect: to bestow a gift is to convey one's goodwill and, hopefully, to cultivate the same in another, to the end that some sort of peaceful alliance be formed.[16] If we rebuff such overtures, he points out,

all beneficence and trust, together with all kind of benevolence, would be taken from among men, neither would there be aught of mutual assistance among them, nor any commencement of gaining grace and favour; by reason whereof the state of war would necessarily remain, contrary to the fundamental law of nature.[17]

So if one is to avoid perpetuating war, one must respond to other people's benevolence and compassion—their peaceable gestures—with visible, if affected, gratitude rather than a truculent lack of appreciation.

In a similar vein, the fifth law of nature requires "*[t]hat every man strive to accommodate himselfe to the rest*" (L 15:209). That is, when interacting with others, one must not try to hold on to "those things which to himselfe are superfluous, and to others necessary," which is to say that one must give way to others when doing so does not result in harm to oneself. Such "compleasance," or mutual accommodation, is necessary if one is to convey to others a desire to live in peace. Indeed, Hobbes cautions that any person who "by asperity of Nature" and "stubbornness of his Passions" refuses to adapt himself in such a conciliatory manner is "to be left, or cast out of Society, as combersome thereunto" (209).

Hobbes goes on to explain that, according to the sixth law of nature, part of what such "compleasance" entails is the pardoning of offenses. To pardon is "nothing but granting of Peace" (L 15:210). And one should pardon another's offenses when someone repents "*the offences past*," asks for pardon, and gives "*caution of the Future time*" (210). Not to forgive someone under such circumstances is, Hobbes says, a "signe of an aversion to Peace; and therefore contrary to the Law of Nature" (210). In other words, it is to appear to be obstinately combative in the face of assurances about one's security.

Similarly, mutual accommodation requires that when one seeks revenge, one must "*look not at the greatnesse of the evill past, but the greatnesse of the good to follow*" in the future (L 15:210). According to Hobbes's elaboration of the seventh law of nature, to seek to avenge an offense with an eye only to the past "tendeth to the introduction of Warre . . . and is commonly stiled by the name of *Cruelty*" (210). The only peaceable aims for punishment are the "correction of the offender, or direction of others," both of which are concerned to affect others' future behavior. To punish according to the strictures of the seventh law of nature is to present oneself as someone who prefers peace over war.

The eighth law of nature is explicit in its requirement that people cultivate a peaceable public affect. In Hobbes's telling, it enjoins "*[t]hat no man by any deed, word, countenance, or gesture, declare Hatred, or Contempt of another*" (L 15:211). That is, when one finds oneself among people that one scorns or abhors, one must decline from expressing one's true opinions through one's words, gestures, or actions. Although defamation and the casting of aspersions may be—and indeed was in seventeenth-century England—an effective way to force shifts in policy, Hobbes contends that such "signs of hatred and contempt provoke most of all to brawling and fighting," since "most men would rather lose their lives (that I say not, their peace) than suffer slander" (DC 3:142).[18] Consequently, he explains, in the interest of peace one must try to tailor one's affect, gestures, and actions so that they do not insult or undermine people's reputations, "either direct in their Persons, or by reflexion in their Kindred, their Friends, their Nation, their Profession, or their Name" (L 13:185). Even if one thinks one's interlocutor a cad, an idiot, or an insufferable bore, for the sake of peace one must keep one's scorn to oneself and feign, at the very least, a modicum of respect.

The necessity that one not publicly scorn one's interlocutors is reiterated in the ninth law of nature, which stipulates that because "men that think themselves equall, will not enter into conditions of Peace, but upon Equall termes, such equalitie must be admitted" (L 15:211). In other words, when confronted with those whom one believes to be inferior to oneself, one must keep that evaluation from appearing in one's manner of engagement and instead act as if one believes in their equal worth. Explaining this stipulation, Hobbes points out that whatever status, aptitude, or achievements one enjoys, "every man looketh that his companion should value him, at the same rate he sets upon himselfe" and will fight to "extort a greater value from his contemners, by dommage; and from others, by the example" (L 13:185). So in order to avert conflicts and reprisals arising from perceived condescension or insolence, each individual must act as if he or she believes in the fundamental equality of all others. Whether or not one truly believes in the natural equality of each and every person is, in this account, of small consequence. If one is to make one's behavior accord with the injunction to seek peace, one must "*acknowledge other for his Equall by Nature*" in one's gestures, bearing, and actions (L 15:211). Those recalcitrant few who lack the "humility, and patience, to suffer the rude and combersome points of their present greatnesse to be taken off" (L 29:363), "who through their pride, will not stoop to equal conditions, without which there can be no society" (DC 1:110n), will show themselves to be belligerents and thereby run the risk of the social and political exile that is the lot of enemies at war.

The remaining laws of nature specify that one must be amenable to various institutional mechanisms and procedures that promote an environment in which concern for equity and conciliation appears to be at the fore. The tenth draws on the ninth, specifying that no one may reserve rights for herself that she will not grant to others. The eleventh demands equity in judgments resolving controversies between individuals. The next three concern equitable ways to divide common property. The fifteenth requires that conflict mediators be given safe passage. And the remainder elaborate ways to make arbitration of conflicts as fair as possible. As even this précis makes clear, the aim of these latter laws of nature is to secure ahead of time the peaceful resolution of potential discord.

Hobbes's elaboration of the laws of nature suggests that when the primary law of nature commands that we seek peace (L 15:210), it requires that we hold peace—or the pursuit of peace—as a primary commitment in all our doings. The purpose and content of each law of nature point to the demand that peace be the value or goal that orients and directs each of our interactions with one another (216). So we should keep our promises, respond positively to peaceful gestures, contain our irascibility, forgive, and so on, because these create the appearance of an affinity for peace and consequently foster the cause of peace.

If we consider the laws of nature against the backdrop of Hobbes's account of the determination of desire and imagination, they quite clearly draw on his claim that individuals' actions have a causal bearing on one another's desires and actions. The laws of nature suggest that when we abide by the injunction to seek peace, our actions constitute an intersubjective arena visibly dominated by our peace-oriented desires and aims. Our actions bear an immediate effect as actions: we are not immediately selfish, condescending, or vicious, which means that we do not provoke an immediate defensive or vindictive reaction in our interlocutors. But perhaps more importantly, they communicate those of our desires and dispositions that bear the most weight in our deliberations: we signal that we do not intend to be partial or violent in the future, which means that our interlocutors will not feel compelled to orient themselves toward us as if toward a threat. The idea here is that when the peaceableness of our actions prompts others to be peaceable, their peaceableness in turn enables us to be peaceable.

Of course, Hobbes does not pretend that through our adherence to the laws of nature we will be able to control or direct other people's actions narrowly. Rather, his argument proposes that our peaceable actions will produce something akin to a culture of peace, which is to say that they will be among the causes that contribute to the formation of other people's dispositions and intentions. Each peace-oriented act has an effect on the social environment, each works on people's dispositions and passions, each augments the parameters of the processes of deliberation. Together they affect the movements of people's imagination and inflect people's judgments as they consider a course of action for themselves. Indeed, the greater the number of people who engage in such practices, the more seemingly peaceable the collection of relationships in which we all live. So, rather than being a form of direct control over others' actions, our pacific actions and behavior work to deflate the distrust or "diffidence" that Hobbes believes is one of the causes of "warre" (L 13:185). We could say, then, that each individual's adoption of these peace-oriented precepts is a causal antecedent of future peaceable interactions. In fact, Hobbes describes each of the laws of nature he elaborates after the first, fundamental one as "Articles of Peace" (188), as if each were a particle or element of peace that contributes to or transforms a causal series engendering peace. Here we might paraphrase Hobbes's claim in *Of Liberty and Necessity* that "[t]o make the *law,* is . . . to make a *cause* of *justice*" (LN, 253) and say instead that, in his view, to follow the laws of nature is to make a cause of the pursuit of peace.

As mentioned at the beginning of this section, Hobbes's account of the laws of nature can be seen as a part of a larger ethical vision—or as trying to convey or articulate an ethical orientation that is broader than is explicit in the injunction to seek peace. Before exploring that larger vision, however, we should return briefly to the question of lying that opens the chapter. As we have seen, Hobbes is acutely aware of the ways in which our actions and affects influence other people's affects and actions. Drawing on this insight in articulating the laws of nature, he argues that in our public and social interactions, our words, actions, gestures, and anything else that signals our attitudes and intentions must communicate a desire to live in peaceful coexistence. And importantly, when we make our behavior adhere to the third through ninth laws of nature, our gestures, expressions, and actions constitute a form of lying: we promote peace when, by lying, we avoid conveying the contemptuous feelings we may have toward others in our social environment; we promote peace when, by lying, we cover our distaste, contain our hatred, and rein in our evangelistic impulse to broadcast and actualize those among our truths that entail aggression or worse toward those we despise. Whatever our true feelings or opinions about our interlocutors may be, peace can be served only by our not publicly stating those feelings or offering those opinions up for public discussion.[19] When we comply with the demands of the laws of nature, our actions need not—and indeed may not—reflect our beliefs, our creed, or our conviction about the worth of our interlocutors. In fact, what we truly think does not really matter. For according to Hobbes's account of the determination of the imagination and desire, even a rote and fairly unconvincing recitation of the equality or worthiness of those we despise is better than an explicit articulation of our true feelings. The commitment to peace made visible in even a poorly told lie contributes to a broader culture of peace. It provides a form of "assurance to the contrary" of war generative of a social context in which each can anticipate interactions that, however competitive or contestatory they might be, are underwritten by an assurance that violent conflict is not the desired or intended outcome. Lying is ethical, then, when with it we signal or convey to our interlocutors not our disparaging judgments or beliefs but rather our overriding desire for and disposition toward peace.

It is important to emphasize here that Hobbes's ethics does not require that we actually like one another or that we truly respect or appreciate one another. When the laws of nature dictate peace, they do not demand that we be loving and generous in our hearts. Rather, they teach us that the minimum condition of our interactions is a perceptible or visible commitment to ending overt hostility.[20] To specify the character of the ethical practices more precisely: They do not constitute a form of toleration in which the troubling existence of odious interlocutors is passively granted. The laws of nature require an active effort to convey a peace-oriented disposition.[21] Further, the ethical practices outlined by Hobbes do not constitute an art of self-cultivation according to which one endeavors to *become* the kind of person who respects and values each among her interlocutors. They do not require that we each become the object of one another's authentic or heartfelt appreciation. Indeed, the state of one's soul in the face of the other is not what is at stake in Hobbes's ethics. Through the laws of nature, Hobbes does not ask us to attend to how we feel about the other. Rather, he asks us to attend to how we appear to the other in the face of the other. Or to put the point in terms that capture the complexity of the social world inhabited by thinking-bodies: he asks us to attend to how we appear to and affect the many others whose appearances and behavior affect us so profoundly.

As mentioned at the opening of this chapter, the broad ethical vision that informs Hobbes's articulation of the laws of nature concerns just this complex intersubjective form of existence. When he urges us to conceive of ourselves as individuals whose words, actions, and visible attitudes have significant causal bearing upon the dispositions and desires of others, he asks us to imagine ourselves as the constituent elements of a collective, or more particularly, to see ourselves in relationship to the collective of which we are inescapably a part. Hobbes's insight here is that, however hostile we may be toward one another, we are inevitably interrelated. We are always and inescapably social even if we are not sociable. More than this, our actions are always and ineluctably bound up or entangled with the actions of others. In fact, this latter point about the interrelatedness of our actions comes closest to expressing the ethical self-understanding that Hobbes endeavors to articulate in his ethical theory more generally. As we shall see in the final section of this chapter, through his ethics Hobbes tries to get us to think of our individual actions in terms of their intersubjective causes and implications. The idea is not that individuals should think of themselves as part of an integrated whole. Rather, it is that individuals should conceive of themselves as inevitably part of a collective whose constitutive relations have a significant bearing on the possibilities for peace, security, and prosperity that each individual can imagine and pursue.

Ethics and the Collective

Hobbes's elaboration of the laws of nature is not the only occasion on which he argues that intersubjectivity has ethical entailments. In his account of how we should respond to activities that contribute to social and political disorder, he invokes the broader social context that constitutes the conditions of people's actions. More specifically, in his discussions of crime and punishment, he suggests that in assessing an individual's responsibility for a particular action, we should look to the range of that action's causal antecedents. For example, in his analysis of when a fact against the law is to be seen as a crime and when not, Hobbes contends that the circumstances under which the act was committed may either excuse it or mitigate its legal and moral gravity. He claims that a man "is totally Excused" of a crime when he is "destitute of food, or other thing necessary for his life, and cannot preserve himselfe any other way, but by some fact against the Law" (L 27:346). Similarly, he contends that the laws of nature demand lenience in the case of what he calls "Crimes of Infirmity; such as are those which proceed from great provocation, from great fear, great need, or from ignorance" (L 30:389–90). In the case of both excuse and extenuation, then, Hobbes refers us to the conditions formative of desire and imagination. What is at issue is whether the circumstances that condition and are the context of an individual's action are such that we can conceive of that individual as being able to obey the law that his actions contravene. If those conditions are such as to work against the specific individual's being able to perceive obedience as conducive to his self-preservation, that is to say, if obedience is for all intents and purposes impossible, then that individual is absolved of his obligation to obey the law "because no Law can oblige a man to abandon his own preservation" (L 27:345). In fact, Hobbes goes so far as to say that for individuals in those circumstances in which an "accident . . . hath taken away the means to take notice of any particular Law," we must acknowledge that "that Law is no Law to him" and that therefore he "is excused, if he observe it not" (L 26:318). In other words, an individual's obligation to obey the law—and his or her responsibility for infractions against it—extends only as far as the conditions under which deliberation occurs make it possible for that particular thinking-body actually to observe the law in his or her actions.[22]

There are a couple of interesting things about Hobbes's contention that, in the context of crime and punishment, we should consider the conditions formative of the individual's passions, imagination, and deliberative processes precedent to the offensive action in question. The first is that, contrary to the argument that Hobbes's work prefigures a Kantian deontic account of duty, there is a distinctly casuistic character to his thinking.[23] Throughout chapter 27 of *Leviathan* (whose title is "Of Crimes, Excuses, and Extenuations), Hobbes explains the situations and contexts that either aggravate or attenuate individuals' responsibility for crimes they have committed. Included in the circumstances that affect desire and reasoning in such a way as to either extenuate or excuse a crime are fear of immediate physical harm (L 27:343), captivity (345), "terrour of present death" (345), famine (346), evil or misleading teachers (347), examples of crimes committed with impunity (348), and the tacit approval of authorities for formally illegal acts (349). If we take Richard Miller's recent mapping of casuistic moral reasoning as a standard for comparison, Hobbes's focus on the circumstances of an event that might affect our judgment of an action, his formulation of maxims or rules of thumb that should inform our judgment, and his demand that we devise punishments with an eye specifically to their future effects together suggest that he is a casuist in his ethical or moral thinking.[24]

Bolstering the impression that he is a casuist in his ethical and moral thinking, Hobbes evinces an awareness of and an evident discomfort with the disrepute into which Jonsen and Toulmin claim the practice of casuistic reasoning had fallen by the seventeenth century.[25] As if responding to anticipated objections about the corruption facilitated by the flexibility characteristic of casuistic moral reasoning, Hobbes takes special care to distinguish the circumstances that he believes excuse and extenuate a crime from those that do not but might nevertheless be invoked by some individuals. He notes, for instance, that people who are rich or popular or who consider themselves wiser than others may "adventure on Crimes" or "take courage to violate the Lawes" because they presume that "the punishments ordained by the Lawes, and extended generally to all Subjects, ought not to be inflicted on them, with the same rigour they are inflicted on poore, obscure, and simple men" (L 27:341). That is, some people may claim that their particular superiority or distinctiveness shields them from having to be held legally responsible for their actions. Against such arguments, Hobbes insists that the demand for equity found throughout the laws of nature requires that "Justice be equally administred to all degrees of People" and that consequently "the rich, and mighty, . . . [and] the great, may have no greater hope of impunity, when they doe violence, dishonour, or any Injury to the meaner sort, than when one of these, does the like to one of them" (L 30:385). In other words, although the casuistic sensitivity to the importance of the conditions under which people act may relieve some people of complete responsibility for their actions, the conditions that call for such sensitivity do not include great riches, high social status, or proximity to the sovereign power. The casuistic dimensions of Hobbes's ethical and moral thinking are limited to attending to the conditions that make it possible or impossible—quite literally—for a thinking-body to obey the law.

The second interesting thing about Hobbes's argument that we consider the conditions antecedent to and formative of nominally illegal acts is his explicit inclusion of social actors—or social causes more broadly—among those conditions. In the list of extenuating conditions recounted above, he contends that actions committed by teachers, visible public figures, and the sovereign and its officers might and sometimes should be seen as contributing causes to a crime committed by an individual. Significantly, in including such figures as among the causes of an individual's actions, he broadens the cast of actors who might be held responsible for particular acts. In fact, in places he suggests that this collection of accountable persons may extend to include the entire populace or the entire commonwealth.

For instance, in his discussion of the causes of war, Hobbes points out that people who believe that they live in a condition of dire inequity often disturb the peace in their endeavor to recast the political conditions that dealt them such a poor hand. As he puts it, "needy men, and hardy, not contented with their present condition . . . are enclined to continue the causes of warre; and to stirre up trouble and sedition: for there is no . . . such hope to mend an ill game, as by causing a new shuffle" (L 11:162). Now, in Hobbes's general schema, to "continue the causes of warre" when others are coordinating their actions with one another for the sake of peace is to go against the imperative that organizes the laws of nature.[26] To break a *civil* law in order to initiate a figurative reshuffle is to reserve rights to oneself that one does not grant to others, a reservation that is not permitted by the laws of nature that call for equity. However, in the case of "needy men, not contented with their present condition," Hobbes appears to withhold his (and our) censure: for as we saw above, Hobbes believes that there may be circumstances and social causes that make it impossible to act in accordance with the law and indeed that abrogate one's obligation to do so. According to this line of reasoning, to break the peace with the aim of rectifying a situation in which living itself is impossible is something for which individuals should not be condemned or punished.

This particular point of Hobbes's argument would seem to make him a supporter if not an advocate of revolution—an appearance that is certainly contrary to the Hobbes of our commonplace understanding.[27] However, he makes such claims not as an advocate of revolution but as an analyst of action undertaken by thinking-bodies, an analyst of those conditions that affect whether we are able to do one thing rather than another. Hardly a champion of order-breaking, peace-disturbing revolution, Hobbes is making the point that if miserable conditions of existence compel people to try to reshuffle the political order, then the political collective must take responsibility for those conditions. In fact, he claims that "whereas many men, by accident unevitable, become unable to maintain themselves by their labour; they ought not to be left to the Charity of private persons; but to be provided for, (as far-forth as the necessities of Nature require,) by the Lawes of the Common-wealth" (L 30:387). When such assistance or protection from the commonwealth is not forthcoming, he argues, individuals cannot rightly be censured for acting so as to defend against perceived threats to their lives.[28] Or to put the point differently, since the collective has a real interest in fostering an orientation toward peace rather than conflict, the commonwealth must attend actively to the material and social conditions within which people's dispositions are formed, which is to say that it is responsible for ensuring that each individual's need for "food, or other thing necessary for life" is somehow met.

The characterization of the relationship between the individual and the collective that emerges through Hobbes's casuistic discussion of crime and punishment is the same as that he forwards through his account of the laws of nature. Individuals always act in a field whose material and social elements are significant factors in the development of the dispositions and judgments that lead to action. Every individual's behavior is a causal factor in other individuals' behavior. To be aware of one's own and others' actions as moments in these complex causal chains is to be better able to anticipate the possibilities for and consequences of particular activities and interactions. It is to be able to imagine what kinds of behavior and interactions might lead to peace and to be able to prepare the conditions for the pursuit of peace in oneself as well as in others. So, in arguing that we must conceive of actions both in terms of the social relations that are their context and partial cause and in terms of the contribution they make to the conditions for future actions, Hobbes tries to do two things: to capture the complexity of each individual's relationship to the collective and to compel us to be cognizant of that relationship when we act.

Conclusion

There are a number of insights I would like to draw from the ethics that Hobbes develops through his materialist determinism. The first is that we are inevitably related to one another through the happenstance of our cohabitation. That is to say, individuals are always embedded in and a part of a collective, whether the relations that constitute that collective are harmonious, fractious, or violent, transient, temporary, or permanent. Hobbes's portrayal of our unavoidable interrelationship means that we cannot conceive of ourselves as solitary actors: our actions are never self-contained, either in their causes or in their effects. In his view, then, the simple and undeniable fact of intersubjectivity must be at the center of any account of ethical action. In other words, when we consider the moral imperatives that should guide our actions, we must think of ourselves as elements of a social collective that unavoidably has an effect upon our actions, while our actions unavoidably shape it in turn.

A second insight concerns the relationship between the self and the ethical injunction to seek peace. In Hobbes's argument, to orient oneself to others in the peaceful manner he enjoins does not require a surrender of the self to the collective. That is, it does not entail that individuals abjure their own desires for the sake of promoting the collective well-being. Now, Hobbes's refusal to demand such self-sacrifice does not derive from a stipulation that thinking-bodies are driven by a raw egoism that makes selflessness impossible. Rather, the account of intersubjectivity that is a corollary of his deterministic materialism disrupts the binary opposition between self-interest and a regard for others. What emerges instead is an ethical self-understanding that rests on a self-regard routed through a regard for the many others—or for the many relationships—that constitute the context of our existence. The idea Hobbes forwards here is that the interest we have in our own security and preservation and the care we take to foster them are inextricably bound up with the responsibility we assume for the quality of the relationships that constitute the context for our actions. This is not to say that he believes that there is a coincidence between the common good and the private good. In fact, he is quite clear that the artificiality of the collective and the diversity of objects of desire are such that there can be no identity between the common good and individual goods (L 17:226). His insight, rather, is that we cannot pursue our own security without also attending to the assemblage of relationships that constitute the context for that pursuit. Or to put the point the other way around, the responsibility we assume for those relationships is integral to our effort to look after ourselves.

The third and final insight is related to the first two, and it concerns the status or character of the desire for peace that Hobbes portrays as the very foundation of his ethics. In his elaboration of his injunction that we seek peace, Hobbes seems to presume that we genuinely hold the desire for peace that we convey through our behavior. Or, at least, his demand that we contrive to appear as if we desire peace above all raises the question of whether or not that appearance is or must be an expression of an authentic, heartfelt disposition. What is at stake in such a question is whether the ethical subject values peace as a good in itself or whether she values it merely as a means to another end. However, this question presses as a question when we assume that the ethical moment can lie only in the self's attitude or orientation toward a principle. And as mentioned at the outset of this chapter, and as we have seen in the discussion throughout, Hobbes is concerned not with the state of our souls but rather with the consequences of individuals' interactions for the quality of the relationships that constitute the determinative context for future interactions. In other words, for him, the true feelings and thoughts of an ethical subject are less important than her interactions and their effects. Of course, the desire for peace must be pragmatically or actively genuine; if subjects were not actually to have the desire for peace, peaceable actions would themselves be impossible. But for Hobbes, the question of whether someone desires peace in principle or whether she desires peace for instrumental reasons does not really matter. What does matter is whether an individual's actions contribute to the production of a culture in which peace seems to be everyone's primary disposition.

If such a response to the query about the authenticity of the desire for peace seems to sidestep the question rather than answer it, that is because the ethics Hobbes derives from his materialist determinism does not proceed on the assumption that self-regard and ethical regard for the other are necessarily mutually opposed. Indeed, the very fact of intersubjectivity makes any such opposition difficult to sustain. For Hobbes, when individuals produce a culture of peace, they produce social conditions favorable to their own individual preservation. In fact, in his view, peaceful relations in the collective of which they are inescapably a part are a condition for individuals' pursuit of their own security.

But of course Hobbes's point is not simply that we must try to get along peacefully. Admittedly, he does portray "continuall feare, and danger of violent death" as among the worst consequences of the ongoing insecurity incident to the condition of war (L 13:186). To follow his ethics, then, is to mitigate the fearfulness that plagues individuals who live under the seeming threat of imminent hostility. However, in Hobbes's view, there are other costs to war as well: industry, culture, the arts and letters, philosophy, science, and so forth (186). In other words, acutely and uncomfortably aware of how war squanders individual lives and desolates individual livelihoods, Hobbes also appreciates that war is just a terrible and tragic waste of the collective goods that arise as a consequence of individuals' pursuit of their specific goals and happiness. In social conditions in which ongoing peace is not an assured aim, a society cannot thrive and prosper. The reason for such stultification is that, in conditions of insecurity, "the fruit" of individuals' activities "is uncertain" (186). And what makes the fruit of individual initiative so hopelessly uncertain is not the possibility of theft—although theft is indeed a possibility (184–86). Rather—and importantly—uncertainty about what individuals can accomplish rests on the inability of individuals to act alone. According to Hobbes's materialist account of causation, it is not simply the case that individuals shape one another's desires and thoughts through their encounters and engagements. They also share the conditions for action, which is to say that they cannot act effectively but with the coincidence or support of others' actions. In other words, as we shall see in the discussion of Hobbes's theory of power in the next chapter, we must elevate the pursuit of peaceful social relations to priority of place because we are profoundly interdependent in our actions.

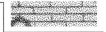

The Action and Passion of Politics

Hobbes on Power

When one proposes to talk about Hobbes and power, two images—and a problem—spring to mind. The first image is of the notorious Hobbesian individual, a solitary and rapacious warrior driven by self-interest to pursue power relentlessly and to destroy anyone who stands in the way. In the plural, these individuals are drawn ineluctably into a conflict that cannot but escalate into a freewheeling, chaotic war of all against all. Indeed, in the nightmarish scenario that a population of such individuals promises, violence is the only certainty, insecurity is the commonplace, and no one can be counted as a friend. The second image is of the equally notorious Hobbesian sovereign, frequently figured as a monarch, the sole possessor of an absolute power that serves as the instrument for the imposition of order on the unruly, bellicose individuals described above. Positioned outside of the law, constitutively incapable of committing injustice, and beyond recall or accountability, this awful sovereign uses the threat of his punishment to inspire and compel each individual to obedience. And the problem, of course, is how these mutually antagonistic individuals could possibly pause their fighting for long enough collectively to constitute the sovereign, whose formidable power will force them to hold their warring impulses in check. To be clear, the problem is not *why* they might do this—why they might give up their tumultuous and fear-ridden liberty and subject themselves to the fearful yet ordering power of a sovereign. Hobbes famously says that fear and reason suggest that both order and peace are more desirable than war (L 15:216). Rather, the problem consists in imagining the initial transition from war to sovereign-constituting covenant to order and peace: how might these hostile and mutually estranged individuals possibly be brought into relation with one another?

That this is the problem posed by both the destructive pursuit of power by individuals and the terrible power of the sovereign is, on the face of it, the result of Hobbes's not offering us, as Locke did, a narrative of the transition from war to peace: he does not tell the tale of how these monstrous individuals come to exercise the fundaments of cooperation to authorize a sovereign to rule over them all.[1] This seeming aporia in Hobbes's political theory has inspired many a fine text. However, the moment of the covenant remains somewhat murky in some of the best analyses and often is glossed over through the linguistic fiat of the interpreter or teacher: "and so they covenant." In this chapter, I want to suggest that the coordination problem that is seemingly produced by a narrative insufficiency is not actually the problem that grips Hobbes's theoretical imagination and orients his political thinking.[2] In fact, this particular formulation of the political problem posed and addressed by Hobbes misses the insights about intersubjectivity and interdependence generated by his materialist metaphysics. In what follows, then, I won't so much resolve the puzzle of the original agreement as put it aside and suggest that, for Hobbes, a different question is at stake.

What is at issue for Hobbes is the nature of power. That is, he seeks to come to grips with how we should understand the workings of political power and authority once they have been denaturalized and secularized and are seen as the product of human artifice (L intro.: 82). To pose the issue in terms informed by our analysis of Hobbes's materialism: how are we to conceptualize political power and authority in the context of heteronomy?

In the preceding chapters of this book, I have argued that Hobbes's materialist acknowledgment of the fact of intersubjectivity requires that we attend to the temporality of our self-knowledge, of our desires and thoughts, and of our effects upon one another in our social interactions. Hobbes's account of power also requires that we attend to the temporality of actions. As we shall see, in his philosophical arguments, Hobbes conceives of power as prospective cause, which is to say that it is the collection of causes that together will produce an act in the future. And when he moves from his philosophical to his political account of power, he likewise portrays power as the conditions for future action: the fact of interdependence—the fact that we are contributing causes to one another's actions—means that to think about power is to take into account our future interdependence.

Hobbes's proposal that power entails an orientation toward the future is at the center of his analysis of the pursuit of power more generally as well as his analysis of sovereign power. In both analyses, he suggests that power seekers are not just aware of the ways in which events and interactions occurring in the present produce and circumscribe the possibilities for future success. They also deliberately foster the conditions for future actions in the course of their current undertakings. Hobbes's aim in elucidating the attention to the future that is implicit in the effort to acquire power is not to persuade us to consider long-term rather than short-term interest—as if what is at issue is the hardship and reward of delayed gratification. Rather, his aim is to get us to recognize that when we seek to foster the conditions for the possibility of future actions, we must recognize that enduring peace is foremost among those conditions. In other words, for Hobbes, because we act under conditions of heteronomy, because we are interdependent, the pursuit of peace is integral to the pursuit of power.

Cause and Power

The most enduring fable about Hobbes's account of power is the notion that, for the individual and the sovereign alike, power is a crass instrument used to bend the world to the one's will, to forcibly extract resources for the satisfaction of desire, to bludgeon people into obedient submission. In other words, it is a tool for domination—of the earth, of women, of individuals—and indeed, for many queasy readers of Hobbes—of vibrant political life and the human spirit itself.[3] However, to characterize what we might term "Hobbesian power" as something like "offensive and defensive strength against others" (Macpherson, 37) is to subscribe to a conception of the subject as the origin of her action; the notion that a subject is an agent who might "use" power to compel others to do what she wishes is tied up implicitly with the conception of free will that is part of the dualist framework that Hobbes rejects with his materialism. To put the point differently, the common impression of Hobbes's description of power comes from a reading that does not give enough weight—if it gives any at all—to his materialist metaphysics and to the accounts of causation, power, and action that it entails.

One of the most striking features of Hobbes's definition of power is his focus on the conditions that coalesce to produce an act or an event. That is to say, he discusses power in the same terms as he does cause and effect. In fact, to say that he discusses them in the same terms is not strong enough, for he actually claims that power is the very same thing as cause, "though, for divers considerations, they have divers names" (DCO 10:127).

The diverse names we give to the phenomena we know as cause and power come from temporal considerations. Hobbes explains that we use the term "cause" "in respect of the effect already produced, and power in respect of the same effect to be produced hereafter; so that *cause* respects the past, *power* the future time" (127–28). In other words, we use the terms "cause" and "effect" retrospectively to talk about what has already taken place; we use the terms "power" and "act" prospectively to talk about what we anticipate will happen. However, despite this difference in temporal perspective, cause and effect are essentially equivalent to power and act. This equivalence is important, for it means that Hobbes's analyses of cause and effect hold for his analyses of power and act—and not simply his more technical metaphysical analyses of the power and action of physical objects, but also, as we shall see, his analyses of social and political power, that is, the power of individuals, groups, and the sovereign.

As we saw in our discussion of causality in Chapter 3, for Hobbes, any event is the product of a complex series of causal factors. In other words, every event or act is effected by the confluence of numerous conditions at a particular moment. What is pertinent for this particular discussion, however, is that in his discussion of cause and effect in *De Corpore*, Hobbes analytically resolves an event or act into two distinguishable elements. On the one hand, there is the body whose movement "generates motion" in another body (DCO 9:120). This "generative" body is what Hobbes calls the agent of an act; its motion is "action." On the other hand, there is the body in which the movement is generated. This moved body is what Hobbes calls the patient; its motion is "passion." (Let me note that this term "passion" is better than the term "passive" since we tend to think of or hear "passivity" as inactivity or lack of movement. The term "passion" better captures Hobbes sense of "being moved," a responsive motion, or a susceptibility to reactive movement.)

There are a couple of interesting things to point out about Hobbes's mapping of an event here. The first is his suggestion that when we consider events more broadly, every body is both an agent and a patient. Hobbes states that if an agent and a patient are contiguous or next to one another, then the relationship between the agent and patient is immediate (in the sense of being unmediated) (DCO 9:120). However, if the two bodies are not contiguous, then the relationship between agent and patient is mediated. The body that mediates the agent and patient is itself considered to be both an agent and a patient, "an agent in respect of the body next after it, upon which it works, and a patient in respect of the body next before it, from which it suffers" (DCO 9:121). Hobbes's claim that a body is both an agent and a patient with respect to the other agents and patients around it is important, for it recapitulates aspects of the argument we encountered in Chapter 3—namely, that we must think about specific acts not simply in terms of their immediate causes and immediate intended effects but rather in terms of the chains of causal antecedents as well as the "long chaynes of consequences" that continue to unfold after a particular act can be said to have taken place.[4] For a body to be only an agent, it would have to be a first cause, which according to Hobbes is a speculative inference to which we sometimes give the name "God."[5] In other words, in the mundane world in which we live, an agent simpliciter simply does not exist: a causal agent is always and inevitably also a patient, acted upon and compelled to act by other causal forces. Similarly, for a body to be only a patient, the act that proceeded from it would have to be the final act, the last effect, an event after which there is no other event or act. Such a last effect is as yet unthinkable, except perhaps for those who might subscribe to some apocalyptic vision of the end of the world. The prospects of apocalypse aside, suffice it to say that every patient is always and inevitably also an agent, acting upon other bodies and compelling further movement. To put the point shortly, in remarking that every body is both agent and patient, Hobbes prompts us to remember that although we may be inclined to isolate events and think of them in terms of their immediacy, every event is produced by and contributes to manifold and complex causal chains.

A second interesting aspect of Hobbes's claim that an event consists in the motion of an agent and a patient is his contention that both agent and patient are necessary for the event to occur. As we saw in Chapter 3, the causes that produce a particular effect are manifold rather than singular. Accordingly, Hobbes contends that an agent's motion is generated by a collection of factors that together constitute what he calls the "efficient cause." Likewise, the patient's passion—its movability with respect to the agent, or rather its being-moved when acted upon by the agent—is the product of the coalescence of a range of factors that together constitute what Hobbes calls the "material cause." And importantly, the cause of any event is "the sum or aggregate of all the accidents, as well in the agent as in the patient, which are requisite for the production of the effect" (DCO 10:128). That is, what makes an event occur is the coincidence of all the necessary factors, both in the acting body as well as in the body acted upon, in the agent as well as in the patient. In fact, Hobbes defines all these factors together as the "whole cause" or the "entire cause": neither the efficient cause nor the material cause alone but rather the entire cause produces an effect.

This notion of an entire cause is crucial to understanding Hobbes's account of an act or event, for he argues that if just one factor among either the efficient or the material causes is missing, then the effect will not be produced. As he puts it, "the efficient and material causes are severally and by themselves parts only of an entire cause, and cannot produce any effect but by being joined together" (129). In short, all the factors constituting the motion of both the agent and the patient must be present in order to produce an effect: each is the necessary supplement of the other. As with Hobbes's point that each body is both agent and patient, Hobbes's insistence that agents and patients each require the other in all their fullness if a specific act is to occur reminds us not to narrow our analytic focus to consider only the immediate agent of an event or act (as is our wont) but rather to attend to the broad array of efficient and material causes that together—and only together—produce any event.

When Hobbes claims that cause and effect are equivalent to power and act—with the latter two distinguished from the former two only by an orientation toward the future—he requires that we think about power in terms of the efficient and material causes that will coalesce to occasion an act. In doing so, Hobbes rejects the idea that power is a characteristic or accident of something or someone (131). That is, he denies that power could inhere in a body as if it "had" power or could be said to "be" powerful irrespective of the conditions around it. To the contrary, in specifying that power consists in the spectrum of causes that will coincide at a particular moment to occasion an act, Hobbes suggests that power is not a property of a body but rather a situation in which a body finds itself: power consists in a particular configuration of numerous causal factors in a given context.

When Hobbes talks about the power of agents and patients, he describes the causal motion of agents as "active power" and the causal motion of patients as "passive power." Correspondingly, just as an effect requires both efficient and material causes—action and passion—so an act requires both active and passive power. As Hobbes explains, "the power of the agent and patient together, which may be called entire or *plenary power,* is the same thing with *entire cause;* for they both consist in the sum or aggregate of all the accidents, as well in the agent as in the patient, which are requisite for the production of the effect" (128). Hobbes's claim that "plenary" power is "requisite for the production of the effect" is important, for it means that active power and passive power are conditioned by one another. Active power can do its work only if there is an appropriate patient to be acted upon; likewise, passive power can do its work of being acted upon only if there is action from an appropriate agent. In fact, Hobbes contends that just as "the efficient and material causes are severally and by themselves parts only of an entire cause, and cannot produce any effect but by being joined together, so also power, active and passive, are parts only of plenary and entire power; nor, except they be joined, can any act proceed from them" (129). In other words, if any of the elements that constitute a patient are not present at a particular moment, then at that moment there is no "active power" for a particular prospective act, even if the agent is missing nothing in the collection of factors that would constitute its efficient cause. Likewise, if any of the factors that constitute the agent are not present at a particular moment, then at that moment there is no "passive power" for a specific prospective act, even if the patient is missing nothing in the collection of factors that would constitute its material cause. The active power of an agent depends upon the passive power of a patient to make an act take place; the passive power of the patient depends upon the active power of an agent to produce an effect. According to Hobbes, then, when we think about power, we need to consider all of the active and passive powers that together constitute the "plenary and entire power" to generate an event. Here, again, he suggests that we eschew the tendency to think of acts in terms of an agent whose energy and power are both self-originating and the single cause of an act. Instead, Hobbes pushes us to think of acts in terms of the broad conditions for their occasion.

The Action and Passion of Power: Individuals

In what may come as a surprise to many of his readers, when Hobbes discusses power that people have or pursue, he continues to define it in terms of the broad array of conditions that will occasion an act. And as I shall argue below, when he takes account of the conditions that contribute to the possibility of individuals acting—not just the prospective efficient causes but also the prospective material causes, not just the active power but also the passive power—Hobbes gives us an unexpected picture of the social relations generated by the generalized pursuit of power. If we read Hobbes's account of power through his materialism, we disrupt the iconographic image of hostile strangers coming to arms. Indeed, as we have found in previous chapters, it turns out that the Hobbesian subject is not the isolated belligerent of political theory lore. Rather, it is an anxious, watchful person ineluctably embedded in a tangle of tense and fragile relationships that serve as the conditions for possible action: a lonely subject perhaps, but not alone. In Hobbes's telling, then, the pursuit of power does not necessarily or only tear us apart. It also brings us together. That is to say, the pursuit of power both depends upon and produces a form of sociality characterized by mobile relations of hierarchically patterned interdependence.

Before I can elaborate Hobbes's account of "people power," however, I must address the possible objection that it might be both philosophically and politically suspect to claim that an analysis of power and act among objects explains equally well the power and actions of people. The concern here centers on the question of whether Hobbes's contention that power is prospective causality reduces social and political action to a kind of vectorial physics—something no more interesting than a mere series of movements determined by the event of people bumping into one another. As Hanna Pitkin points out, we tend to want to distinguish between the actions of objects and the actions of humans. According to this philosophical stance, the actions of objects are properly described as events subject to and determined by the laws of physical causation. Things "happen" and objects are simply caught up in the various flows of causal necessity. In the case of humans, to the contrary, we talk of choice, self-determination, and free will—a constellation of concepts that marks our freedom from the laws of physical causation and that signals our status as agents. In this view, choosing defines the capacity to act and "distinguishes man from the rest of nature. Only human beings can act."[6] However, as we saw in Chapter 3, the notion that our agency or our capacity to choose and act can be explained only via recourse to free will is bound up with a dualist philosophical framework. More particularly, it springs from a conception of determinism that is beholden to a dualism in which matter is essentially inert. As we have seen, Hobbes rejects both a conception of matter as inert and an account of determinism as unilinear or unitemporal. To the contrary, within the terms of his materialism, he elaborates a temporally complex determinism in which it is possible both to distinguish between the actions of inanimate and animate forms of matter—or objects and people—and yet to draw on the same account of causation when explaining both. Indeed, it is through his analysis of the material, intersubjective, and temporal aspects of perception that he explains how the pursuit of power, conceived as the conditions for action, produces and is the product of complex social and symbolic formations.

Hobbes's description of perception is crucial to his account of power. In fact, as we shall see, he argues that perceptual evaluations combine with their expression in practices of honoring and dishonoring to make both the pursuit of power and the actions made possible by power not simply a social physics derived from chains of material causality but, rather, complex social symbolic processes. As we saw in Chapter 1, in Hobbes's analysis the very process of perception involves a reaction or evaluation on the part of the perceiving thinking-body (L 1:85). A perceptual evaluation is an affective response of the thinking-body to the object before it—a motion toward or away from the object according to whether the perceptual motions it generates in the thinking-body are experienced as threatening or beneficial to the thinking-body's well-being (L 6:118–20). The motion that constitutes that perceptual evaluation—or what Hobbes rather unsurprisingly calls the passion—transforms the thinking-body, altering physical movements, redirecting thought patterns, precipitating new gestures or complexions, and generally reorienting the body within the context of its activities. Indeed, as Stephen Darwall has pointed out, for Hobbes's subject, a perceptual evaluation does not take the form of an intellectual cognition linguistically registered as "this object is good" that provokes the subject to make a decision and to formulate a deliberate response. Rather, an evaluation is composed of all the reactions and adjustments precipitated through the process of perceiving itself.[7]

Many of Hobbes's insights about power turn on the significance he attributes to people's observation of one another, that is, to their status as both agents and objects of a public gaze. As we saw in Chapter 4, this ability to imagine oneself as the object of a public gaze is the key to Hobbes's account of ethics. He enjoins us to be aware of how other people's perceptions of our actions and intentions might shape their dispositions toward us and suggests that the presentation of a pacific orientation will generate a likewise peaceable disposition in our interlocutors. In his analyses of power, Hobbes extends his insight that the very process of perception entails evaluation to contend that one of the critical factors generative of power is individuals' perceptions of one another's opinions about who is powerful. Depicting power, again, as a matter of the conditions for action, he observes that individuals evince a keen awareness of the significance of their visibility and of public opinion for people's perception of their power. In other words, he claims that, in considerably large part, power is an effect of perception and reputation. But before we can explore how and why this is so, we must examine his argument that, for thinking-bodies as for objects, power is a matter of the conditions that coalesce to produce an act.

Hobbes contends that "the object of mans desire, is not to enjoy once onely, and for one instant of time; but to assure for ever, the way of his future desire" (L 11:160–61). In his view, people are not content with the mere satisfaction of a desire in the present moment. Rather than being occupied by the pleasures of immediate sensual gratification and the simple avoidance of pain, Hobbes's subjects are bound to the future. That is, they are driven by a combination of experience, foresight, and the very basic desire to persevere to ensure that they can realize their future desires. Hobbes's sense, here, that humans find themselves "in a perpetuall solicitude of the time to come" (L 12:169) is important, for it marks again the peculiar temporality of subjects conceived as thinking-bodies: individuals conceive of their actions not in terms of immediate circumstances and singular events but rather in terms of retrospective and prospective chains of causation. Indeed, Hobbes claims that it is because every individual wants to "assure for ever, the way of his future desire" that each is inclined to "a perpetuall and restlesse desire of Power after power" (L 11:161). If the desire to assure the way of future desire leads to the "desire of Power after power," then the "perpetuall and restlesse desire of Power after power" must be portrayed, generally, as the desire to secure the conditions for the future realization of future desires—which is exactly how Hobbes portrays it. In his view, the pursuit of the power necessary to assure the way of future desire is not a brutish and violent clash of interests but rather a project requiring a complex temporal orientation and attention to the many social and material conditions that will provide for the occasion of acting in the future.

When Hobbes discusses "the Power of a Man," he essentially recapitulates his philosophical account of power as the conditions that coalesce to produce an effect. In a statement that echoes his claim that power is prospective causality, he declares that "[t]he Power *of a Man*, (to take it Universally,) is his present means, to obtain some future apparent Good" (L 10:150). At a first reading, this depiction of power as someone's "present means" suggests that power is something personal—particular to and possibly the possession of a specific person. However, as Hobbes elaborates upon this claim, it becomes clear that a person's "power" consists in the conditions that enable him or her to realize a desire—and that those conditions are largely social. According to Hobbes's argument, as in the case of physical objects, so with people; power comprises the collection of both efficient and material causes—the actions and the passions—that together will produce an act. Indeed, Hobbes describes people as both the efficient causes of their own actions and the material causes of one another's actions. Or to be more specific, he portrays the material conditions for each individual's successful action as constituted in large part by other people's characteristics, skills, and actions. He characterizes power as the ability to gather those people and their skills and energies together for the purpose of realizing a specific desire. And he depicts individuals' pursuit of power as the effort to ensure that the material causes—or other people's passions—are prepared to respond to and move with some future active initiative.

When Hobbes defines power, he divides it analytically into *"Naturall Power"* and *"Instrumentall"* power. Natural power is "the eminence of the Faculties of Body, or Mind," or qualities peculiar to a specific agent that contribute to the production of a desired effect (L 10:150). And what is remarkable about those faculties or qualities is that their power lies in their social effects. That is, when Hobbes describes the various natural powers, which include "Strength, Forme, Prudence, Arts, Eloquence, Liberality, [and] Nobility" (150), they turn out to be those qualities of body and mind that dispose people well to one another and incline them to association, friendship, and assistance (150–51). As Hobbes explains it, "forme," or beauty, is power because it seems to promise something good and "recommendeth men to the favour of women and strangers"; eloquence is power because "it is seeming Prudence," a characteristic that makes people willing to "commit the government" of themselves to the prudent person; liberality is power because, combined with riches, "it procureth friends, and servants"; and affability is power because "it gaineth love" (150–51). As even this small number of examples suggests, natural powers are important because they enable the well-endowed individual to gather other people together for the purpose of getting something done. Or to put the point in the more technical language of Hobbes's philosophical account of power, an individual's natural powers solicit and work with the passive powers of others, appealing to their sense of possibility and their aspiration to succeed in what they do in such a way that those others become the agents of the individual's action.

It is because they make other people into agents that Hobbes contends that natural powers enable individuals to acquire instrumental power (L 10:150). Hobbes defines instrumental power as the "means and Instruments to acquire more" power (150). Such means and instruments are resources that an agent acquires or can draw upon in order to produce a desired effect. And again, in his description, they are particularly social in character. For example, Hobbes explains that riches are power because wealth "procureth friends, and servants"; servants and friends are power, "for they are strengths united"; and prior success is power "because it maketh reputation of Wisdome, or good fortune; which makes men either feare him, or rely on him" (150–51). In fact, Hobbes contends, "what quality soever maketh a man beloved, or feared of many . . . is Power; because it is a means to have the assistance, and service of many" (151). So, instrumental power is the array of conditions that earn an individual the assistance and obedience of others in his or her projects and undertakings. Here, again, Hobbes's emphasis is on the ability to solicit or win the skills, cooperation, or compliance of others.

It is important to stress here that in his recounting of both natural and instrumental power, Hobbes defines power in terms of relationships of assistance, cooperation, and service. In doing so, he suggests that the "Power of a Man," or "his present means, to obtain some future apparent Good" (L 10:150), consists not just in an individual's personal skills and efforts but also in the receptiveness to his action present in the conditions in which he endeavors to act, in the willingness or propensity of others to take up the initiative and to see it through to its realization. To put the point shortly, an individual's power to act consists not simply in the action of that individual agent but also in the passion of others. In discussing people power, then, Hobbes clearly draws upon his contention that the plenary power that makes something happen consists in the combination of active and passive power: although an individual may have the initiative, skills, and energies constitutive of active power, he or she will not be able actually to "act," or be effective in realizing a particular desire, without the various social conditions and resources constitutive of that act's passive power.

With power conceived as prospective passion as well as prospective action, the pursuit of power identified by Hobbes must be seen as including the effort by individuals to figure out how to acquire or harness other people's characteristics, skills, and actions for their own ends. And of course, such an effort requires an attentiveness to others, and to one's relationships with others, through time. That is, in specifying the importance of passive power for any act, Hobbes suggests that the conditions for the future realization of one person's future desires are bound up with the conditions for the future realization of other people's future desires. The characteristics, skills, and energies that belong to other people and that constitute, in part, the passive power for one individual's act also, at the same time, constitute the active power of those other people, active power that derives its direction from those people's various desires and that depends in turn upon other passive powers to be effective. This imbrication of individuals' active and passive powers requires that, in the pursuit of power, individuals be concerned about more than the present moment and immediate gain. Instead, they must orient themselves within a horizon of time and consider the array of conditions that, over time, will enable them to realize their desires. That is, in their relentless pursuit of power, in their effort to secure the conditions for their future realization of their future desires, they must concern themselves with the passions of others and with the effects of their own and other people's actions upon those passions in the future. More than this, since, collectively, individuals' active and passive powers are mutually dependent upon one another, each individual must take into account and even work to enhance the conditions for other people's successful action as part of their effort to enhance the conditions for their own. So, as we see in Hobbes's description of the various forms of alliances that constitute power, we get an ironic twist on the Hobbes story we generally tell: the ineluctable orientation toward the future combines with the pursuit of power to bind Hobbesian subjects to one another.

Of course, in arguing that the pursuit of power involves this mutual attention and engagement, Hobbes does not suggest that people engage in their efforts in unified harmony. To the contrary, he acknowledges explicitly that the conditions for one person's success sometimes contravene those of another. Hobbes states quite clearly that "[c]ompetition of Riches, Honour, Command, or other power, enclineth to Contention, Enmity, and War: Because the way of one Competitor, to the attaining of his desire, is to kill, subdue, supplant, or repell the other" (L 11:161). In other words, sometimes individuals collide in their efforts to gain power or to secure the conditions for the future realization of future desires. When they do so, conflicts arise. It is this observation by Hobbes that informs the familiar account of the pursuit of power as characterized by mutual efforts to kill and destroy.

However, in his analyses of power, Hobbes also tells another story—one that is often overlooked—in which not conflict but instead (at least grudging) cooperation is the outcome of the pursuit of power. Hobbes contends that although "all men, tend, not only to the procuring, but also to the assuring of a contented life," they "differ . . . in the way," or in the figurative paths they take, both because of "the diversity of passions, in divers men" and because their different experiences lead them to different conclusions about "the causes, which produce the effect desired" (L 11:161). That is, even though every one of us wants to ensure our continued well-being, the diversity of our desires and the differences in our opinions about how to realize them do not necessarily put our paths into direct conflict. As is implied in the patterns of friendship and service that Hobbes claims characterize different kinds of people power, even though individuals may not share objects of desire, their assessments about the conditions for successful action may coincide. And when the pursuit of power requires people to take advantage of the same conditions for action, people enter into associations—and I am speaking here not of the covenant that constitutes the sovereign, but rather of lesser associations wrought of the interdependence of the conditions for individuals' success. So, in addition to compelling us to "kill, subdue, supplant, or repell" one another, the pursuit of power also requires that we endeavor to win friends and servants, through various means, who might provide the assistance, support, or "passive power" that can transform an initiative into an accomplishment.

And of course, this point about winning friends and servants can be told from a different perspective. Just as for some the pursuit of power entails *recruiting* others, so for those others, the pursuit of power entails being *recruited*. That is, the effort to secure the conditions for the future realization of future desires may involve *giving* assistance and obedience—being the friend or the servant—in exchange for the support and protection that such a relationship might provide. In an anticipatory reflection that accounts for chains of complex causality, such individuals consider the ways in which their current characteristics, skills, and actions might contribute to the conditions for other people's actions in such a way that those people's actions will enhance the conditions for their future realization of their own future desires. Their passion may combine with another's action to create the passions for their own future actions. Accordingly, as Hobbes's account of the relationships formed through the pursuit of power suggests, some people hitch their proverbial horses to other people's carts. Or to be less metaphorical, they work with and for other people as a way to enhance the possibility of succeeding in their own future endeavors.

Such a move is not quite the paradox that it might appear to be. Hobbes is quite clear that each person considers himself or herself best able to govern his or her own affairs (L 13:183–84). But his discussion of power suggests that if someone has the wisdom, prudence, wealth, friends, or servants that enable her to succeed in her endeavors, that is to say, if someone is powerful, then others may decide to "commit the government" of themselves to that person as part of their efforts to secure the conditions for their own future success (151). Hobbes explains in a different context that "the motive, and end" that prompts such a transference of the right to govern oneself "is nothing else but the security of a mans person, in his life, and in the means of so preserving life, as not to be weary of it" (L 14:192). Or as he observes in a yet different discussion, "[t]he end of Obedience is Protection; which, wheresoever a man seeth it, either in his own, or in anothers sword, Nature applyeth his obedience to it, and his endeavour to maintain it" (L 21:272). In other words, people "commit the government" of themselves to powerful others when the alliance enhances the conditions for their future actions. Again, and crucially, this is not to say that the more powerful and the less powerful in the relationship are united in an effort to attain shared goals or common objects of desire. Rather, it is to say that for each, the other's powers or conditions for action constitute at least some of the conditions for his or her own action. Through the relationship, each individual augments her power; each enhances the conditions for the future realization of her future desires.

Now, in addition to laying out the different kinds of power manifested in various forms of relationship, Hobbes also provides insight into how those relationships and the power they promise are disrupted, transformed, or augmented. In fact, in his discussion of power, reputation, and honor he suggests that the relationships that serve as the conditions for people's future actions are not at all static but rather are continually under challenge and constantly in flux.

According to Hobbes, many of the conditions for action that constitute an individual's power to realize a desire have something to do with reputation. For example, in addition to claiming that "what quality soever maketh a man beloved, or feared of many . . . is Power," he also asserts that "the reputation of such quality, is Power; because it is a means to have the assistance and service of many" (L 10:151). Accordingly, when he lists the various forms of power, he includes as power the reputation of those qualities. So the reputation of being a patriot (of loving one's country), of being successful, affable, well supported, lucky, prudent, or wise is power because "it draweth with it the adhaerence of those that need protection" or "makes men either feare him, or rely on him" (150–52). In other words, because power is, for Hobbes, a matter of the conditions for action—and people's perceptions of those conditions—to be reputed as powerful is much the same thing as to be powerful. Importantly, in making this claim, Hobbes proposes that the cultivation of reputation is a significant component of the effort to garner and have ready for one's use the skills and energies of as many people as possible. That is, individuals' attention to the ways their past and present actions might affect the conditions for action in the future includes the endeavor to craft, protect, and enhance any reputation they may have for being powerful in a particular way.[8] As a consequence, the pursuit of power involves not only the elaboration of a complex of social relationships but also what we might call a semiotics of power, an economy of gestures and behaviors that symbolize and generate power.[9]

In a claim that explicitly links power with our perceptions of one another, Hobbes observes that "[t]he *Value,* or Worth of a man, is as of all other things, his Price; that is to say, so much as would be given for the use of his Power" (L 10:151). Thanks to C. B. Macpherson's reading of Hobbes as a protocapitalist or an apologist for the emerging early modern bourgeois culture of possessive individualism, this observation is often thought to presage the commodification of the individual and an economistic or exchange model of social interaction: rather than having any kind of intrinsic (we might say, human) value, a person is worth as much as others would pay to purchase him or her in the marketplace.[10] However, if we read Hobbes's remark about "the Value, or Worth of a man" while mindful of the relationships and alliances that he says are elaborated in the generalized pursuit of power, the question "what would you give for the use of this person's power?" can be answered without having to make recourse to the monetary concepts central to a capitalist market economy. As we saw in Hobbes's description of power above, for the use of another's power, people often give friendship, service, assistance, loyalty, protection, or obedience. That is to say, they enter into relationships with one another through which they can take advantage of one another's skills and resources and thereby enhance the conditions for the future realization of their future desires. When an individual assesses another's worth, then, what is at issue is not that other's possible labor market value but rather what contribution the conditions for her interlocutor's actions will make to the conditions of her own future actions. And the social relations produced through that assessment and the development of the relationship are not orchestrated and mediated through the imperatives of individuals' distinctive desires, preferences, and choices (as in the logic of supply and demand) but rather are shaped by, as well as expressive of, individuals' profound interdependence.

As is implied in the claim that someone's value rests on whether or not her skills and resources can make a positive contribution to the conditions for another's future action, Hobbes argues that someone's value or worth "is not absolute; but a thing dependant on the need and judgement of another" (L 10:151–52). In his subsequent elaboration of this point, Hobbes portrays "need" as broadly circumstantial, remarking, for instance, that a skilled commander of soldiers is valuable in wartime but not during peacetime: the commander's power, which is to say his ability to elicit loyalty, obedience, and effective action from a collection of other people, may enhance someone else's conditions for action during war but may not be so appealing or useful in a peaceful civil setting (152). However, in specifying that someone's value depends on "the need and judgement of another," Hobbes suggests that need is not confined to broad social circumstances but may also be a matter of the particular plans and desires of particular individuals. As he notes, when someone rates another as valuable or not valuable, "high, and low, in this case, is to be understood by comparison to the rate that each man setteth on himselfe" (152). In other words, one individual's power is useful—and valuable—relative to another person's assessment of the conditions for future action that she herself may have secured or yet need. Hobbes suggests, then, that in assessing one another's worth, individuals try to ascertain which among their interlocutors' skills, characteristics, and resources might possibly serve as the passive power that could combine with their own active power to produce an act. People are more or less socially valuable, depending upon the desires, plans, and prospects of those around them.

Importantly, Hobbes claims that when a thinking-body perceives an object or person, some of the attunements and adjustments that together constitute the perceptual evaluation are visible and can be read by others as a manifestation or "signe" of that evaluation. He remarks that "[t]he best signes of Passions present, are either in the countenance, motions of the body, actions, and ends, or aimes, which we otherwise know the man to have" (L 6:129). For example, Hobbes says that when we dislike something and anticipate that it will harm us, the internal responsive motion or passion is "Feare" (L 6:123). Accordingly, the gestures, winces, grimaces, and gross physical movements that proceed from fear express—and can be read as expressing—our anticipation of imminent harm. Similarly, when at once we perceive an object that we want and believe that we can acquire it, the feeling or passion is "Hope. The same, without such opinion, Despaire" (6:123). So the countenance, attitude, physical bearing, and actions that proceed from our hope or despair express—and can be read as expressing—our assessment of the likelihood of success in action. When the passion fear is modified by the passion hope, the resulting passion expresses something else again: When we are fearful "with the hope of avoyding that Hurt by resistance," the passion is "Courage. Sudden *Courage,* Anger" (123). When we act angrily, our actions express and signal our hope that we can avoid injury in the face of sudden danger.[11] In Hobbes's analysis, then, we convey or reveal our passions—the perceptual responses and evaluations raised by our perceptions of others—through our facial expressions, gestures, physical demeanor, and actions. Our doing so is integral to the generation of power via honoring and reputation.

According to Hobbes, when our perception and evaluation of someone's power are revealed through our behavior, affect, or actions, that signification or "manifestation of the Value we set on one another, is . . . commonly called Honouring, and Dishonouring" (L 10:152). As he explains in a different context, "Honour consisteth in the inward thought, and opinion of the Power, and Goodnesse of another" (L 31:399–400). So when someone promotes another's good, flatters him, gives way to or praises him, believes or trusts him, relies on him, asks his advice, or heeds his counsel, that individual's behavior can be described as honoring the one flattered or praised. That is, the individual's affect and actions signal to others that she feels a great love for or fear of that other, or that she recognizes or approves of some ability, talent, or power (L 10:152). Likewise, when someone neglects another person, is arrogant or contemptuous, when she reviles, mocks, or pities another, when she is rash, obscene, or slovenly in another's presence, or when she distrusts or disagrees with another, her behavior can be described as dishonoring the one neglected or reviled. The individual's affect and actions express her unfavorable assessment of that person's power (152).

Of course, in the case of either honoring or dishonoring, the behavior that expresses the perceptual evaluation may directly help or hinder that other person in pursuing a particular course of action—giving way or not, being helpful or slovenly, constitute the conditions for the actor's prospective action. But perhaps more importantly, the activities of honoring and dishonoring have a broader social effect: according to the logic of Hobbes's argument, people perceive the honoring and dishonoring and infer that the cause of the evaluator's behavior is the evaluator's perception of the power of the person observed. This inference and perceptual evaluation cause the observers to reassess their own power vis-à-vis the power of the various figures in the scene. And that reassessment itself entails the kind of attunements, adjustments, and actions that constitute any evaluative perception, which is to say that it effects shifts in who is perceived as powerful and who, as a consequence, can garner the conditions necessary for the future realization of future desires. To make the point differently, when people behave toward a particular person in a manner that exhibits their opinion of that person's power, their actions and behaviors produce the popular opinion—or the generally shared perceptual evaluation—that constitutes reputation. In a sense, the honoring produces the passions—or the passive power—that enables the person in question to act. For Hobbes, then, there is a relay between individuals' evaluative perception of someone's power and others' evaluative perception of that evaluation, a dynamic that reflects, reinforces, and augments the power of the person observed. As he says it so nicely, "the nature of Power, is in this point, like to Fame, increasing as it proceeds" (L 10:150).[12]

As Hobbes's discussion of honoring suggests, one of the ways people assess their own and others' power or "value" is through observing people interact with one another and attending to how they themselves are treated by others. For just as a particular person's appraisal of others and her own self-estimation can be read out of her actions, attitudes, and gestures, so others' behavior will be inflected by their own evaluations and self-regard. What this means is that social interactions among Hobbesian subjects are characterized not only by fairly straightforward evaluations of one person by another but also by the responses of individuals to one another's evident evaluations of each other. Indeed, in his account of what kinds of responses dishonoring provokes, Hobbes provides an eloquent illustration of the complex social orientation and the keen sense of the social map produced and required by the pursuit of power. He contends that "every man looketh that his companion should value him, at the same rate he sets upon himselfe: And upon all signes of contempt, or undervaluing, naturally endeavours, as far as he dares . . . , to extort a greater value from his contemners, by dommage; and from others, by the example" (L 13:185).

Here, Hobbes draws on insights from his analysis of honoring to argue that individuals perceive and react to the passions and appraisals legible in other people's actions. The reaction in question proceeds from that individual's perception of whether such appraisals are well founded, given her assessment of her own "value" relative to all those involved. If the appraisals others display are not what that individual expects, she may try to correct the misperception. Such a correction can be made by forcing some kind of injury or loss ("dommage") with respect to the "contemner" or the offending undervaluer. By the logic of the play of power, this would diminish the power of the contemner and, in that forced diminution, comparatively increase the power of the offended. Alternatively—or, Hobbes suggests, additionally—the correction can be undertaken with an eye to the public gaze by making an example of the contemner in the face of any observers. Such a spectacle detracts from the contemner's public value or reputation and ratchets up the reputation of the offended in the eyes of others.[13]

Now, when Hobbes observes that an individual will try to make an example of the contemner in the face of perceived undervaluing, he implicitly recognizes that individuals are equally concerned with the opinions of the observing/perceiving audience of their power as with those of their direct interlocutors. Indeed, the effort of the offended individual to contain the broader effects of the offending undervaluation points to the complexity of the social world wrought of and negotiated in the pursuit of power: It is not simply the case that every person's reputation contributes to a general economy of power. More than this, a transformation in one person's reputation effects a shift, or has ripple effects, throughout the network of relationships that constitute the social context.

An important insight to draw out of Hobbes's recounting of this example is that when the cultivation of reputation is a part of the pursuit of power, individuals do not simply express their opinions about one another's power passively as they interact, but rather, they make a concerted effort to behave and appear in ways that shift the general economy of reputation to their advantage. The practices of honoring and dishonoring by which reputations are augmented and undermined are not just the natural, spontaneous expression of passions or our being moved but rather are strategically performed as part of the pursuit of power itself. In fact, the strategic dimensions of the cultivation of reputation combine with the concern for a broad audience to make for practices of honoring that are quite complex.

According to Hobbes, individuals concern themselves with others' reputations as much as they concern themselves with their own. That is to say, just as individuals' efforts to secure the conditions for the future realization of their future desires entail taking into consideration the conditions for other people's actions—forming alliances or relationships where they enhance powers—so in the tense and watchful choreography by which reputations are negotiated, individuals attend to and work upon other people's reputations as a means of fostering their own power. And importantly, when Hobbesian individuals work to foster, protect, negotiate, and undermine the reputations of others in their efforts to craft, manipulate, amend, and augment their own, the practices of honoring and dishonoring they undertake may involve a kind of triangulation or a splitting of the manifest addressee of these practices from the person whose power is actually acknowledged and affirmed.

This is a complicated point about the semiotics of power, about what and how people communicate through practices of honoring and dishonoring, so let me try to elaborate it clearly. Hobbes explains that the specific behaviors that are to be counted as honoring are not simply natural— although they might be—but can also be customary, scripted, or commanded (L 10:154). He notes, for example, that "[t]o do those things to another, which he takes for signes of Honour, or which the Law or Custome makes so, is to Honour; because in approving the Honour done by others, he acknowledgeth the power which others acknowledge" (153). Here Hobbes suggests that when an individual acknowledges another's power, the practices of honoring with which he does so may be not a natural expression of his perceptual evaluation but rather a practice that has been designated by the honored or by others as the proper form of acknowledgment. When an individual honors another in such a concerted manner, his performance not only communicates his opinion of the power of the honored but also his recognition that others also perceive the honored as powerful. That is, the practice functions as an indication of an explicitly or expressly shared perception of a particular person's power. The communication of this particular indication both enhances the power of the honored and provides important information to observers and participants alike about the distribution or economy of power—or about the conditions for action.[14]

In a similarly complex and strategic play of honor and power, an individual might honor one person as a way to honor another. Hobbes remarks that "[t]o honour those another honours, is to Honour him; as a signe of approbation of his judgement" (L 10:154). In this case, there are two registers to the honorific practice as well as two persons honored. On one register, one person expressly honors another in such a way as to acknowledge and augment the honored's power. On another register, the person engaged in that honorific practice does so in order actually to honor a third, whose perceptions of the honored's power are acknowledged and affirmed through that very practice. In such a case, the explicit addressee of the honoring practice is different from the intended addressee. Or to be more precise, although the explicitly honored person might very well be perceived as powerful by the person engaged in the honoring practice, it is the third person whose power is seen as useful and is affirmed and solicited by the worshiper. So the worshiper acknowledges the one's power strategically, with an eye to signaling her perception of the other's power and securing his favor or assistance.[15] And importantly, through this effort to secure the conditions for successful future action, the worshiper bolsters the relationship between the two persons honored, with the effect that the power of both is augmented, in turn boosting the passive power available for the worshiper's initiatives.

As in other dimensions of his materialism, what is particularly important in Hobbes's analysis of the action and passion of power among individuals is the double displacement of the individual. First, when Hobbes proposes that we conceive of power as the conditions for action, he displaces the individual as the single source of action. Arguing that an individual can act only to the degree that the extant passive powers or social conditions allow, he points to individuals' fundamental interdependence: any individual's success in acting—or in realizing a particular desire—is the product of a complex of material and social factors, and particularly of a distinctively social process involving the intentional and unintentional assistance, cooperation, or participation of other individuals in the endeavor. The pursuit of power both rests upon and reconfigures this interdependence. Second, and correspondingly, in portraying people power as relations of subordination and superordination that constitute the conditions for realizing desires, Hobbes displaces the individual as the unit of analysis in thinking about action and politics. In arguing that the power to act is the product of relations of interdependence, Hobbes suggests that any analysis of power, of political action, or of politics must take as its focus of analysis those very relationships. That is, seemingly recapitulating his ethical argument that individuals must conceive of themselves and their actions in terms of their relationship to the collective, Hobbes pushes us to conceive of the pursuit of power in terms of the manifold complicated relationships that constitute the conditions for the future realization of future desires.

To clarify this point: In arguing that Hobbes's account of power effects a double displacement of the individual, I do not mean to suggest that he does not appreciate our individuality. As we can see in his analysis of subjectivity, Hobbes quite clearly conceives of thinking-bodies as irreducibly individual in the sense of being singular: we cannot but be unique given our singular constitution, the singular history we each bear, and the singular trajectory we each take in the common world in which we live. However, I do not think this appreciation amounts to a celebration or advocacy in the way that Richard Flathman suggests.[16] Rather, it is something akin to an acknowledgment of an ontological fact. And, again, I am not suggesting that Hobbes effectively erases the individual by focusing primarily on or drawing our attention most forcefully to the collective conceived as a single entity. Although I think Rosamond Rhodes is right to argue that the social and political collective itself is an important and often overlooked conceptual category for Hobbes, I am not sure I agree that the notion of the collective supersedes the notion of the individual.[17] Instead, Hobbes's analysis of power suggests that we should think about power and action, not in terms of the individual *or* the collective as distinct entities, but rather in terms of the relationship *between* the individual and the collective.

The Action and Passion of Power: The Sovereign

In the opening paragraphs of this chapter, I suggested that to engage the problem of power in Hobbes's political theory is to raise the issue of the sovereign's power as well as the problem of the pursuit of power by individuals. As we saw above, if we examine Hobbes's account of power mindful of his materialism, we see a displacement of the individual as a unit of analysis and a focus instead on the perceptions, judgments, relationships, and practices within the collective that constitute the conditions for individuals' actions. In the case of his analyses of the sovereign, we see a similar shift. Hobbes's account of power suggests that we should conceive of the sovereign not as an autonomous actor but rather as an entity whose ability to act is conditioned by the same perceptions, judgments, relationships, and practices that enable individuals to act. What emerges from this analysis is Hobbes's sense that the figure of the sovereign must be concerned with those very conditions for action—not in the sense of engaging in a coarse and disingenuous manipulation of desire and fear but rather, as we saw in the discussion of the casuistic dimensions of his ethics in Chapter 4, in the sense of appreciating, nourishing, and working with the fact of interdependence.

When Hobbes shifts his attention to expound upon the power of the sovereign, the details of his analysis suggest that the sovereign power is an elaboration and product of the pursuit of power more generally. That is, the relationships and practices generative of the sovereign's power are closely related to the sovereign's ability to appear to others as the "passive power" they need in order to act. And as in the play of power we saw in the prior section, the ability to appear so shapes the passions or the "passive power" necessary for the sovereign's initiatives to effect actions. Interestingly, in *Behemoth,* Hobbes references his insights into the relationship between power and reputation in his contention that the power of the sovereign rests on nothing "but . . . the opinion and belief of the people."[18] He does so more explicitly in *Leviathan* when he observes that "the Actions of men proceed from their Opinions; and in the wel governing of Opinions, consisteth the wel governing of mens Actions, in order to their Peace, and Concord" (L 18:233). And indeed, in his discussions about the rights of sovereignty and the various ailments that might weaken or destroy a commonwealth, he points again and again to the importance of enhancing and protecting the appearance of the sovereign's power—the prerogatives, privileges, accessories, and such that mark the supremacy of the power of the sovereign and generate the reputation or opinion of that power in the general populace. In fact, it is through attending to his recounting of the sovereign's power that we come to see that Hobbes is telling not so much an origins story—a tale of how an ordered polity might come to be out of chaos—but rather a constitutional story about how a polity works and about the conditions for successful action both every day and into the future.

Much as in other relationships in which an assessment about the conditions for success in future action provoke one person to give obedience in exchange for protection, Hobbes argues that the purpose of the sovereign, or the end "for which he was trusted with the Soveraign Power," is the *salus populi*, or "the procuration of *the safety of the people*" (L 30:376). The only significant difference is that, according to Hobbes, civil order demands that the sovereign's power be "greater, than that of any, or all the Subjects" (L 18:238), for their obligation to obey the sovereign lasts "as long, and no longer, than the power lasteth, by which he is able to protect them" (L 21:272). Indeed, Hobbes explains that if the sovereign is not powerful enough to make security the benefit of obedience—if there is another figure who appears to be equally as powerful as the sovereign, if not more so—then people may determine that "their obedience to the Soveraign Power, will bee more hurtfull to them, than their disobedience" and feel justified in disdaining the sovereign's commands (L 42:567). In Hobbes's view, such a predicament would assuredly precipitate the downfall of the commonwealth and introduce "confusion, and Civill war, for the avoiding whereof, all Civill Government was ordained" (567).

Hobbes argues that the rights of sovereignty work to ensure that the sovereign appears to be powerful enough to command the obedience and assistance necessary to the task of protecting the people. These particular rights are "the markes, whereby a man may discern in what Man, or Assembly of men, the Soveraign Power is placed, and resideth" (L 18:236). In other words, as marks that distinguish the person who fills the office of the sovereign from other subjects and that denote his preeminence, the rights of sovereignty both designate and signal the sovereign's power.[19] That is, they make visible the sovereign's power, a visibility that—as we might surmise from the analysis of power above—creates the reputation of power that actually affirms and reconstitutes the sovereign's power. Among the rights Hobbes enumerates that grant the sovereign the power to make laws, to declare war, to punish criminals, and such are rights to institutionalize rituals in which individuals publicly and collectively acknowledge the sovereign power. What is so interesting about such rituals is that they quite clearly draw on Hobbes's analyses of power and reputation: they comprise practices that foster the appearance of the sovereign's power and that thereby augment or consolidate the sovereign power itself.

As he discusses the various rights of sovereignty, Hobbes proposes that following upon weekly civil religious services, subjects should be assembled together and taught the rights of sovereignty and their corresponding civil duties. The aim of such teaching is to put the people "in mind of the Authority that maketh them Lawes" (L 30:381). Generally speaking, the idea is that if subjects are taught and required to acknowledge the rights of the sovereign, they will not only appreciate his power but also recognize their duties toward him—and more particularly the importance of obedience for peace and prosperity.[20] In his recounting of such lessons and remonstrances, Hobbes clearly draws on his understanding of the generative relationship between reputation and power. For example, included in the list of duties to be taught to the assembled people is an injunction against allowing their admiration for "the vertue of any of their fellow Subjects, how high soever he stand, nor how conspicuously soever he shine in the Common-wealth," to lead them to "deferre to them any obedience, or honour, appropriate to the Soveraign onely" (380). In other words, they cannot behave toward people other than the sovereign in any way that might convey an opinion about the sovereign's not being the supremely powerful figure. Following Hobbes's analysis of the play of power and reputation, the danger in such a deferral of obedience or honor lies in the possibility that it might actually diminish the power of the sovereign. In another example, Hobbes says that the gathered people must also be taught "how great a fault it is, to speak evill of the Soveraign Representative, . . . or to argue and dispute his Power, or any way to use his Name irreverently, whereby he may be brought into Contempt with his People, and their Obedience . . . slackened" (381). Here, again, Hobbes is concerned to ensure that the sovereign maintain his reputation so that his ability to be effective is not undermined.

But what is equally as important as the actual content of the lessons is the power-generative effects of the ritual of the lessons themselves. If we consider Hobbes's analysis of the ways that practices of honoring both acknowledge and produce power, then the weekly ritual of gathering in public for instruction about the sovereign's power can be seen as accomplishing both. In the very course of participating in such compulsory civic rituals, everyone engages in a form of honoring or worship that conveys to everyone else their recognition of the sovereign's power. By the logic of the play of perception, reputation, and power, such a public acknowledgment generates a perception of a general opinion about the sovereign's power, a perception that in turn produces and consolidates the sovereign's power. In fact, in his account of this power-producing dynamic, Hobbes draws on his insights about the semiotics of power discussed above.

Hobbes describes the purpose of worship as the simultaneous acknowledgment and production of power. In obvious recognition of the relationship between reputation and power, he contends that "[t]he End of Worship amongst men, is Power. For where a man seeth another worshipped, he supposeth him powerfull, and is the readier to obey him; which makes his Power greater" (L 31:401). In other words, to see someone worship another leads one to the presumption that the person worshiped is powerful. And as the dynamic of reputation and power goes, the supposition that someone is powerful affects one's own actions in such a way as to actually make that person powerful: one is willing to obey his commands or his calls for assistance. And crucially, Hobbes explains that even if the worship is commanded, it reflects and regenerates power, for when worship is commanded, "not the words, or gesture, but the obedience is the Worship" (400). As he elaborates in a different context, "to Pray to, to Swear by, to Obey, to bee Diligent, and Officious in Serving: in summe, all words and actions that betoken Fear to Offend, or Desire to Please, is *Worship,* whether those words and actions be sincere, or feigned" (L 45:666–67).

According to this account of worship, when subjects congregate to be taught about and to acknowledge the sovereign power, they engage in worship. Their activities of praying to, swearing by, obeying, and serving the sovereign while assembled together generate an environment in which people act as if they believe in the supremacy of the sovereign's power. The generalized performance of this belief reproduces the appearance of the sovereign's supremacy. This visible public opinion in turn affects people's perceptions of the sovereign, increasing the probability that individual subjects will recognize the sovereign's power and obey him: seeing everyone else worship the sovereign, each individual "supposeth him powerfull, and is the readier to obey him; which makes his Power greater." In fact, we could say that when individuals participate in the rituals of civil worship that Hobbes advocates, when they publicly and conspicuously acknowledge the rights and power of the sovereign, they constitute and reconstitute the sovereign power.

We can clarify this dynamic if we think about this mandatory form of civil worship in terms of the semiotics of power explored above. For in these compulsory rituals of civic teaching, the intended addressee of these worshipful activities is not primarily the sovereign. To be sure, the sovereign is the explicit addressee. However, even though the worshipful activities are ostensibly about or directed at the sovereign figure, the primary addressee for the worshipful activities is, collectively, the other subjects. As Hobbes argues, worship is best done "in Publique, and in the sight of men: For without that, (that which in honour is most acceptable) the procuring of others to honour him, is lost" (L 31:405). So when individuals honor the sovereign by participating in mandatory civil worship, their behavior indicates to the gathered crowd that they consider the sovereign to be extremely powerful. Individuals in the assembly who apprehend the volume of evident opinions about the sovereign power find themselves developing a similar opinion—one that is similarly expressed and thereby contributes to the general appearance of power that confronts and moves everyone else. In short, when individuals obediently and conspicuously subject themselves to that one sovereign figure through weekly civil "teachings," when they observe others and are in turn observed doing so, their actions generate a political environment in which one particular person or group of persons (the sovereign) is produced as and perceived by everyone to be the most powerful of all.

Of course, such power-generative forms of honoring or worship are highly formal organized events. Interestingly, though, Hobbes specifies another right of sovereignty that both takes advantage of the complex ways in which practices of honoring generate and consolidate power and, in a sense, makes those practices more mundane. He claims that it is both a right and a duty of the sovereign to institute "Lawes of Honour, and a publique rate of the worth of such men as have deserved, or are able to deserve well of the Common-wealth" (L 18:235). Rather than court the detrimental effects that attend the untrammeled competition for status and public regard, Hobbes says the sovereign must institutionalize "the precedence, place, and order of subjects in the Common-wealth" (L 10:159). Working against the possibility that the effects of personal talent, riches, and free public approbation might propel particular individuals or groups to the kind of potent popularity and political prominence that could detract from the appearance of the sovereign's singularly supreme power, the sovereign should bestow honorific titles upon select individuals. That is, the sovereign should establish "a publique rate of . . . worth" that appoints "what Order of place, and dignity, each man shall hold; and what signes of respect, in publique or private meetings, they shall give one another" (L 18:235–36). And again, if we examine this sovereign right to make some people's power derive from and dependent upon the sovereign's will and command while keeping in mind the semiotics of power described above, we can see how Hobbes's materialist understanding of how power is generated shapes his account of the sovereign's power. When the sovereign creates laws designating how the distinctions among the designated honored and other subjects should be observed and made manifest, he not only contains the ongoing pursuit of power from which his own power derives but also secures his supremacy.

According to Hobbes's argument, the sovereign, as the official "fountain of Honour," awards titles such as "Lord, Earle, Duke, and Prince" to those who are valuable—one can read "loyal"—to the commonwealth (L 18:238). Such "signes of favour" elevate those individuals in the public eye, giving official recognition to both their worth in the eyes of the sovereign and their proximity to the sovereign power (L 10:154). Since these titles granted by the sovereign must be "taken for a signe of his will to Honour" the individuals of his choosing, other subjects must acknowledge the sovereign's power by showing respect for and giving way to such dignitaries as the sovereign commands (154). That is, they show their obedience to the sovereign by honoring, "in publique or private meetings," the place and dignity of those exceptional individuals (L 18:236).

Now, when the sovereign formalizes relations of interdependence in this way, he enhances the conditions for future action not only for himself and for the honored but also for the friends and followers of the honored, that is, those whose conditions for action are bound up with the conditions for action of the honored. Since to "honour those another honours, is to Honor him; as a signe of approbation of his judgement" (L 10:154), the sovereign's honoring of a particular person can be taken as "approbation" of or agreement with those who are that person's friends or servants. Like them, the sovereign recognizes the power or worth of the individual in question. In approving and affirming their judgment in this way, the sovereign secures their esteem: his judgments appear wise to them, an appearance that generates power. In other words, in honoring a particular person, the sovereign enhances the power relationship between himself and that person's friends and followers. Likewise, these friends and followers of the honored subject honor him by honoring or acknowledging the power of the sovereign whom he honors and upon whom his power depends. In other words, they secure their relationship with the honored individual by acknowledging the power that he acknowledges. Thus the formalization of power relations via the granting of official honors builds upon the power-generative effects of the pursuit of power more generally and has a similar but more stable socially binding force.

Throughout his analysis of the rights and duties of the sovereign, Hobbes suggests that sovereign power is generated through subjects' pursuit of power. That is to say, the sovereign's power as an agent is produced through the interplay of the action and passion that defines individuals' activity under conditions of interdependence. And importantly, just as the dynamic relations of interdependence among power-seeking individuals are the "patients," or material causes of the sovereign's effective action, so may they be the sovereign's undoing. Hobbes elaborates upon this possibility in his analysis of the "diseases" that might undermine the power of the sovereign. In fact, in his view, many of the threats to the sovereign power are situations, persons, or institutions that detract from the power-generative effects of the rights of sovereignty examined just above.

Hobbes points out, for example, that fanciful ideas about which form of government is most conducive to freedom and prosperity and doctrines disputing the sovereign as the proper location of spiritual authority threaten the integrity and internal coherence of the sovereign's power (L 30:380). Shared sovereignty, whether spiritual or institutional, jeopardizes the body politic: if there is more than one locus of power and authority from which individuals take their bearings, then no one knows to whom they owe their obedience. In his oft-cited formulation, Hobbes observes that sovereignty shared is sovereignty divided, and "what is it to divide the Power of a Common-wealth, but to Dissolve it; for Powers divided mutually destroy each other" (L 29:368). Elaborating upon another possible threat, Hobbes explains that because military leaders command the loyal obedience of large numbers of armed soldiers—thereby appearing immensely powerful—those leaders may also pose a challenge to the seeming supremacy of the sovereign power. He points out that, of course, no matter who is "made Generall of an Army, he that hath the Soveraign Power is alwayes Generallissimo" (L 18:235). But a mere title is not necessarily enough: to have the general's apparent power contribute to the production of the sovereign's power, his loyalty to the sovereign must be secured. In other words, "the safety of the People" requires not only that military leaders "be good Conductors" of the armies committed to their command but also that they be "faithfull Subjects" (L 30:393). Hobbes notes that the growth of cities may pose a similar problem. If a town becomes immoderately great, it might be "able to furnish out of its own Circuit, the number, and expence of a great Army" (L 29:374–75). Since a large city might be able to generate the kind of military power that could undermine the power of the sovereign, cities should be limited in their size. Most generally, Hobbes cautions that individuals who are powerful and who have a popular following must be prevented from becoming a "dangerous Disease; because the people (which should receive their motion from the Authority of the Soveraign,) by the flattery, and by the reputation of an ambitious man, [may be] drawn away from their obedience to the Lawes, to follow a man, of whose vertues, and designes they have no knowledge" (L 29:374). So unless the sovereign has "very good caution of his fidelity," an individual should not be allowed to become so popular that his reputation and apparent power could undermine the effectiveness and visibility of the sovereign's apparent power (374).

Hobbes's insights about the action and passion of sovereign power are interesting in a number of respects. His contention that the bustling, pulsing interactions that characterize the pursuit of power by individuals not only produce the sovereign's apparent supremacy but also constitute the conditions for the sovereign's actions suggests that the order instituted by the sovereign is characterized not by stasis but rather by flux. To put the point differently, because sovereign power depends upon the ongoing pursuit of power by individuals, the relationships of inequality that are both integral to and the aim of individuals' interdependent actions must have the space or the room to change. In other words, relations of inequality must be disrupted so that they may be pursued and reconstructed anew. The sovereign's dependence upon the continual regeneration of the relationships of interdependence among individuals means that the sovereign must strike a balance between formalizing the relationships and activities through which sovereign power is produced—stabilizing them so as to prevent the displacement of the sovereign from his focal position—and allowing them to transform and flourish in ways that make possible the sovereign's actions through time. To permit a particular configuration of inequality to persist would not merely invite the kind of hostility foreseen and countered by the laws of nature. With such a consolidation of inequality, the dynamism of the pursuit of power would stagnate in such a way as to diminish and render more fragile the sovereign power.

Hobbes's suggestion that the sovereign must provide the conditions for the generalized pursuit of power to flourish has another corollary. For although Hobbes incontestably claims that sovereign power must be supreme and that in its supremacy it is a cause of the fear that compels lawful obedience, his analysis of sovereign power suggests that the sovereign cannot rule effectively—or for long—through fear alone. In his view, the effectiveness of sovereign power does not lie in its threat to "dammage, or weaken[ ]" its subjects; rather, the "strength and glory" of "Soveraign Governours" consist in the "vigor" of those subjects (L 18:238). So, in the pursuit of power—that is, in the effort to produce the conditions for the future success in action—the sovereign must to do more than conjure a fearsome image. As we saw in Hobbes's discussion of desperate rebels in Chapter 4, the sovereign must provide for his subjects in such a way that they can actually serve as the passion for his action.

To be sure, this vision of Hobbes's sovereign—as constitutively dependent upon subjects' own pursuit of power, as concerned to ensure that inequalities are more mobile than not, as provider of the economic and social sustenance that makes obedience possible—is at odds with the grisly monster we generally associate with Hobbes's political imagination. And yet, this vision is entirely consonant with Hobbes's insights into the facts of intersubjectivity and interdependence. Moreover, it also makes sense of—while calling upon us to reconsider—his account of the covenant.

The Action and Passion of Politics: The Daily Covenant

Hobbes's analysis of the action and passion of politics—of the pursuit of power by individuals and by the sovereign—demands that we rethink the covenant or agreement that both constitutes the commonwealth and establishes the sovereign as sovereign. His analysis of power suggests that it might not make sense to conceptualize the agreement that establishes the sovereign power as a singular, temporally finite event. To the contrary, if we take seriously Hobbes's argument that individuals' acknowledgment of the power of the sovereign in the course of their interactions produces and reproduces the reputation of power that is itself power, then we must conceive of the covenanting process as composed of just this dynamic— a continuous, daily, ongoing process. This argument is not akin to Jean Hampton's claim that "there is no one-time contract either among the subjects or between every subject and the sovereign that is necessary to empower the sovereign."[21] In Hampton's rationalist reading, the contract is something like a literal verbal agreement entered into reluctantly because of the sacrifices and compromises it entails. Some individuals do find themselves compelled to enter into a contract agreeing to obey the sovereign, she says, but everyone else obeys the sovereign because it is in their interest to do so—the idea here being that if obedience is in someone's interest, then it is done voluntarily and without a contract. The virtue of Hampton's argument is its claim that there is no single original agreement. However, in its rationalist presumptions, it misses Hobbes's important insights about power. If we read Hobbes's discussion of the covenant through his analysis of both the pursuit of power and the semiotics of honor and reputation through which people convey their opinions about power, then everyone covenants—and all the time. Of course, to make such a claim is to counter the long-standing commonplace that Hobbes is telling us a story about the origins of society. So let me elaborate the argument in more detail.

According to Hobbes, the hallmark of the covenanting process is the transference of the right to govern oneself to another. As he articulates it, the covenant consists in an agreement among individuals in which each effectively declares, "*I Authorise and give up my Right of Governing my selfe, to this Man, or to this Assembly of men, on this condition, that thou give up thy Right to him, and Authorise all his Actions in like manner*" (L 17:227). Several interesting facets of this covenant come to light when it is analyzed alongside the account of power explored above. The first concerns the authorization of the sovereign—the "Man, or . . . Assembly of men" to whom the right of governing is given up. According to Hobbes, to authorize is to transfer one's right to act to another: another becomes the actor of deeds that one owns or for which one takes responsibility (L 16:218). In other words, another becomes the active agent of one's actions, realizing one's desires in one's stead. The nature of this transference of the right to act requires some elucidation. Hobbes explains that to transfer a right is not to give to another something he did not have before. Rather, it is to "stand[ ] out of his way, that he may enjoy his own originall Right, without hindrance from him" (L 14:191). In other words, it is a "diminution of impediments" (191), the impediments that might "take away part of a mans power to do what hee would" (189). To transfer a right, then, is to make oneself not be an obstacle to another's action. Indeed, we could say that it is to make oneself into the passion of another's action, into the conditions that enable another's initiatives to result in an act. But if this is what constitutes the transference of a right, what does it mean to transfer the right to govern oneself? It is to let another govern one's actions; it is to not resist being (made into) one of the causes that contribute to the realization of another's desires. In short, it is to obey. And of course, as we saw above in Hobbes's analysis of power, to obey is both to recognize and to produce power.

In addition to the interesting notion that the authorization of the sovereign consists in obedience is Hobbes's description of the nature of the agreement or covenant itself. In describing the covenant, Hobbes does not specify that it must be explicitly made—as if a document were to be drawn up or a convention held. To the contrary, he suggests that some contracts might simply be implicitly made: that a contract or agreement has been made can be inferred from the way people behave. As he puts it, "Signes of Contract . . . by Inference, are sometimes the consequence of Words; sometimes the consequence of Silence; sometimes the consequence of Actions; sometimes the consequence of Forbearing an Action: and generally a signe by Inference, of any Contract, is whatsoever sufficiently argues the will of the Contractor" (L 14:193–94). Hobbes appears to draw on this claim that someone's will—and by extension a contract—can be "read" from his or her behavior when he portrays the sovereign-constituting covenant as an agreement that is made "in such manner, as if every man should say to every man, *I Authorise* . . ." (L 17:227). The qualifying phrase "in such manner, as if every man should say" suggests that the agreement and authorization in question are implicit, conveyed in the manner by which the covenant is made even if not explicitly declared.

Finally, and importantly, there is the condition at the heart of the covenant: "*I Authorise and give up my Right . . . to this Man, or to this Assembly of men, on this condition, that thou give up thy Right to him . . . in like manner"* (L 17:227). Hobbes specifies that in the covenant that authorizes and constitutes the sovereign power, individuals do not transfer the right to govern to just any person. Rather, each individual transfers his or her right to one particular (sovereign) figure. In other words, everyone must transfer the right to the same individual or group. In fact, the covenant involves a splitting of the audience of the transfer (other individuals) from the addressee of the transfer (the sovereign): the agreement is made among individuals about their mutual transfer of a specific right to a single (presumptive) sovereign.

If we consider these three of Hobbes's points together, then we come up with a fascinating picture: if someone behaves visibly or publicly in such a way as to be seen by others as surrendering the right to govern herself to the presumptive sovereign figure, then that person can be presumed to have authorized the sovereign. That is, if someone obeys—or otherwise recognizes the power of—the sovereign, her authorization of the sovereign can be inferred. If she does this in the view of and in concert with others, the covenant implicitly has been made.

Drawing on Hobbes's analyses of power, we could say, then, that the covenant through which the sovereign is authorized and granted power consists in public displays of obedience. That is, it consists in the rituals, activities, and gestures with which individuals signal their opinion of the sovereign's power—whether in the weekly public teachings that Hobbes recommends or in various practices of honoring others in the myriad "publique or private meetings" that attend daily intercourse (L 18:236). To make the point differently, the actions and behaviors through which individuals acknowledge to one another their apprehension of the sovereign's power, the play of reputation, honor, and power through which the sovereign's power is made visible and effective—these together constitute the covenant that establishes the sovereign as the supremely powerful figure to whom each transfers the right of government. In other words, the covenant is not really a distinct and distinctive event. Rather, it resembles and replicates the complex social choreography by which power and reputation are negotiated and produced in the generalized pursuit of power by individuals.

The argument that the covenant consists in the daily activities through which individuals obey, affirm, and reproduce the sovereign power might seem to point to specious reasoning on Hobbes's part: Hobbes presumes the sovereign has the power (or power enough) to solicit or provoke the obedience that is promised or authorized through the covenant. Logically, the sovereign's power seems to preexist the covenant that is supposed to produce and secure it. However, the objection that Hobbes's analysis of power seems to present us with a difficulty in developing a coherent account of the institution of the sovereign rests on the presumption that Hobbes is out to tell us about the initial creation of the commonwealth. The queries "Which came first? Power or the covenant?" are predicated on an implicit narrative of development about how the "Artificiall man" that is civil society is initially composed from the "*Matter*" of man (L intro.: 82). But as the reading I have developed here suggests, Hobbes does not forward a story about the origins of society. Rather, he presents an analysis of politics that rests upon a recognition of our profound interdependence.

Conclusion

In conceiving of power as the conditions for future action, in developing an account of political power and authority upon the materialist premise that we are ineluctably interdependent, Hobbes does two things: he installs the pursuit of peace at the center of social and political life, and he prompts us to adopt an ecological mind-set as we consider how to secure the conditions for our future effectiveness or success.

To take the issue of peace first: In his analyses of power, Hobbes points out that individuals' ability to secure the conditions for the future realization of their future desires is bound up with others' like ability. In order to foster the relations of assistance and cooperation that *are* power, individuals must think of themselves and their actions in terms of their relationships with others now and into the future. And importantly, the intersubjective nature of the patterns of thought and desire that cause individuals' actions requires that this exercise of imagining oneself in relation to others have a specific character. In order to foster the kinds of relationships that constitute power, individuals must behave in such a way as to assure one another that violent conflict is not the aim of the relation, which is to say they need to convey their commitment to peace. Indeed, according to his analysis, to make war is to have to brook war. To persist in war is to fail to recognize our fundamental intersubjectivity and our profound interdependence and to lay down the conditions for one's future failure and misery. Conversely, Hobbes's argument suggests that we must seek peace because of our interdependence. According to his analysis, to pursue peace is not to forsake power. To the contrary, to seek peace is the only way successfully to pursue the power we desire.

Hobbes opens his chapter on the commonwealth by stating that "The finall Cause, End, or Designe of men . . . in the introduction of that restraint upon themselves, (in which wee see them live in Commonwealths,) is the foresight of their own preservation, and of a more contented life thereby" (L 17:223). Explicitly linking peace to the possibility of such contentment, he contends that the aim of people choosing to live in a commonwealth is to "get[ ] out from that miserable condition of Warre" and to live in "observation of those Lawes of Nature set down in the fourteenth and fifteenth Chapters" (223). In other words, people live in a commonwealth in order to ensure the peaceful relations necessary to secure the conditions for the future realization of their future desires.[22] In fact, Hobbes suggests that one of the distinguishing features of commonwealths is their use of the peace-oriented laws of nature as structuring principles.

As noted at the end of the last section, the play of perception, reputation, and honor that characterizes individuals' pursuit of power more generally bears a remarkable resemblance to the play of perception, reputation, and honor through which the sovereign power is authorized and secured. What distinguishes them is that, in the latter, individuals deliberately and in concert try to recognize and produce a single locus of superior power. That is to say, in the unbridled pursuit of power, individuals may make different assessments about who is powerful and troth themselves and their skills and resources to different personalities and alliances. In a commonwealth, to the contrary, they constitute a power in common, or "a Common Power" (L 17:226–27).

Hobbes explains that "in all places, where men have lived by small Families, . . . men observed no other Lawes therein, but the Lawes of Honour; that is, to abstain from cruelty, leaving to men their lives, and instruments of husbandry" (L 17:224). But families, and indeed cities and kingdoms, that live according to the laws of honor tend to foster insecurity in the very process of trying to ensure their security. Recalling his analysis of the social dynamics produced through the pursuit of power, Hobbes points out that in order to protect against the possibility of invasion, "upon all pretences of danger" they endeavor either to "enlarge their Dominions" by preemptive invasion or to "subdue, or weaken their neighbours" who might have plans to invade (224). In other words, to live according to the laws of honor in the process of trying to enhance security is to participate in an expansionary dynamic in which war or conflict is the predominant mode of living.[23]

According to Hobbes, a desire to live in peace and security—a desire to live according to the laws of nature—is not in itself sufficient to bring about peace and security (L 17:223–24). The only way to halt the escalation of power-seeking competition characteristic of the pursuit of power, the only way to forestall the instability and insecurity that are the product of the shifting loyalties attendant to having two or more powerful figures make a bid for our allegiance, is for everyone to agree upon and thereby produce a single supremely powerful person or assembly. Such a singularly powerful figure would give a common focus to individuals' efforts to pursue power after power. And as the focal point of the shifting relationships and activities that constitute its power, this singular figure would also be positioned to ensure that those living in the polity interact not according to the laws of honor, which inevitably foster conflict, but rather according to the laws of nature, whose aim is peace. So people covenant, Hobbes says, "to the end, to live peaceably amongst themselves, and be protected against other men" (L 18:229).

As this discussion begins to demonstrate, contrary to the popular association of his name with the brutality and inevitability of war, Hobbes is something of a peacenik. In his view, peace must be a prominent characteristic of our interactions and a defining feature of the polity. Because intersubjectivity and interdependence are simply facts of our existence, and because contest and negotiation are integral to any effort to produce the conditions for future action, peace cannot be construed simply as an abstract value. Quite emphatically to the contrary, for Hobbes, peace is the material, living condition of possibility for social and political life itself.

Interestingly, when Hobbes forwards his materialist accounts of determinism, intersubjectivity, and interdependence, he does more than highlight the urgent necessity for peace. When he elaborates these aspects of his materialism to depict power as the conditions for future action, his work serves as a caution or even a warning. Recall that, for Hobbes, the desires that move our thoughts, make possible our plans, and propel our actions are determined by the confluence of a broad swath of factors: body, experience, habit, luck, self-image, and culture. In specifying these determinants of desire, he ties each to our ability to imagine possible futures, to feel inspired to act, and to engage one another skillfully. In doing so, Hobbes suggests that to consider the conditions for future action is to have to include in our considerations those determinants and the effects of current actions upon them. To begin to specify: we must attend to the effects of our current pursuits upon the matter of our bodies, for the state of the stuff of which we are constituted affects our perceptions, our memories, our experience, our self-perception, and so the movements of desire and imagination. We must attend to the matter of the world that we absorb, inhale, consume, and exploit, for the material environment that we purposefully and accidentally ingest becomes a constituent element of our bodies. We must attend to the matter of the resources we use to live, to grow, and to flourish, for their continued existence is a condition of our lives. To put the point differently, Hobbes's materialism suggests that to appreciate our intersubjective and interdependent existence is to have to think ecologically.

Formally speaking, ecology is the study of "the relations of living organisms to their surroundings, their habits and modes of life."[24] But as Jane Bennett has recently argued, rather than restricting its meaning to segments of the natural environment, we can also construe ecology as the "network of relations" in the "natural-cultural-technological assemblages" in which we are embedded.[25] Hobbes is so skilled at specifying the complexities of the relations, "assemblages," and interdependencies that constitute our existence as material beings that we can characterize his work as a kind of political ecology. Indeed, we might see his use of bodily metaphors and similes throughout his political theory as his effort to convey the quality and significance of our interdependence even as we understand that politics is the product of convention.[26] If we conceive of his arguments as a political ecology, then not only does Hobbes require that we strive to create peace in all our interactions. He also demands that we consider carefully the kinds of futures that we make possible—and that we foreclose—if we persist in the myopic fantasy of autonomy and self-sovereignty.

Notes

INTRODUCTION

1. I draw here on Linda Zerilli's discussion of Wittgenstein's notion of "aspect-dawning" in *Feminism and the Abyss of Freedom*, 54–58.

2. For some recent notable exceptions to this pattern, see Bennett, "The Force of Things"; Brennan, *Transmission of Affect;* Connolly, *Neuropolitics;* Connolly, *Pluralism;* Coole, "Rethinking Agency"; Grosz, *Nick of Time;* Massumi, *Parables of the Virtual.*

3. For a similar effort, although one that gets waylaid by its focus on the primacy of the linguistic, see Zarka, *Décision métaphysique.* For my critique, see Frost, "Hobbes out of Bounds." For a thorough and insightful examination of the historical and philosophical background against which Hobbes's materialism emerges, see Tuck, *Philosophy and Government.*

4. For a kindred effort to think about subjectivity in terms of the movement of material atoms (albeit an effort with a completely different intellectual genealogy), see Massumi, *Parables of the Virtual.*

5. Wolin, "Political Theory as a Vocation," 1071.

6. Derrida, *Limited Inc,* 147.

7. Kroll, *Material Word.*

8. Popkin, *History of Skepticism;* Burnyeat, *Skeptical Tradition.*

9. Tuck, *Philosophy and Government,* esp. chap. 7, "Thomas Hobbes."

10. Overhoff, *Hobbes's Theory of the Will.*

11. Tuck, *Philosophy and Government,* esp. chaps. 5 and 6, "Hugo Grotius" and "English Revolution."

12. See "Hobbes's Theological Defense of His Theory of the Will" and "Further Religious Implications of Hobbes's Theory of the Will: His Materialist Eschatology," in Overhoff, *Hobbes's Theory of the Will.*

13. Overhoff, *Hobbes's Theory of the Will,* 54.

14. See Malcolm, *Aspects of Hobbes;* Bowle, *Hobbes and His Critics;* Mintz, *Hunting of Leviathan;* Bramhall, *Defence of True Liberty.*

15. Israel, *Radical Enlightenment,* 14.

16. On the philosophical, religious, and political conditions that contributed

to the ascendancy of Descartes's philosophy, see Israel, *Radical Enlightenment*. On the philosophical questions eclipsed by the continuing dominance of Cartesianism, see James, *Passion and Action*.

17. See, for example, Watkins, "Philosophy and Politics in Hobbes"; Watkins, *Hobbes's System of Ideas;* Gert, "Hobbes, Mechanism, and Egoism"; Gert, "Hobbes's Psychology"; Peters, *Hobbes;* Peters and Tajfel, "Hobbes and Hull"; Spragens, *Politics of Motion;* Sorell, *Hobbes*.

18. See, for example, Searle, *Rediscovery of the Mind;* E. Wilson, *Neural Geographies;* Damasio, *Feeling of What Happens;* Howes, *Empire of the Senses*.

19. See, for example, Butler, *Bodies That Matter;* Butler, *Psychic Life of Power;* Braidotti, *Metamorphoses;* Connolly, *Neuropolitics;* Foucault, *Essential Works*.

20. Most notably in this regard, see the reassessments of Spinoza in Israel, *Radical Enlightenment;* Deleuze, *Spinoza;* Gatens and Lloyd, *Collective Imaginings*.

21. Hobbes, *Leviathan,* chap. 46, 689. All italics in quotations from Hobbes are his.

22. Peters, *Hobbes;* Peters and Tajfel, "Hobbes and Hull."

23. Gert, "Hobbes's Psychology"; Sorell, *Hobbes;* Watkins, "Philosophy and Politics in Hobbes."

24. Cavell, *Claim of Reason,* 494.

25. Hobbes uses the notion of a "thinking-body" in *De Corpore,* chap. 3, 34.

26. Macpherson, *Political Theory*.

27. Hampton, *Hobbes,* 9 (italics in original).

28. Thanks to James Martell for pointing this out to me so clearly.

29. For a notable exception to this tendency, see John Searle's suggestion that we should conceive of thinking in the body as "a natural biological phenomenon" rather than a characteristic that is somehow "added" to the body. Searle, *Mystery of Consciousness,* xiii–xiv.

30. Connolly, *Neuropolitics,* 62; MacIntyre, *Dependent Rational Animals,* 4–6; Wolin, "Hobbes." For a more extended elaboration of this concern with regard to Hobbes in particular, see Sorell, *Hobbes*.

31. Thanks to Jane Bennett for this language.

32. For an insightful analysis of the historical and ideological context that made Hobbes's argument comprehensible to his contemporaries, see Overhoff, *Hobbes's Theory of the Will*.

33. See, for example, Ackerman, "Two Concepts of Moral Goodness"; and Bertman, "Hobbes on 'Good.'" See also Deigh, "Reason and Ethics."

34. See, for example, A. E. Taylor, "Ethical Doctrine of Hobbes." See also Warrender, *Political Philosophy of Thomas Hobbes*.

35. See, for example, Nagel, "Hobbes's Conception of Obligation." See also Bobbio, *Thomas Hobbes*.

36. Interestingly, this account of action is similar to that articulated by Judith

Butler in her discussion of agency and prerogative in "Contingent Foundations,"
12–14. It is also remarkably similar to Hannah Arendt's account of action in chapter 5 of *Human Condition,* esp. 183–92. For an extended contemplation of this latter similarity, see Martell, "Radical Promise of Thomas Hobbes."

37. Pateman, *Sexual Contract;* DiStefano, *Configurations of Masculinity.* For an
extended analysis of their arguments about the femininity or femaleness of the
body in Hobbes's philosophy, see my "Reading the Body."

38. For a notable exception to naturalized visions of gender in Hobbes's political theory, see Slomp, "Hobbes and Equality." Also helpful in this regard is Susan
James's observation that although the binarisms and associations that feminists
have relied upon were initially enormously useful interpretive tools, we have
reached a point at which we can now think and read critically without having to
circumscribe our analyses with these tried but now overly worn political truisms.
See James, *Passion and Action,* 18–20.

39. For an analysis of feminist humanists' wariness about thinking about the
body as an organism, see Martin, "Success and Its Failures," 102–31. For a fascinating effort to think beyond such wariness, see Grosz, *Nick of Time.*

40. Clearly, then, I take issue with Jean Hampton's claim that Hobbes forwards "a very strong brand of individualism, one that regards individual human
beings as conceptually prior not only to political society but also to *all* social interactions" (Hampton, *Hobbes,* 6).

41. Flathman, *Thomas Hobbes.*

42. For an analysis of Hobbes's account of how we constitute and reconstitute
the world daily, see Orlie, *Living Ethically, Acting Politically.*

CHAPTER I

1. Letter to Colvius, 14 November 1640, in Descartes, *Correspondence,* 159. For
biographical information on Colvius, see ibid., 387.

2. Ibid., 159; Descartes's italics.

3. For several exemplary efforts to answer such questions, see Chalmers, *Conscious Mind;* Nagel, *Other Minds;* Dennett, *Consciousness Explained;* Searle, *Minds,
Brains and Science;* Ryle, *Concept of Mind.*

4. The language cited in the text that refers to Descartes's account of self-
consciousness comes from Cottingham, *Descartes,* 25.

5. Descartes observes, "Even those who have the weakest souls could acquire
absolute mastery over all their passions if we employed sufficient ingenuity in
training and guiding them" (*Passions of the Soul,* 348).

6. Richard Tuck discusses Mersenne's role in coordinating the correspondence
between Hobbes and Descartes in his *Philosophy and Government.* For the philosophical exchanges between Hobbes and Descartes, see Descartes, *Meditations on*

First Philosophy and *Objections and Replies,* in *The Philosophical Writings of Descartes,* vol. 2, trans. Cottingham, Stoothoff, and Murdoch (cited hereafter in the text as CSM II, with page numbers). For the correspondence, see Hobbes, *Correspondence;* and Descartes, *Correspondence.*

7. This is Hobbes's term. In *De Corpore,* Hobbes castigates "philosophers" who are so befuddled by the techniques of abstract thinking that they deny that the thing that thinks is "a thinking-body" (chap. 3, 34). *De Corpore* is cited hereafter in the text as DCO, with chapter and page numbers.

8. Damasio, *Descartes' Error;* Damasio, *Feeling of What Happens;* Damasio, *Looking for Spinoza.*

9. Damasio, *Descartes' Error,* 250.

10. For a very dismissive version of these complaints, see McGinn's review of Damasio's *Looking for Spinoza* in "Fear Factor." For a more measured version of these complaints, see Hacking's review of the same book in "Minding the Brain."

11. See Deleuze, *Spinoza.*

12. See Israel, *Radical Enlightenment.* For an example of a similar portrayal of Hobbes with respect to Spinoza, see Gatens and Lloyd, *Collective Imaginings.* For a similar albeit more respectful and less gestural comparison, see Geismann, "Spinoza." For a comparative analysis of Hobbes's and Spinoza's accounts of the passions, thought, and action that is notably measured and not disparaging of Hobbes, see chap. 6 in James, *Passion and Action.*

13. For arguments that aspects of Spinoza's metaphysics are strikingly similar to if not strongly influenced by Hobbes's, see Sacksteder, "Spinoza's Attributes, Again"; Parrochia, "Science de la nature corporelle"; Boss, "La conception de la philosophie"; Sacksteder, "How Much of Hobbes?"

14. Connolly, "Spinoza and Us," 593n8.

15. Connolly, *Neuropolitics,* III. See also Connolly, *Why I Am Not a Secularist.*

16. White, *Sustaining Affirmation,* 131.

17. For a recent such account, see Malcolm, "Hobbes's Science of Politics and His Theory of Science," in *Aspects of Hobbes.* See also Johnston, *Rhetoric of Leviathan,* ix and chap. 6; Sorell, *Hobbes;* Watkins, *Hobbes's System of Ideas;* Peters, *Hobbes.*

18. Wolin, "Hobbes," 25.

19. For fascinating accounts of the passions and desire, see esp. Darwall, "Normativity and Projection"; Gert's argument for the ineluctable normativity of reason in "Hobbes on Reason"; and Hoekstra's careful account of the drive toward self-preservation in "Hobbes on Law, Nature, and Reason." For concerns about whether Hobbesian thinking qualifies as thinking, see Gert, "Hobbes on Language"; Sorell, "Sense, Thought and Motivation," in *Hobbes.*

20. Gert, "Hobbes on Language," 51–53; Sorell, *Hobbes,* 84–87.

21. For overviews of the political significance of materialist philosophies, see

Israel, *Radical Enlightenment;* Overhoff, *Hobbes's Theory of the Will;* Tuck, *Philosophy and Government;* Zarka, *Décision métaphysique.*

22. Hobbes, *Of Liberty and Necessity,* 274; Cheah, "Rationality of Life," 15.

23. Hobbes, *Leviathan,* introduction, 81. *Leviathan* is cited hereafter in the text as L, with chapter and page numbers.

24. If we read this passage closely, it is clear that Hobbes's aim in using this metaphor is not to give us an account of what it is to be a human being. Rather, it is to propose that humans can create humanlike machines in imitation of God's creation. That is, he compares automata ("Engines that move themselves by springs and wheeles as doth a watch") and the humans who might create them in order to introduce the idea that the commonwealth is a human contrivance, "an Artificiall man" created by the people whom it will govern (L intro.: 81–82).

25. In *De Corpore,* Hobbes describes vital motion as "the motion of the blood, perpetually circulating (as hath been shown from many infallible signs and marks by Doctor Harvey, the first observer of it) in the veins and arteries" (DCO 25:407).

26. In a similar discussion in *Leviathan,* Hobbes explains that when we consider "*Matter, or Body*" as "*living, sensible, rationall, hot, cold, moved, quiet,*" we understand that although what we perceive are the accidents "living, sensible, rational," and so forth, what we are talking about is matter—living matter, sensible matter, rational matter (L 4:107). Now, by dint of abstraction, we can consider by themselves the accidents by which we perceive matter and give them their own names, and so "for *living* put into account *life;* for *moved, motion;* for *hot, heat;* for *long, length,*" and, one might add, for thinking, thought (107). But, he cautions, even though these abstract names take the form of nouns rather than adjectives, we need to remember that "all such Names, are the names of the accidents and properties, by which one Matter, and Body is distinguished from another" (107). For Hobbes, then, abstract names such as "life," "motion," and "thought" always and necessarily imply the different kinds of matter or body that are the subject of the accidents "living," "moving," and "thinking." They do not name "things themselves." Abstract names are called "*Abstract;* because severed (not from Matter, but) from the account of Matter" (107). That is, abstract names such as "life," "motion," and "thought" are to be understood only as abstracted from our *discussion* of matter and not as abstracted from *matter itself.*

27. In "Normativity and Projection," Stephen Darwall argues that we should see this drive toward self-preservation not as a belief or intention but as a tendency expressed in behavior, thought, and speech.

28. For an elaboration of this point, see Tuck, *Philosophy and Government,* 279–302; and also chap. 2 of Zarka, *Décision métaphysique.*

29. Gert, "Hobbes on Language," 52.

30. We could say, then, that for Hobbes the experience of perception itself produces the intentionality of perceptual objects.

31. For an extended analysis of the difference between marks and signs, and more particularly for an argument that Hobbes's theory of language is essentially about communication rather than meaning, see Hungerland and Vick, "Hobbes's Theory."

32. Hobbes, *Human Nature,* chap. 5, 34; cf. *Leviathan,* chap. 3. *Human Nature* is cited hereafter in the text as HN, with chapter and page numbers.

33. I say "ideally" here because, of course, Hobbes is all too aware that language can be polyvalent and lead to deceit, misunderstanding, absurdity, and conflict. On possible abuses of language, see L 4:102; on the inconstancy of the meaning of language created by our passions and interests, see L 4:109.

34. Ross, "Hobbes and Descartes," 224.

35. Hobbes, *Questions Concerning Liberty,* 34.

CHAPTER 2

1. I borrow the term "upheavals" here from Nussbaum, *Upheavals of Thought.*

2. For broad surveys on this issue, see ibid. See also James, *Passion and Action.*

3. For surveys on this point, see, for example, Schiebinger, *Nature's Body;* Fausto-Sterling, *Myths of Gender;* Haraway, *Simians, Cyborgs, and Women;* Norton, *Bloodrites of the Post-Structuralists.*

4. Thanks to Patchen Markell for helping me develop this particular point.

5. Sorell, *Hobbes,* 74. Cited hereafter in the text.

6. In *De Corpore,* Hobbes comments that "though all sense, as I have said, be made by reaction, nevertheless it is not necessary that every thing that reacteth should have sense. . . . For unless those bodies had organs, as living creatures have, fit for the retaining of such motion as is made in them, their sense would be such, as that they should never remember the same. And therefore this hath nothing to do with that sense which is the subject of my discourse" (DCO 25:393). In *Leviathan,* Hobbes makes a similar point about the necessity for sensory organs when he explains that sense is the "fancy" caused "by the motion, of externall things upon our Eyes, Eares, and other organs thereunto ordained" (L 1:86). For Hobbes, then, it makes a difference whether one is a stone or a living creature whose body has organs "fit for the retaining of [sensory] motion."

7. Funnily enough, Samuel Mintz makes almost exactly the same observation, claiming that "Hobbes never considered the possibility that the product of mental activity—thought—is different in kind from the physical processes which give rise to it" (*Hunting of Leviathan,* 65).

8. In his essay "Between Acknowledgment and Avoidance" in *The Claim of Reason,* Cavell muses: "I am not this piece of flesh (though perhaps Falstaff was his); I am not in this flesh (though perhaps Christ was in his, but then his body was also bread); nor am I my flesh and blood (though somebody else is); nor am I of my flesh (though I hope somebody is). I am flesh" (398).

9. Elizabeth Grosz begins such an effort in her essay "Bodies and Knowledges: Feminism and the Crisis of Reason," in *Space, Time, and Perversion.*

10. MacIntyre, *Dependent Rational Animals,* 6.

11. McDermott, "Feeling of Rationality," 699; cited hereafter in the text. See also Marcus, Neuman, and Mackuen, *Affective Intelligence and Political Judgment,* in which the authors argue that "[e]motions prepare and direct conscious awareness" (29).

12. See, for example, Damasio, *Descartes' Error;* LeDoux, *Emotional Brain;* Changeux and Ricoeur, *What Makes Us Think?*

13. Connolly, *Neuropolitics;* and Connolly, *Why I Am Not a Secularist.*

14. Damasio, *Looking for Spinoza,* 35.

15. See also the definition he gives at DCO 25:391. Note that a phantasm is not an epiphenomenon of motions; these motions are the phantasms.

16. See also the account Hobbes gives at L 45:657–58.

17. Hobbes writes that "any object being removed from our eyes, though the impression it made in us remain; yet other objects more present succeeding, and working upon us, the Imagination of the past is obscured, and made weak; as the voyce of a man is in the noyse of the day" (L 2:88).

18. Descartes, *Passions of the Soul,* 341, 340. See also Descartes, *Treatise on Man,* 106; and Descartes, *Sixth Meditation,* in CSM II:59.

19. I borrow the definition and the example from *Webster's Encyclopedic Unabridged Dictionary of the English Language* (New York: Portland House, 1989).

20. Silverman, *Subject of Semiotics,* 110–11. Interestingly, in cognitive linguistics, this context of "contiguous things" includes domains of the mind in which concepts are located. Metonymy in this instance is understood both as a relationship that structures the movements between concepts that are associated by category and as an operation in which one area of the mind activates thoughts in a different but contiguous area of the mind. For explanations of this understanding of metonymy, see, for example, Barcelona, "Introduction"; and Ruiz de Mendoza, "Role of Mappings and Domains."

21. Barcelona, "Introduction," 5.

22. In *De Corpore,* Hobbes reiterates this point, remarking that the manner in which thoughts follow upon one another "is not without cause, nor so casual a thing as many perhaps think it" (DCO 25:397–98).

23. Hobbes's examples here are the compounding of "man" and "horse" to create the idea of a centaur, and also of "self" and "another's actions" to create an idea of the self as Hercules or Alexander the Great (L 2:89).

24. Or to recall Hobbes's language from *Human Nature,* the "power motive" of the mind is "the affections and passions" (HN 6:43).

25. For arguments that deny that Hobbes contends that phantasms and thoughts produce appetites and aversions, and desires and fears—and consequently

can have a causative relationship to actions—see Gert, "Hobbes, Mechanism, and Egoism"; and McNeilly, "Egoism in Hobbes."

26. The point here—that desire is what makes reasoning possible in the first place—is broached, albeit not explicitly, in recent arguments about the normativity of reason in Hobbes's philosophy. See Darwall, "Normativity and Projection"; Gert "Hobbes on Reason"; and Hoekstra, "Hobbes on Law, Nature, and Reason."

27. According to Hobbes, it takes "appetite, and judgment to discern" which of these arrayed phantasms are the "means conducing to that end" (DCO 25:398): judgment to distinguish between the phantasms (L 8:135) and appetite to serve as the measure for judgment.

28. For an extended analysis on the difference between marks and signs, and more particularly for an argument that Hobbes's theory of language is essentially about communication rather than meaning, see Hungerland and Vick, "Hobbes's Theory."

29. It is important to note here that since words or names are merely markers of or signs for motions in the thinking-body (i.e., phantasms), they have no intrinsically necessary relationship to the object that instigates the motions. For a thorough analysis of the importance of Hobbes's distinction between objects and words, see Zarka, *Décision métaphysique,* esp. chap. 2, "*L'Annihilatio Mundi.*" See also Guenancia, "Hobbes-Descartes."

30. Of course, the linguistic reconstitution of phantasms does not necessarily follow upon the recitation of the vocal signs, for as Hobbes notes, one might learn to recite a string of words without understanding them, that is, without having the ideas the words signify come to one's notice. As Hobbes notes, "A naturall foole that could never learn by heart the order of numerall words, as *one, two,* and *three,* may observe every stroak of the Clock, and nod to it, or say one, one, one; but can never know what houre it strikes" (L 4:104). It is only through the experience known as learning that the vocal signs and their sequencing come to reconstitute phantasms and their sequencing, thereby producing what Hobbes calls understanding.

31. See Hobbes, *De Corpore,* esp. chaps. 1–6, for Hobbes's explanation and delineation of the numerous possible types of relationships between words.

32. Hobbes lays out this process quite explicitly in L 5:110.

33. According to Hobbes, since "*truth* consisteth in the right ordering of names in our affirmations, a man that seeketh precise *truth,* had need to remember what every name he uses stands for; and to place it accordingly" (L 4:105).

34. Hobbes contends that the affective response elicited by phantasms is variable from moment to moment for individuals themselves because "the constitution of a mans Body, is in continuall mutation" (L 6:120). Such responses also differ from person to person, for "though the nature of that we conceive, be the

same; yet the diversity of our reception of it, in respect of different constitutions of body, and prejudices of opinions, gives everything a tincture of our different passions" (L 4:109).

35. In *Leviathan and the Air-Pump,* Shapin and Shaffer also recognize that, for Hobbes, the conclusions we reach in ratiocination may be oriented toward prudential or instrumental concerns even as we think they are oriented by the concerns of science.

36. Flathman, "Liberalism."

37. For the first point, see Boyd, "Thomas Hobbes." For the second point, see Chapter 5, ahead.

CHAPTER 3

1. DCO, 6:120.

2. Hobbes, *Of Liberty and Necessity,* 274. Cited hereafter in the text as LN, with page numbers.

3. Rogers, introduction to Bramhall, *Defence of True Liberty,* v. For a survey of some of the bitter responses to Hobbes's work, see Bowle, *Hobbes and His Critics;* Mintz, *Hunting of Leviathan;* and Reik, *Golden Lands.* For a more recent analysis of both the context for and the early reception of Hobbes's materialism, see Overhoff, *Hobbes's Theory of the Will.*

4. Skinner, *Reason and Rhetoric,* 328.

5. Tuck, *Philosophy and Government,* 344.

6. I'm thinking here not simply of the frustratingly myopic discussion in contemporary texts such as Ted Honderich's *How Free Are You?* but also of the criticisms often lobbed at theorists such as Michel Foucault and Judith Butler for the "lack of agency" seemingly entailed by their materialist analyses of power and politics. For Butler's response to such accusations, see her "Contingent Foundations." For a brief and recent lay account of both philosophical and scientific concerns about the implications of deterministic theories of action for our sense of agency, see Overbye, "Free Will."

7. Bramhall, *Defence of True Liberty,* 91. Cited hereafter in the text.

8. Mintz, *Hunting of Leviathan,* 113.

9. It is important to acknowledge here that some among Bramhall's arguments focus on scriptural and theological issues, warning that following from Hobbes's argument against the incorporeality of the soul is the blasphemous implication that God is not a spiritual being. Hobbes dismisses these objections, portraying Bramhall's repeated recourse to the question of the nature of God as tiresome and unproductive. Indeed, he likens Bramhall to "Sisyphus in the poet's hell" who "rolls this and other questions with much ado, till they come to the light of Scripture, and then they vanish; and he vexing, sweating, and railing, goes to it

again, to as little purpose as before." See Hobbes, *Answer to a Book,* 349. Without meaning to endorse Hobbes's characterization of Bramhall's scriptural arguments, I shall lay them aside and leave their assessment to another better-suited to the task. See, for example, Mintz, *Hunting of Leviathan,* and Overhoff, *Hobbes's Theory of the Will,* for detailed discussion of the religious implications of Hobbes's materialism.

10. *Passions of the Soul* is cited hereafter in the text as PS, with page numbers.

11. Indeed, Descartes apparently penned *The Passions of the Soul* in an effort to respond to insistent queries about the interaction between the body and the soul put forth by Princess Elizabeth of Bohemia. See the translator's preface to PS, 325. For speculation on how Descartes's argument that the immaterial mind and the material body interact might be philosophically rendered and understood, see Garber, "Understanding Interaction."

12. Descartes, *Principles of Philosophy,* 280; see also PS, 335, 341. *Principles of Philosophy* is cited hereafter in the text as PP, with page numbers.

13. See also Descartes's similar comments in the Fourth Meditation, in *Meditations,* 40–41. For discussions on this point, see Cottingham, *Reason, Will, and Sensation.*

14. Indeed, Cynthia Bryson argues that it is just this implication of Descartes's dualism that underlies early modern feminist Mary Astell's arguments for women's equality. See C. Bryson, "Mary Astell."

15. I owe the language for this particular articulation to Patchen Markell, who posed the issue as a question in an e-mail exchange about thinking.

16. Indeed, Bramhall's sense that such is what we need to do is accentuated in his recounting of a story about the Stoic master Zeno and his slave. Having been caught for petty thievery, Zeno's slave sought to avoid punishment by disingenuously invoking his master's philosophy of necessary destiny. Like the malicious manipulator of Bramhall's worried imagination, the slave protests that he should not be punished for his misdemeanor because he was compelled to do it through the movement of fate. Zeno's response was apparently to claim that he too was compelled by destiny and could not avoid beating his slave. Commenting upon the slave's foolishness for trying to deny that he was free and that in that freedom he chose to do wrong, Bramhall points out that a belief in liberty would make it possible for the slave to argue against the beating. The lesson to be drawn from this tale, Bramhall contends, is that "[h]e that denies liberty is fitter to be refuted with rodds, than with arguments, untill he confess that it is free for him that beates him either to continue striking, or to give over, that is, to have true liberty" (88). In other words, given the possibility of such a beating, we would all choose to believe in liberty.

17. Hobbes writes that "The *influence of the stars* is but a small part of the whole cause, consisting of the concourse of all agents," and later explains that

"neither the stars alone, nor the temperature of the patient alone, is able to produce any effect, without the concurrence of all other agents. For there is hardly any one action, how casual soever it seem, to the causing whereof concur not whatsoever is *in rerum natura,* which because it is a great paradox, and depends upon many antecedent speculations, I do not press in this place" (LN, 246, 267).

18. Hobbes, *Questions Concerning Liberty,* 34. Cited hereafter as QCL, with page numbers.

19. I borrow this specification of the temporal complexity of memory in a material being from Brian Massumi's insightful discussion in his introduction to *Parables of the Virtual,* esp. 15–16.

20. I suppose, then, that one could argue, although I do not do so here, that Hobbes offers an alternative—and possibly more complex—account of the spatial and temporal relations that structure causality than those proffered by either Newton or Hume. See Richmond, "Newton and Hume."

21. See Hobbes, *De Homine,* chap. 13, 63. Cited hereafter in the text as DH, with chapter and page numbers.

22. Hobbes argues that just as the light of the stars is obscured by the light of the sun during the day—"which starrs do no less exercise their vertue by which they are visible, in the day, than in the night"—so the manifold impressions made upon our senses may be obscured yet not despoiled of their effecsts upon us when other objects or events hold our attention (L 2:88). In other words, he suggests, our sensibility of the effects of the world upon us does not constitute the totality of the effects of the world upon us.

23. See Pitkin, "Hobbes's Concept of Representation—I"; and Pitkin, "Hobbes's Concept of Representation—II."

24. Indeed, Hobbes is clear that not all people are persons, which is to say that not all people can be considered the owners or authors of their own actions. For example, he says that "Children, Fooles, and Mad-men that have no use of Reason" are not persons in the sense that they are not considered as the authors or owners of their actions (L 16:219). Hobbes suggests here that because these people do not or cannot know what it might mean to have their actions considered as their own—and hence act on the basis of that insight—their actions are not considered as distinctively theirs for the purposes of law and politics.

CHAPTER 4

1. See Bok, *Lying.*

2. Kant, "On a Supposed Right to Lie Because of Philanthropic Concerns," in *Grounding* (1993), 64.

3. For a comment attributing such a view to Flathman, see the opening paragraph of Tuck, "Flathman's Hobbes," 212.

4. It is important to note here, at the outset, that Hobbes also advocates lying as part of our civil duty. In a discussion of the relationship between faith and civil duty, he claims: "A private man has alwaies the liberty, (because thought is free,) to beleeve, or not beleeve in his heart. . . . But when it comes to confession of that faith, the Private Reason must submit to the Publique" (L 37:478), which is to say that we must profess in public the official religious discourse rather than our own beliefs. This particular form of lying can be seen as a precursor to the kind of Rawlsian liberal mandate that privileges public reason in public discourse. What I am interested in here, though, is not this particular form of civic lying but the kinds of lying that Hobbes deems ethical, as entailed by the laws of nature, which is to say the kinds of lying that are the conditions that make politics possible in the first place. On the role of public reason in politics, see Rawls, *Political Liberalism*.

5. Of course, Hobbes notes in the third law of nature that the keeping of promises is essential for contract making and, by extension, civil society (L 15:201). But then again, he is dubious about the likelihood that we will keep promises without threat of enforcement by a superior power such as the sovereign: "Covenants, without the Sword, are but Words, and of no strength to secure a man at all" (L 17:223).

6. For an argument that also identifies peace as a primary principle in Hobbes's ethics, albeit one that sees Hobbes as quite pessimistic about the prospects for peace, see May, "Hobbes on the Attitude of Pacifism."

7. Although I do think they are different. On this point, I disagree with the deontological readings of Hobbes mentioned in the Introduction, but also with that forwarded by David van Mill in his *Liberty, Rationality, and Agency in Hobbes's Leviathan*. For the specifics of my disagreements with the latter, see my "Hobbes out of Bounds," 257–73.

8. For example, Kant contends that "we must presuppose [freedom] if we want to think of a being as rational and as endowed with consciousness of its causality as regards actions, i.e., as endowed with a will" (*Grounding* [1981], 51). On this point, see also Kant, *Critique of Practical Reason;* and Kant, *Metaphysics of Morals*.

9. Pippin, *Modernism*, 49.

10. See Constant as cited in Kant, "On a Supposed Right to Lie," 63. Page numbers in this paragraph and the next in the text refer to "On a Supposed Right to Lie."

11. Significantly, though, Pippin notes that Kant does not really trust that "we could overcome self-interest sufficiently to make" the moral claim the principle behind our action. Accordingly, "[w]e must settle for legality rather than morality" (*Modernism,* 11).

12. Kant, *Grounding*, 26.

13. Likewise, in his discussion of deliberation, Hobbes explains that the "good

or evill effect" of the actions we consider doing "dependeth on the foresight of a long chain of consequences, of which very seldome any man is able to see to the end" (L 6:129).

14. In an argument that is consonant with the one I develop here, Kinch Hoekstra claims that Hobbes's rebuttal to such contentions is leveled not so much at those "Silent Fooles" whose plots are secret and whose connivance is slight and discrete but rather at those "Explicit Fooles" whose actions and words serve to "incite others to contravene contracts and (therefore) laws, or at least will have the effect of eroding respect for contracts and laws." See Hoekstra, "Hobbes and the Foole," 623–24. Hoekstra contends that, for Hobbes, "[o]ccasional low-risk, low-publicity, silent infringements are for a commonwealth survivable, if not always innocuous; the incitement of infringement, however, is deadly to the commonwealth" (628).

15. Hobbes's discussion of the Foole is, of course, at the center of rational choice treatments of the Prisoner's Dilemma as manifested in Hobbes's arguments. Among these treatments, Jean Hampton comes closest to appreciating the temporal dimensions of Hobbes's argument when she notes that Hobbes's account of conflict makes most sense if we presume that individuals are shortsighted about what is good for them. With this point at hand, she contends that Hobbes can be seen as presenting an "iterated" Prisoner's Dilemma game, which is to say one in which individuals play multiple times, so that cooperation comes to be seen as in their long-term interest. See Hampton, *Hobbes,* 80–89.

16. In various of his discussions of power and honor, Hobbes explains that, in the effort to secure his power, the sovereign awards titles to people whom he trusts, a designation that wins him their fealty (L 18:238). The granting of such titles has a broader socially cementing effect, for "[t]o honour those another honours, is to Honour him; as a signe of approbation of his judgement" (L 10:154).

17. Hobbes, *De Cive,* chap. 3, 140. Cited hereafter in the text as DC, with chapter and page numbers.

18. On the political uses made of slander in Hobbes's contemporary England, see Kaplan, *Culture of Slander.*

19. For a more extensive elaboration upon this particular point, see my "Just Lie."

20. Many thanks to Julie Vogel for conversations clarifying this point.

21. It must be noted here that Hobbes's emphasis on the importance of appearances is directly related to his (admittedly convoluted) advocacy of religious toleration. In what may be seen as a legal codification of his ethics, Hobbes argues that although an individual cannot be compelled "to think any otherwise then my reason perswades me," the sovereign may oblige a subject "to obedience, so, as not by act or word to declare I beleeve him not" (L 32:411). In an analysis that picks up on similar themes, Alan Ryan claims that Hobbes's argument

for religious uniformity is "about manners in public rather than about anything deeper." See Ryan, "A More Tolerant Hobbes?" 50.

22. Hobbes says as much in his claim that a covenant can bind an individual only to what is possible—or at least thought possible—to do. As he explains it, "The matter, or subject of a Covenant, is alwayes something that falleth under deliberation; (For to Covenant, is an act of the Will; that is to say an act, and the last act, of deliberation;) and is therefore alwayes understood to be something to come; and which is judged Possible for him that Covenanteth, to performe. And therefore, to promise that which is known to be Impossible, is no Covenant. But if that prove impossible afterwards, which before was thought possible, the Covenant is valid, and bindeth, (though not to the thing it selfe,) yet to the value; or, if that also be impossible, to the unfeigned endeavour of performing as much as is possible: for to more no man can be obliged" (L 14:197–98).

23. Again, for these deontological arguments, see A. E. Taylor, "Ethical Doctrine of Hobbes"; and Warrender, *Political Philosophy of Thomas Hobbes*.

24. The entirety of chapter 27 of *Leviathan* is devoted to elaborating the circumstances that extenuate or aggravate a crime. Included among the extenuating circumstances are the inability to know or comprehend the law, captivity, the threat of imminent death, and destitution. For Richard Miller's elaboration of the features of casuistic moral reasoning, see his *Casuistry and Modern Ethics, 5*.

25. Jonsen and Toulmin, *Abuse of Casuistry*. Interestingly, in the course of their historical analysis, Jonsen and Toulmin lay some of their blame at Hobbes's feet, claiming that the aspiration toward systematicity that is characteristic of Hobbes's philosophy provided a signal contribution to the decline of casuistic moral reasoning (163).

26. Indeed, Hobbes states, "he that having sufficient Security, that others shall observe the same Lawes towards him, observes them not himself, seeketh not Peace, but War; & consequently the destruction of his Nature by Violence" (L 15:215).

27. Indeed, such a seeming would put my reading starkly at odds with C. B. Macpherson's argument that Hobbes is preeminently a philosopher of the emerging capitalist class. See Macpherson, *Political Theory*. For an extended exploration of the possibility of resistance in Hobbes's work, see Steinberger, "Hobbesian Resistance."

28. Hobbes cautions that "not every Fear justifies the Action it produceth, but the fear onely of corporeall hurt, which we call *Bodily Fear*, and from which a man cannot see how to be delivered, but by the action. A man is assaulted, fears present death, from which he sees not how to escape, but by wounding him that assaulteth him; If he wound him to death, this is no Crime; because no man is supposed at the making of a Common-wealth, to have abandoned the defence of his life, or limbes, where the Law cannot arrive time enough to his assistance. But

to kill a man, because from his actions, or his threatnings, I may argue he will kill me when he can, (seeing I have time, and means to demand protection, from the Soveraign Power,) is a Crime" (L 27:343).

CHAPTER 5

1. Hobbes gestures to this missing part of his narrative himself when he acknowledges that, historically, the state of nature as he describes it has not actually existed, even though both the existence of "savage people" who live in "small Families" and nations among themselves might be said to live as if in a war of all against all (L 13:187).

2. For classic interpretations of Hobbes that seek in particular to elucidate and resolve the coordination problem, see, for example, Gauthier, *Logic of Leviathan;* Hampton, *Hobbes;* Kavka, *Hobbesian Moral and Political Theory;* M. Taylor, *Possibility of Cooperation;* and, more recently, M. Murphy, "Hobbes' Shortsightedness Account of Conflict."

3. See Pateman, *Sexual Contract;* Mills, *Racial Contract;* Orlie, *Living Ethically, Acting Politically;* Kateb, "Hobbes"; Wolin, "Hobbes"; and Israel, *Radical Enlightenment.*

4. For an interesting comparison of Hobbes's account of action and passion with that formulated by Spinoza, see James, *Passion and Action.*

5. Here I paraphrase Hobbes at L 31:406.

6. Pitkin, *Wittgenstein and Justice,* 157.

7. Darwall, "Normativity and Projection."

8. To be clear, Hobbes's claim here about the pursuit of power through reputation is not equivalent to his critical appraisal of the effects of ambition—a socially and politically dangerous "*Desire* of Office, or precedence" (L 6:123)—or of glory—the "*Joy,* arising from imagination of a mans own power and ability" (124–25). What is at stake in the attention to and cultivation of reputation is not craving and feeling happy about one's power and ability but rather the careful cultivation of the social conditions for future actions. For analyses of Hobbes's views on ambition and glory, respectively, see Baumgold, *Hobbes's Political Theory;* and Slomp, *Thomas Hobbes.*

9. In a similar analysis that emphasizes the centrality of the representation of power to the production or generation of power, Yves Charles Zarka contends that Hobbes develops an ethicopolitical semiology, "une sémiologie éthico-politique." See Zarka, "La sémiologie du pouvoir," in *Hobbes et la pensée politique moderne.*

10. See Macpherson, *Political Theory.*

11. Of course, in arguing that our passions can be read in our attitudes, bearing, and actions, Hobbes does not suggest that the latter render us transparent to one another. To the contrary, in the introduction to *Leviathan,* Hobbes poses

our mutual legibility as a problem, indeed as one of the key problems he aims to address through the text (intro., 82). He is not suggesting there is a uniform code or universal key to which we can refer that will render our thoughts and passions wholly visible to one another. He acknowledges that some signs are natural, others cultural, and that both can be feigned as well as simply expressive. The point I want to draw out of his analyses is that we read one another's actions and gestures, and that when we perceive one another's evaluative perceptions, we ourselves respond evaluatively, making inferences about what their responses reveal about the person and what they have perceived. It is this contagion of manifest responses that is generative of power. For an extended exploration of the issue of our mutual intelligibility, see Frost, "Faking It."

12. As Hobbes explains this point in *De Cive,* "because men believe him to be powerful, whom they see . . . esteemed powerful by others; it falls out that . . . by the opinion of power true power is acquired" (DC 15:297).

13. In a different discussion, Hobbes gives us further insight into the vexed character of power relationships, this time among those who are relatively equal. He argues that "[t]o have received from one, to whom we think our selves equall, greater benefits than there is hope to Requite, disposeth to counterfeit love; but really secret hatred; and puts a man into the estate of a desperate debtor, that in declining the sight of his creditor, tacitely wishes him there, where he might never see him more" (L 11:162–63). Interestingly, such a dynamic does not develop if the relationship is one of obvious or recognized inequality, for "to have received benefits from one, whom we acknowledge for superiour, enclines to love; because the obligation is no new depression: and cheerfull acceptation, (which men call *Gratitude,*) is such an honour done to the obliger, as is taken generally for retribution" (163). In other words, to be given great gifts from an individual to whom one is already obliged simply requires in return even more gratitude than is already owed. The expression of love that is part of the manifestation of gratitude is "retribution" because it increases the public esteem or power of the benefactor.

14. Hobbes says that we give the name "*Honourable*" to whatever "possession, action, or quality, is an argument and signe of Power." He goes on to conclude: "To be Honoured, loved, or feared of many, is Honourable; as arguments of Power" (L 10:155).

15. As Hobbes notes, "To be sedulous in promoting anothers good; also to flatter, is to Honour; as a signe we seek his protection or ayde" (L 10:153). Or, again: "To agree with in opinion, is to Honour; as being a signe of approving his judgement, and wisdome" (153).

16. See Flathman, *Thomas Hobbes;* and Flathman, *Reflections.*

17. In her reading of Hobbes, Rhodes argues that we should shift our analytic attention from both the individual and the sovereign to the collective, claiming, "The overlooked commonwealth itself, not the individuals who are its founda-

tion and not the sovereign who is its agent, turns out to be the central conceptual political institution of *Leviathan*" ("Creating Leviathan," 188).

18. Hobbes, *Behemoth,* chap. 1, 16.

19. Hobbes makes a similar claim about the marks or signs of power in *Human Nature,* where he remarks, "The signs by which we know our own power are those actions which proceed from the same; and the signs by which other men know it, are such actions, gesture, countenance and speech, as usually such powers produce" (HN 8:48).

20. Indeed, Hobbes claims that it is against the duty of the sovereign "to let the people be ignorant, or mis-informed of the grounds, and reasons of those his essentiall Rights; because thereby men are easie to be seduced, and drawn to resist him, when the Common-wealth shall require their use and exercise. . . . And the grounds of these Rights, have the rather need to be diligently, and truly taught" (L 39:377).

21. Hampton, *Hobbes,* 185.

22. Hobbes contends that "[t]he Passions that encline men to Peace" are not simply the "Feare of Death"—a claim for which he is notorious—but also "Desire of such things as are necessary to commodious living; and a Hope by their Industry to obtain them" (L 13:188). In other words, the desire for power, in all its complexity, is also a motivating factor in the pursuit of peace.

23. Indeed, Keith Thomas reads Hobbes as trying to effect a shift away from an aristocratic military virtue toward an aristocratic gentlemanly virtue. See Thomas, "Social Origins."

24. Oxford English Dictionary (OED) Online, http://dictionary.oed.com, s.v. "ecology."

25. Bennett, "The Force of Things," 365, 361. For another effort to see ecology as an imbrication of mutually transformative material, social, and political interdependencies, see Latour, *Politics of Nature.*

26. According to the OED, the term "ecology" did not come into use until the late nineteenth century.

Bibliography

Ackerman, T. F. "Two Concepts of Moral Goodness in Hobbes's Ethics," *Journal of the History of Philosophy* 14, no. 4 (1976): 415–25.

Allison, Henry E. *Kant's Theory of Freedom* (Cambridge: Cambridge University Press, 1990).

———. *Kant's Transcendental Idealism: An Interpretation and Defense* (New Haven, CT: Yale University Press, 1983).

Arendt, Hannah. *The Human Condition* (Chicago: University of Chicago Press, 1958).

Aubrey, John. "The Brief Life, John Aubrey: An Abstract of Aubrey's Notes," in *Thomas Hobbes: The Elements of Law Natural and Politic: Human Nature and De Corpore Politico,* ed J. C. A. Gaskin (Oxford: Oxford University Press, 1994).

Aylmer, G. E., ed. *The Interregnum: The Quest for Settlement 1646–1660* (North Haven, CT: Archon Books, 1972).

Baker, Gordon, and Katherine J. Morris. *Descartes' Dualism* (New York: Routledge, 1996).

Barcelona, Antonio. "Introduction: The Cognitive Theory of Metaphor and Metonymy," in *Metaphor and Metonymy at the Crossroads: A Cognitive Perspective,* ed. Antonio Barcelona (New York: Mouton de Gruyter, 2000).

Barnouw, Jeffrey. "Hobbes's Causal Account of Sensation," *Journal of the History of Philosophy* 18, no. 2 (1980): 115–30.

———. "Hobbes's Psychology of Thought: Endeavours, Purpose and Curiosity," *History of European Ideas* 10, no. 5 (1989): 519–45.

Baumgold, Deborah. *Hobbes's Political Theory* (Cambridge: Cambridge University Press, 1988).

Benhabib, Seyla, ed. *Democracy and Difference: Contesting the Boundaries of the Political* (Princeton, NJ: Princeton University Press, 1996).

Bennett, Jane. "The Force of Things: Steps Towards an Ecology of Matter," *Political Theory* 32, no. 3 (2004): 347–72.

Bertman, M. A. "Hobbes on 'Good,'" *Southwestern Journal of Philosophy* 6 (1975): 58–74.

Bobbio, Norberto. *Thomas Hobbes and the Natural Law Tradition,* trans. Daniela Gobetti (Chicago: University of Chicago Press, 1993).

Bok, Sissela. *Lying: Moral Choice in Public and Private Life* (New York: Vintage, 1989).

Bono, James. *The Word of God and the Languages of Man: Interpreting Nature in Early Modern Science and Medicine* (Madison: University of Wisconsin Press, 1995).

Boss, Gilbert. "La conception de la philosophie chez Hobbes et chez Spinoza," *Archives de Philosophie* 48 (1985): 311–26.

Bowle, John. *Hobbes and His Critics: A Study in Seventeenth Century Constitutionalism* (New York: Barnes and Noble, 1969).

Boyd, Richard. "Thomas Hobbes and the Perils of Pluralism," *Journal of Politics* 63, no. 2 (2001): 392–413.

Braidotti, Rosi. *Metamorphoses: Towards a Materialist Theory of Becoming* (Cambridge: Polity, 2002).

Bramhall, John. *A Defence of True Liberty from Antecedent and Extrinsicall Necessity* [1655], ed. G. A. J. Rogers (London: Routledge/Thoemmes Press, 1996).

Brandt, Frithiof. *Thomas Hobbes' Mechanical Conception of Nature* (London: Librairie Hachette, 1927).

Brennan, Teresa. *The Transmission of Affect* (Ithaca, NY: Cornell University Press, 2004).

Brown, Wendy. *Edgework: Critical Essays on Knowledge and Politics* (Princeton, NJ: Princeton University Press, 2005).

———. *Politics Out of History* (Princeton, NJ: Princeton University Press, 2001).

———. *States of Injury: Power and Freedom in Late Modernity* (Princeton, NJ: Princeton University Press, 1995).

Bryson, Anna. "The Rhetoric of Status: Gesture, Demeanour and the Image of the Gentleman in Sixteenth- and Seventeenth-Century England," in *Renaissance Bodies: The Human Figure in English Culture c. 1540–1660,* ed. Lucy Gent and Nigel Llewellyn (London: Reaktion Books, 1990).

Bryson, Cynthia. "Mary Astell: Defender of the 'Disembodied Mind,'" *Hypatia* 13, no. 4 (1998): 40–62.

Burnyeat, Myles, ed. *The Skeptical Tradition* (Berkeley: University of California Press, 1983).

Butler, Judith. *Bodies That Matter: On the Discursive Limits of "Sex"* (New York: Routledge Kegan Paul, 1993).

———. "Contingent Foundations: Feminism and the Question of 'Postmodernism,'" in *Feminists Theorize the Political,* ed. Judith Butler and Joan Scott (New York: Routledge, 1992).

————. *Gender Trouble: Feminism and the Subversion of Identity* (New York: Routledge Kegan Paul, 1990).

————. *The Psychic Life of Power: Theories in Subjection* (Stanford, CA: Stanford University Press, 1997).

Cavell, Stanley. *The Claim of Reason: Wittgenstein, Skepticism, Morality, and Tragedy* (New York: Oxford University Press, 1979).

Chalmers, David. *The Conscious Mind: In Search of a Fundamental Theory* (New York: Oxford University Press, 1996).

Changeux, Jean-Pierre, and Paul Ricoeur. *What Makes Us Think? A Neuroscientist and a Philosopher Argue About Ethics, Human Nature, and the Brain,* trans. M. B. DeBevoise [1998] (Princeton, NJ: Princeton University Press, 2000).

Cheah, Pheng. "The Rationality of Life: On the Organismic Metaphor of the State," *Radical Philosophy* 112 (March–April 2002): 9–24.

Churchland, Paul. *Matter and Consciousness: A Contemporary Introduction to the Philosophy of Mind* (Cambridge, MA: MIT Press, 1988).

Conant, James. "Varieties of Skepticism," in *Wittgenstein and Scepticism,* ed. Denis McManus (New York: Routledge, 2004).

Connolly, William. *Neuropolitics: Thinking, Culture, Speed* (Minneapolis: University of Minnesota Press, 2002).

————. *Pluralism* (Durham, NC: Duke University Press, 2005).

————. "Spinoza and Us," *Political Theory* 29, no. 4 (2001): 583–94.

————. *Why I Am Not a Secularist* (Minneapolis: University of Minnesota Press, 1999).

Coole, Diana. "Rethinking Agency: A Phenomenological Approach to Embodiment and Agentic Capacities," *Political Studies* 53, no. 1 (2005): 124–42.

Cottingham, John. *Descartes* (New York: Basil Blackwell, 1986).

————, ed. *Reason, Will, and Sensation: Studies in Descartes's Metaphysics* (Oxford: Oxford University Press, 1994).

Cottingham, John, Robert Stoothoff, and Dugald Murdoch, trans. *The Philosophical Writings of Descartes,* vols. 1 and 2 (Cambridge: Cambridge University Press, 1985, 1984).

Cottingham, John, Robert Stoothoff, Dugald Murdoch, and Anthony Kenny, trans. *The Philosophical Writings of Descartes,* vol. 3 (Cambridge: Cambridge University Press, 1991).

Coward, Barry. *The Stuart Age: England 1603–1714* (New York: Longman, 1994).

Curley, Edwin. "The State of Nature and Its Law in Hobbes and Spinoza," *Philosophical Topics* 19, no. 1 (1991): 97–117.

Curran, Eleanor. "Hobbes's Theory of Rights—A Modern Interest Theory," *Journal of Ethics* 6 (2002): 63–86.

———. "A Very Peculiar Royalist: Hobbes in the Context of His Political Contemporaries," *British Journal for the History of Philosophy* 10, no. 2 (2002): 167–208.

Damasio, Antonio. *Descartes' Error: Emotion, Reason, and the Human Brain,* 4th ed. (New York: Harper Collins-Quill, 2000).

———. *The Feeling of What Happens: Body and Emotion in the Making of Consciousness* (Orlando, FL: Harcourt, 1999).

———. *Looking for Spinoza: Joy, Sorrow, and the Feeling Brain* (Orlando, FL: Harcourt, 2003).

Daniel, Stephen. "Civility and Sociability: Hobbes on Man and Citizen," *Journal of the History of Philosophy* 18, no. 2 (1980): 209–15.

Darwall, Stephen. "Normativity and Projection in Hobbes's *Leviathan,*" *Philosophical Review* 109, no. 3 (2000): 313–47.

Dear, Peter. "Narratives, Anecdotes, and Experiments: Turning Experience into Science in the Seventeenth Century," in *The Literary Structure of Scientific Argument: Historical Studies,* ed. Peter Dear (Philadelphia: University of Pennsylvania Press, 1991).

———. "*Totius in Verba:* Rhetoric and Authority in the Early Royal Society," *Isis* 76, no. 2 (1985): 144–61.

Deigh, John. "Reason and Ethics in Hobbes's Leviathan," *Journal of the History of Philosophy* 34, no. 1 (1996): 33–60.

Deleuze, Gilles. *Spinoza: Practical Philosophy* (San Francisco: City Lights, 1988).

Dennett, Daniel. *Consciousness Explained* (Boston: Back Bay Books, 1991).

Derrida, Jacques. *Limited Inc,* trans. Samuel Weber (Evanston, IL: Northwestern University Press, 1977).

Descartes, René. *The Correspondence,* in Cottingham et al., *Philosophical Writings,* vol. 3.

———. *Discourse on the Method,* in Cottingham, Stoothoff, and Murdoch, *Philosophical Writings,* vol. 1.

———. *Meditations on First Philosophy,* in Cottingham, Stoothoff, and Murdoch, *Philosophical Writings,* vol. 2.

———. *Objections and Replies,* in Cottingham, Stoothoff, and Murdoch, *Philosophical Writings,* vol. 2.

———. *The Passions of the Soul,* in Cottingham, Stoothoff, and Murdoch, *Philosophical Writings,* vol. 1.

———. *Principles of Philosophy,* in Cottingham, Stoothoff, and Murdoch, *Philosophical Writings,* vol. 1.

———. *Treatise on Man,* in Cottingham, Stoothoff, and Murdoch, *Philosophical Writings,* vol. 1.

Dietz, Mary. "Hobbes's Subject as Citizen," in Dietz, *Thomas Hobbes.*

———, ed. *Thomas Hobbes and Political Theory* (Lawrence: University Press of Kansas, 1990).

Digby, Thomas Foster. "Bodies and More Bodies: Hobbes's Ascriptive Individualism," *Metaphilosophy* 22 (October 1991): 324–32.

DiStefano, Christine. *Configurations of Masculinity: A Feminist Perspective on Modern Political Theory* (Ithaca, NY: Cornell University Press, 1991).

Elias, Norbert. *The Civilizing Process: The Development of Manners; Changes in the Code of Conduct and Feeling in Early Modern Times* [1939], trans. Edmund Jephcott (New York: Pantheon, 1978).

Fausto-Sterling, Anne. *Myths of Gender: Biological Theories About Men and Women,* 2d ed. (New York: Basic Books, 1992).

Ferrell, Lori Anne. *Government by Polemic: James I, the King's Preachers, and the Rhetorics of Conformity, 1603–1625* (Stanford, CA: Stanford University Press, 1998).

Flathman, Richard. "Absolutism, Individuality, and Politics: Hobbes and a Little Beyond," *History of European Ideas* 10, no. 5 (1989): 547–68.

———. "Liberalism: From Unicity to Plurality and on to Singularity," *Social Research* 61, no. 3 (1994): 671–86.

———. *Reflections of a Would-Be Anarchist* (Minneapolis: University of Minnesota Press, 1999).

———. *Thomas Hobbes: Skepticism, Individuality, and Chastened Politics* (Newbury Park, CA: Sage, 1993).

———. *Willful Liberalism: Voluntarism and Individualism in Political Theory and Practice* (Ithaca, NY: Cornell University Press, 1992).

Foster, John. *The Immaterial Self: A Defense of the Cartesian Dualist Conception of the Mind* (New York: Routledge, 1991).

Foucault, Michel. *Essential Works of Foucault, 1954–1984,* 3 vols., ed. Paul Rabinow and James Faubion (New York: New Press, 1997, 1998, 2000).

Friedman, Jeffrey, ed. *The Rational Choice Controversy: Economic Models of Politics Reconsidered* (New Haven, CT: Yale University Press, 1996).

Frost, Samantha. "Faking It: Hobbes's Thinking-Bodies and the Ethics of Dissimulation," *Political Theory* 29, no. 1 (2001): 30–57.

———. "Hobbes out of Bounds," *Political Theory* 32, no. 2 (2004): 257–73.

———. "Just Lie: Lessons from Hobbes on the Cultivation of Peace," *Theory and Event* 7, no. 4 (2004).

———. "Reading the Body: Hobbes, Body Politics, and the Vocation of Political Theory," in *Vocations of Political Theory,* ed. Jason Frank and John Tambornino (Minneapolis: University of Minnesota Press, 2000).

Garber, Daniel. "Understanding Interaction: What Descartes Should Have Told Elizabeth," in *Descartes Embodied: Reading Cartesian Philosophy Through Cartesian Science* (Cambridge: Cambridge University Press, 2001).

Gary, R. "Hobbes' System and His Early Philosophical Views," in *Texts and Contexts,* vol. 1 of *Thomas Hobbes: Critical Assessments,* ed. Preston King (New York: Routledge, 1993).

Gatens, Moira, and Genevieve Lloyd. *Collective Imaginings: Spinoza, Past and Present* (New York: Routledge, 1999).

Gauthier, David. "Hobbes: The Laws of Nature," *Pacific Philosophical Quarterly* 82, nos. 3–4 (2001): 258–84.

———. "Hobbes's Social Contract," in *Perspectives on Thomas Hobbes,* ed. G. A. J. Rogers and Alan Ryan (Oxford: Oxford University Press, 1988).

———. *The Logic of Leviathan: The Moral and Political Theory of Thomas Hobbes* (Oxford: Oxford University Press, 1969).

Gauthier, David, and Robert Sugden, eds. *Rationality, Justice and the Social Contract: Themes from Morals by Agreement* (Ann Arbor: University of Michigan Press, 1993).

Geismann, Georg. "Spinoza—Beyond Hobbes and Rousseau," *Journal of the History of Ideas* 52, no. 1 (1991): 35–53.

Gert, Bernard. "Hobbes, Mechanism, and Egoism," *Philosophical Quarterly* 15, no. 61 (1965): 341–49.

———. "Hobbes on Language, Metaphysics, and Epistemology," *Hobbes Studies* 14 (2001): 40–58.

———. "Hobbes on Reason," *Pacific Philosophical Quarterly* 82, nos. 3–4 (2001): 243–57.

———. "Hobbes's Psychology," in *The Cambridge Companion to Hobbes,* ed. Tom Sorrel (Cambridge: Cambridge University Press, 1996).

Goffman, Erving. *Interaction Ritual: Essays on Face-to-Face Behavior* (New York: Anchor, 1967).

Gorham, Geoffrey. "Mind-Body Dualism and the Harvey-Descartes Controversy," *Journal of the History of Ideas* 55, no. 2 (1994): 211–34.

Green, Donald, and Ian Shapiro. *Pathologies of Rational Choice Theory: A Critique of Applications in Political Science* (New Haven, CT: Yale University Press, 1994).

Grosz, Elizabeth. *The Nick of Time: Politics, Evolution, and the Untimely* (Durham, NC: Duke University Press, 2004).

———. *Space, Time, and Perversion* (New York: Routledge, 1995).

Guenancia, Pierre. "Hobbes-Descartes: Le nom et la chose," in *Thomas Hobbes: Philosophie Première, Theorie de la Science Politique,* ed. Yves Charles Zarka and Jean Bernhardt (Paris: Presses Universitaires de France, 1988).

Hacking, Ian. "Minding the Brain," *New York Review of Books* (June 24, 2004): 32–36.

Hampton, Jean. *Hobbes and the Social Contract Tradition* (Cambridge: Cambridge University Press, 1986).

———. "Hobbesian Reflections on Glory as a Cause of Conflict," in *The Causes of Quarrel: Essays on Peace, War, and Thomas Hobbes,* ed. Peter Caws (Boston: Beacon Press, 1989).

Hanson, Donald. "Science, Prudence, and Folly in Hobbes's Political Theory," *Political Theory* 21, no. 4 (1993): 643–64.

Haraway, Donna. *Simians, Cyborgs, and Women: The Reinvention of Nature* (New York: Routledge, 1991).

Herbert, Gary. "Thomas Hobbes's Counterfeit Equality," *Southern Journal of Philosophy* 14, no. 3 (1976): 269–82.

Hill, Christopher. *Change and Continuity in 17th-Century England.* Rev. ed. (New Haven, CT: Yale University Press, 1991).

Hobbes, Thomas. *An Answer to a Book Published by Dr. Bramhall, Late Bishop of Derry; Called the "Catching of Leviathan"* [1668], in Molesworth, *English Works,* vol. 4.

———. *Behemoth, or the Long Parliament* [1668], ed. Stephen Holmes (Chicago: University of Chicago Press, 1990).

———. *The Correspondence of Thomas Hobbes,* 2 vols., ed. Noel Malcolm (New York: Oxford University Press, 1994).

———. *De Cive, Thomas Hobbes: Man and Citizen* [1642], ed. Bernard Gert (Indianapolis, IN: Hackett, 1991).

———. *De Corpore,* [1655] in Molesworth, *English Works,* vol. 1.

———. *De Homine,* in *Thomas Hobbes: Man and Citizen* [1642], ed. Bernard Gert (Indianapolis, IN: Hackett, 1991).

———. *Human Nature,* in *Thomas Hobbes: The Elements of Law Natural and Politic: Human Nature and De Corpore Politico* [1640], ed. J. C. A. Gaskin (Oxford: Oxford University Press, 1994).

———. *Leviathan* [1651], ed. C. B. Macpherson (New York: Penguin, 1968).

———. *Of Liberty and Necessity* [1655], in Molesworth, *English Works,* vol. 4.

———. *The Questions Concerning Liberty, Necessity, and Chance,* in Molesworth, *English Works,* vol. 5.

Hoekstra, Kinch. "Hobbes and the Foole," *Political Theory* 25, no. 5 (1997): 620–54.

———. "Hobbes on Law, Nature, and Reason," *Journal of the History of Philosophy* 41, no. 1 (2003): 111–20.

———. "Tyrannus Rex vs. Leviathan," *Pacific Philosophical Quarterly* 82, nos. 3–4 (2001): 420–46.

Hoffman, Paul. "Three Dualist Theories of the Passions," *Philosophical Topics* 19, no. 1 (1991): 153–200.

Holmes, Stephen. "Political Psychology in Hobbes's *Behemoth*," in Dietz, *Thomas Hobbes*.

Honderich, Ted. *How Free Are You? The Determinism Problem* (Oxford: Oxford University Press, 1993).

Honig, Bonnie. *Political Theory and the Displacement of Politics* (Ithaca, NY: Cornell University Press, 1993).

Honneth, Axel. *The Struggle for Recognition: The Moral Grammar of Social Conflicts* (Cambridge, MA: MIT Press, 1996).

Horton, John, and Susan Mendus, eds. *Aspects of Toleration: Philosophical Studies* (New York: Methuen, 1985).

Houten, Art Vanden. "Prudence in Hobbes's Political Philosophy," *History of Political Thought* 23, no. 2 (2002): 288–302.

Howes, David, ed. *Empire of the Senses: The Sensual Culture Reader* (New York: Berg, 2005).

Hungerland, Isabel, and George Vick. "Hobbes's Theory of Language, Speech, and Reasoning," in *Thomas Hobbes: Computatio Sive Logica / Part I of De Corpore,* ed. Isabel Hungerland and George Vick (New York: Abaris Books, 1981).

Hunter, Graeme. "The Fate of Thomas Hobbes," *Studia Leibnitiana* 21, no. 1 (1989): 5–20.

Israel, Jonathan. *Radical Enlightenment: Philosophy and the Making of Modernity 1650–1750* (Oxford: Oxford University Press, 2001).

James, Susan. *Passion and Action: The Emotions in Seventeenth-Century Philosophy* (Oxford: Oxford University Press, 1997).

Johnston, David. *The Rhetoric of* Leviathan: *Thomas Hobbes and the Politics of Cultural Transformation* (Princeton, NJ: Princeton University Press, 1986).

Jonsen, Albert R., and Stephen Toulmin. *The Abuse of Casuistry: A History of Moral Reasoning* (Berkeley: University of California Press, 1988).

Kahn, Victoria, Neil Saccamano, and Daniela Coli, eds. *Politics of the Passions, 1500–1850* (Princeton, NJ: Princeton University Press, 2006).

Kant, Immanuel. *Critique of Practical Reason,* 3d ed., trans. Lewis White Beck (New York: Macmillan, 1993).

———. *Critique of Pure Reason,* trans. Norman Kemp Smith (New York: St. Martin's Press, 1965).

———. *Grounding for the Metaphysics of Morals,* trans. James W. Ellington (Indianapolis, IN: Hackett, 1981).

———. *Grounding for the Metaphysics of Morals,* with *On a Supposed Right to Lie Because of Philanthropic Concerns,* 3d ed., trans. James W. Ellington (Indianapolis, IN: Hackett, 1993).

———. *The Metaphysics of Morals,* ed. Mary Gregor (Cambridge: Cambridge University Press, 1996).

———. *Political Writings,* ed. Hans Reiss (Cambridge: Cambridge University Press, 1991).

Kantorowicz, Ernst. *The King's Two Bodies: A Study in Mediaeval Political Theology* (Princeton, NJ: Princeton University Press, 1957).

Kaplan, M. Lindsay. *The Culture of Slander in Early Modern England* (Cambridge: Cambridge University Press, 1997).

Kateb, George. "Hobbes and the Irrationality of Politics," *Political Theory* 17, no. 3 (1989): 355–91.

Kavka, Gregory. *Hobbesian Moral and Political Theory* (Princeton, NJ: Princeton University Press, 1986).

———. "Hobbes's War of All Against All," *Ethics* 93 (January 1983): 291–310.

Kidder, Joel. "Acknowledgements of Equals: Hobbes's Ninth Law of Nature," *Philosophical Quarterly* 33, no. 131 (April 1983): 133–46.

Knowlson, James. *Universal Language Schemes in England and France, 1600–1800* (Toronto: University of Toronto Press, 1975).

Knox, Dilwyn. "Ideas on Gesture and Universal Languages, c.1550–1650," in *New Perspectives on Renaissance Thought: Essays in the History of Science, Education and Philosophy; In Memory of Charles B. Schmitt,* ed. John Henry and Sarah Hutton (London: Duckworth, 1990).

Krieger, Leonard. *The German Idea of Freedom: History of a Political Tradition* (Chicago: University of Chicago Press, 1957).

Kristeva, Julia. *Powers of Horror: An Essay on Abjection* (New York: Columbia University Press, 1982).

Kroll, Richard. *The Material Word: Literate Culture in the Restoration and Early Eighteenth Century* (Baltimore, MD: Johns Hopkins University Press, 1991).

Kronman, Anthony. "The Concept of an Author and the Unity of the Commonwealth in Hobbes's *Leviathan,*" *Journal of the History of Philosophy* 18, no. 2 (1980): 159–75.

Latour, Bruno. *Politics of Nature: How to Bring the Sciences into Democracy* (Cambridge, MA: Harvard University Press, 2004).

Lazzeri, Christian. "Politics of Reason or Politics of Passions? Hobbes and Spinoza Revisited," *Philosophy and Social Criticism* 28, no. 6 (2002): 661–86.

LeDoux, Joseph. *The Emotional Brain: The Mysterious Underpinnings of Emotional Life* (New York: Simon and Schuster, 1996).

Lloyd, S. A. *Ideals as Interests in Hobbes's Leviathan: The Power of Mind over Matter* (Cambridge: Cambridge University Press, 1992).

Lott, Tommy. "Hobbes's Mechanistic Psychology," in *Thomas Hobbes: His View of Man,* ed. J. G. van der Bend (Amsterdam: Rodopi, 1982).

Mabbot, Gilbert, ed. *King Charles His Speech Made upon the Scaffold at Whitehal-Gate immediately before his Execution. Tuesday, January 30. 1648* (London, 1649).

————. *King Charls his Tryal: or A perfect Narrative of the whole Proceedings of the High Court of Justice in the Tryal of the King in Westminster Hall. Begun Saturday Jan. 20 and ended on Saturday Jan. 27 1648* (London, 1649).

MacIntyre, Alasdair. *Dependent Rational Animals: Why Human Beings Need the Virtues* (Peru, IL: Carus, 1999).

Macpherson, C. B. *The Political Theory of Possessive Individualism: Hobbes to Locke* (Oxford: Oxford University Press, 1962).

Malcolm, Noel. *Aspects of Hobbes* (New York: Oxford University Press, 2002).

Marcus, George, W. Russell Neuman, and Michael Mackuen. *Affective Intelligence and Political Judgment* (Chicago: University of Chicago Press, 2000).

Markell, Patchen. *Bound by Recognition* (Princeton, NJ: Princeton University Press, 2003).

Martell, James. "The Radical Promise of Thomas Hobbes: The Road Not Taken in Liberal Theory," *Theory and Event* 4, no. 2 (2000).

Martin, Biddy. "Success and Its Failures," *Women's Studies on the Edge,* special issue, *Differences: A Journal of Feminist Cultural Studies* (Fall 1997): 102–31.

Mascuch, Michael. "Social Mobility and Middling Self-Identity: The Ethos of British Autobiographers, 1600–1750," *Social History* 20, no. 1 (1995): 46–61.

Massumi, Brian. *Parables of the Virtual: Movement, Affect, Sensation* (Durham, NC: Duke University Press, 2002).

May, Larry. "Hobbes on the Attitude of Pacifism," in *Thomas Hobbes de la métaphysique à la politique,* ed. Martin Bertman and Michel Malherbe (Paris: Vrin, 1989).

McDermott, Rose. "The Feeling of Rationality: The Meaning of Neuroscientific Advances for Political Science," *Perspectives on Politics* 2, no. 4 (2004): 691–706.

McGinn, Colin. "Fear Factor," *New York Times* (February 23, 2003): http://www.nytimes.com.

McNeilly, F. S. *The Anatomy of Leviathan* (New York: St. Martin's Press, 1968).

————. "Egoism in Hobbes," in *Ethics,* vol. 2 of *Thomas Hobbes: Critical Assessments,* ed. Preston King (New York: Routledge Kegan Paul, 1993).

Miller, Richard. *Casuistry and Modern Ethics: A Poetics of Practical Reasoning* (Chicago: University of Chicago Press, 1996).

Miller, Ted. "Thomas Hobbes and the Constraints That Enable the Imitation of God," *Inquiry* 42, no. 2 (1999): 149–76.

Mills, Charles. *The Racial Contract* (Ithaca, NY: Cornell University Press, 1997).

Mintz, Samuel. *The Hunting of Leviathan: Seventeenth Century Reactions to the Materialism and Moral Philosophy of Thomas Hobbes,* 2d ed. (Bristol, UK: Thoemmes Press, 1996).

Mitchell, Joshua. "Hobbes and the Equality of All Under the One," *Political Theory* 21, no. 1 (1993): 78–100.

Molesworth, William, Sir, ed. *The English Works of Thomas Hobbes,* vols. 1, 4, and 5 (London: John Bohn, 1839, 1840, 1841).

Montag, Warren. "Beyond Force and Consent: Althusser, Spinoza, Hobbes," in *Postmodern Naturalism and the Future of Marxist Theory: Essays in the Althusserian Tradition,* ed. Antonio Calleri and David Ruccio (Hanover, NH: Wesleyan University Press, 1996).

Murphy, Mark. "Hobbes' Shortsightedness Account of Conflict," *Southern Journal of Philosophy* 31, no. 2 (1993): 239–53.

Nagel, Thomas. "Hobbes's Concept of Obligation," *Philosophical Review* 68, no. 1 (1959): 68–83.

———. *Other Minds: Critical Essays, 1969–1994* (New York: Oxford University Press, 1995).

Norton, Anne. *Bloodrites of the Post-Structuralists: Word, Flesh and Revolution* (New York: Routledge, 2002).

Nussbaum, Martha. *Upheavals of Thought: The Intelligence of Emotions* (Cambridge: Cambridge University Press, 2001).

Oakeshott, Michael. *Hobbes on Civil Association* (Berkeley: University of California Press, 1975).

———. *Rationalism in Politics and Other Essays* (Indianapolis, IN: Liberty Press, 1991).

Okin, Susan Moller. *Women in Western Political Thought* (Princeton, NJ: Princeton University Press, 1979).

O'Neill, Onora. *Constructions of Reason: Explorations of Kant's Practical Philosophy* (Cambridge: Cambridge University Press, 1989).

Orlie, Melissa. *Living Ethically, Acting Politically* (Ithaca, NY: Cornell University Press, 1997).

Osler, Margaret. "Baptizing Epicurean Atomism: Pierre Gassendi on the Immortality of the Soul," in *Religion, Science, and Worldview: Essays in Honor of Richard Westfall,* ed. Margaret Osler and Paul Lawrence Farber (Cambridge: Cambridge University Press, 1985).

Overbye, Dennis. "Free Will: Now You Have It, Now You Don't," *New York Times* (January 2, 2007): http://www.nytimes.com.

Overhoff, Jürgen. *Hobbes's Theory of the Will: Ideological Reasons and Historical Circumstances* (Lanham, MD: Rowman and Littlefield, 2000).

Pacchi, Arrigo. "Hobbes and the Passions," *Topoi* 6, no. 2 (September 1987): 111–19.

Parrochia, Daniel. "La science de la nature corporelle," *Studia Spinozana* 3 (1987): 151–73.

Patellis, Ioli. "Hobbes on Explanation and Understanding," *Journal of the History of Ideas* 62, no. 3 (2001): 445–62.

Pateman, Carole. *The Sexual Contract* (Stanford, CA: Stanford University Press, 1988).

Patton, Paul. "Nietzsche and Hobbes," *International Studies in Philosophy* 33, no. 3 (2001): 99–116.

Pécharman, Martine. "Le discours mental selon Hobbes," *Archives de Philosophie* 55, no. 4 (1992): 553–73.

Peterfreund, Stuart. "Scientific Models in Optics: From Metaphor to Metonymy and Back," *Journal of the History of Ideas* 55, no. 1 (1994): 59–73.

Peters, Richard. *Hobbes,* 2d ed. (New York: Penguin, 1967).

Peters, Richard, and Henri Tajfel. "Hobbes and Hull: Metaphysicians of Behaviour," in *Hobbes and Rousseau: A Collection of Critical Essays,* ed. Maurice Cranston and Richard Peters (Garden City, NY: Anchor, 1972).

Pippin, Robert. *Modernism as a Philosophical Problem: On the Dissatisfactions of European High Culture,* 2d ed. (Malden, MA: Blackwell, 1999).

Pitkin, Hanna. *The Concept of Representation* (Berkeley: University of California Press, 1967).

———. "Hobbes's Concept of Representation—Part 1," *American Political Science Review* 58, no. 2 (1964): 328–40.

———. "Hobbes's Concept of Representation—Part 2," *American Political Science Review* 58, no. 4 (1964): 902–18.

———. *Wittgenstein and Justice: On the Significance of Ludwig Wittgenstein for Social and Political Thought* (Berkeley: University of California Press, 1972).

Polin, Raymond. *Politique et Philosophie chez Thomas Hobbes* (Paris: Presses Universitaires de France, 1953).

Popkin, Richard. *The History of Skepticism from Erasmus to Descartes* (New York: Humanities Press, 1964).

Rawls, John. *Political Liberalism* (New York: Columbia University Press, 1993).

Reik, Miriam M. *The Golden Lands of Thomas Hobbes* (Detroit: Wayne State University Press, 1977).

Rhodes, Rosamond. "Creating Leviathan: Sovereign and Civil Society," *History of Philosophy Quarterly* 11, no. 2 (1994): 177–90.

———. "Reading Rawls and Hearing Hobbes," *Philosophical Forum* 33, no. 4 (2002): 393–412.

Richmond, Samuel. "Newton and Hume on Causation: Alternative Strategies of Simplification," *History of Philosophy Quarterly* 11, no. 1 (1994): 37–52.

Rogers, G. A. J. Introduction to *A Defence of True Liberty from Antecedent and Extrinsicall Necessity,* by John Bramhall [1655] (London: Routledge / Thoemmes Press, 1996).

Ross, George MacDonald. "Hobbes and Descartes on the Relation Between Language and Consciousness," *Synthese* 75, no. 2 (1988): 217–29.

Royce, Josiah. *Lectures on Modern Idealism* (New Haven, CT: Yale University Press, 1919).

Ruiz de Mendoza Ibáñez, Francisco José. "The Role of Mappings and Domains in Understanding Metonymy," in *Metaphor and Metonymy at the Crossroads: A Cognitive Perspective,* ed. Antonio Barcelona (New York: Mouton de Gruyter, 2000).

Rushworth, John, ed. "The Nineteen Propositions" and "His Majesty's Answer to the Nineteen Propositions of both Houses of Parliament, tending towards a Peace," in *Historical Collections. The Third Part; in Two Volumes. Containing the Principle Matters Which happened from the Meeting of the Parliament, November the 3d, 1640. To the End of the Year 1644* (London, 1721).

Russell, Conrad. *The Causes of the English Civil War: The Ford Lectures Delivered in the University of Oxford 1987–1988* (Oxford: Clarendon, 1990).

Ryan, Alan. "A More Tolerant Hobbes?" in *Justifying Toleration: Conceptual and Historical Perspectives,* ed. Susan Mendus (Cambridge: Cambridge University Press, 1988).

Ryle, Gilbert. *The Concept of Mind* (Chicago: University of Chicago Press, 1949).

Sacksteder, William. "How Much of Hobbes Might Spinoza Have Read?" *Southwestern Journal of Philosophy* 11 (1980): 25–40.

———. "Spinoza's Attributes, Again: An Hobbesian Source," *Studia Spinozana* 3 (1987): 125–49.

Schiebinger, Londa. *Nature's Body: Gender in the Making of Modern Science* (Boston: Beacon Press, 1993).

Schneewind, J. B. "Autonomy, Obligation, and Virtue: An Overview of Kant's Moral Philosophy," in *The Cambridge Companion to Kant,* ed. Paul Guyer (Cambridge: Cambridge University Press, 1992).

Schochet, Gordon. "Intending (Political) Obligation: Hobbes and the Voluntary Basis of Society," in Dietz, *Thomas Hobbes.*

———. "Patriarchalism, Politics and Mass Attitudes in Stuart England," *Historical Journal* 12, no. 3 (1969): 413–41.

Searle, John. *Minds, Brains, and Science* (Cambridge, MA: Harvard University Press, 1984).

———. *The Mystery of Consciousness* (New York: New York Review of Books, 1997).

————. *The Rediscovery of the Mind* (Cambridge, MA: MIT Press, 1992).

Sepper, Dennis. "Imagination, Phantasms, and the Making of Hobbesian and Cartesian Science," *Monist* 71, no. 4 (1988): 526–42.

Shapin, Steven, and Simon Schaffer. *Leviathan and the Air-Pump: Hobbes, Boyle, and the Experimental Life* (Princeton, NJ: Princeton University Press, 1985).

Shulman, George. "Metaphor and Modernization in the Political Thought of Thomas Hobbes," *Political Theory* 17, no. 3 (1989): 392–416.

Silverman, Kaja. *The Subject of Semiotics* (Oxford: Oxford University Press, 1983).

Skinner, Quentin. "The Ideological Context of Hobbes's Political Thought," *Historical Journal* 9, no. 3 (1966): 286–317.

————. *Reason and Rhetoric in the Philosophy of Thomas Hobbes* (Cambridge: Cambridge University Press, 1996).

Slomp, Gabriella. "Hobbes and the Equality of Women," *Political Studies* 42, no. 3 (1994): 441–52.

————. *Thomas Hobbes and the Political Philosophy of Glory* (New York: St. Martin's Press, 2000).

Somerville, Johann P. "The 'New Art of Lying': Equivocation, Mental Reservation, and Casuistry," in *Conscience and Casuistry in Early Modern Europe,* ed. Edmund Leites (Cambridge: Cambridge University Press, 1988).

————. *Thomas Hobbes: Political Ideas in Historical Context* (New York: St. Martin's Press, 1992).

Sorell, Tom. "Descartes, Hobbes and the Body of Natural Science," *Monist* 71, no. 4 (1988): 515–25.

————. *Hobbes* (New York: Routledge Kegan Paul, 1986).

————. "Hobbes and the Morality Beyond Justice," *Pacific Philosophical Quarterly* 82, nos. 3–4 (2001): 225–42.

Spragens, Thomas. *The Politics of Motion: The World of Thomas Hobbes* (Lexington: University Press of Kentucky, 1973).

Springborg, Patricia. "Hobbes's Biblical Beasts: *Leviathan* and *Behemoth,*" *Political Theory* 23, no. 2 (1995): 353–75.

Stanlick, Nancy. "Hobbesian Friendship: Valuing Others for Oneself," *Journal of Social Philosophy* 33, no. 3 (2002): 345–59.

Steinberger, Peter. "Hobbesian Resistance," *American Journal of Political Science* 46, no. 4 (2002): 856–65.

Strauss, Leo. *The Political Philosophy of Hobbes: Its Basis and Its Genesis,* trans. Elsa M. Sinclair (Chicago: Phoenix / University of Chicago Press, 1963).

————. "The Spirit of Hobbes's Political Philosophy," in *Hobbes Studies,* ed. K. C. Brown (Cambridge, MA: Harvard University Press, 1965).

Strong, Tracy. "How to Write Scripture: Words, Authority, and Politics in Thomas Hobbes," *Critical Inquiry* 20 (Autumn 1993): 128–59.

Taylor, A. E. "The Ethical Doctrine of Hobbes," *Philosophy* 13 (October 1938): 406–24.

Taylor, Michael. *The Possibility of Cooperation* (Cambridge: Cambridge University Press, 1987).

Ter Hark, Michel. *Beyond the Inner and the Outer: Wittgenstein's Philosophy of Psychology* (Boston: Kluwer, 1990).

Thomas, Keith. "The Social Origins of Hobbes's Political Thought," in *Hobbes Studies,* ed. K. C. Brown (Cambridge, MA: Harvard University Press, 1965).

Tricaud, François. "Hobbes's Conception of the State of Nature from 1640–1651: Evolution and Ambiguities," in *Perspectives on Thomas Hobbes,* ed. G. A. J. Rogers and Alan Ryan (Oxford: Clarendon, 1988).

———. "Le roman philosophique de l'humanité chez Hobbes et chez Locke," *Archives de Philosophie* 55, no. 4 (1992): 631–43.

Tuck, Richard. "Flathman's Hobbes," in *Skepticism, Individuality, and Freedom: The Reluctant Liberalism of Richard Flathman,* ed. Bonnie Honig and David Mapel (Minneapolis: University of Minnesota Press, 2002).

———. "Optics and Sceptics: The Philosophical Foundations of Hobbes's Political Thought," in *Conscience and Casuistry in Early Modern Europe,* ed. Edmund Leites (Cambridge: Cambridge University Press, 1988).

———. *Philosophy and Government: 1572–1651* (Cambridge, MA: Harvard University Press, 1993).

———. "Scepticism and Toleration in the Seventeenth Century," in *Justifying Toleration,* ed. Susan Mendus (Cambridge: Cambridge University Press, 1988).

van Mill, David. *Liberty, Rationality, and Agency in Hobbes's* Leviathan (Albany: State University of New York Press, 2001).

Waldron, Jeremy. "Hobbes and the Principle of Publicity," *Pacific Philosophical Quarterly* 82, nos. 3–4 (2001): 447–74.

Warrender, Howard. *The Political Philosophy of Thomas Hobbes: His Theory of Obligation* (Oxford: Clarendon, 1957).

Watkins, J. W. N. *Hobbes's System of Ideas: A Study of the Political Significance of Philosophical Theories* (London: Hutchinson University Library, 1965).

———. "Philosophy and Politics in Hobbes," in *Hobbes Studies,* ed. K. C. Brown (Cambridge, MA: Harvard University Press, 1965).

White, Stephen. *Sustaining Affirmation: The Strengths of Weak Ontology in Political Theory* (Princeton, NJ: Princeton University Press, 2000).

Williams, Bernard. *Ethics and the Limits of Philosophy* (London: Fontana, 1985).

Wilson, Elizabeth. *Neural Geographies: Feminism and the Microstructure of Cognition* (New York: Routledge, 1998).

Wilson, James Q. "Resolving Hobbes's Metaphorical Contradiction: The Role of the Image in the Language of Politics," *Philosophy and Rhetoric* 29, no. 1 (1996): 15–32.

Wilson, Margaret D. "Descartes on the Origin of Sensation," *Philosophical Topics* 19, no. 1 (1991): 293–323.

———. *Ideas and Mechanism: Essays on Early Modern Philosophy* (Princeton, NJ: Princeton University Press, 1999).

Wittgenstein, Ludwig. *On Certainty,* ed. G. E. M. Anscombe and G. H. von Wright, trans. Denis Paul and G. E. M. Anscombe (New York: Harper, 1972).

———. *Philosophical Investigations,* 3d ed., trans. G. E. M. Anscombe (Englewood Cliffs, NJ: Prentice-Hall, 1958).

Wolin, Sheldon. "Hobbes and the Culture of Despotism," in Dietz, *Thomas Hobbes.*

———. "Political Theory as a Vocation," *American Political Science Review* 63, no. 4 (1969): 1062–82.

Wrightson, Keith. *English Society: 1580–1680* (New Brunswick, NJ: Rutgers University Press, 1982).

Yolton, John W. *Perception and Reality: A History from Descartes to Kant* (Ithaca, NY: Cornell University Press, 1996).

Zagorin, Perez. "Hobbes's Early Philosophical Development," *Journal of the History of Ideas* 54, no. 3 (1993): 505–18.

Zarka, Yves Charles. *Hobbes et la pensée politique moderne* (Paris: Presses Universitaires de France, 1995).

———. *La décision métaphysique de Hobbes,* 2d ed. (Paris: Vrin, 1999).

———. "Liberty, Necessity, and Chance: Hobbes's General Theory of Events," *British Journal for the History of Philosophy* 9, no. 3 (2001): 425–37.

Zerilli, Linda M. G. *Feminism and the Abyss of Freedom* (Chicago: University of Chicago Press, 2005).

———. *Signifying Woman: Culture and Chaos in Rousseau, Burke, and Mill* (Ithaca, NY: Cornell University Press, 1994).

Index

and, 35, 42–43, 63; Spinoza and, 18–19; theory of the subject and, 2, 7–8, 17; transference of right to self-governance and, 133–34, 147–48, 158, 166–68; will and, 70. *See also* Sovereign

Power: active, 139–40, 145; cause and, 136–40; conditions of, 143–45, 149, 157; cooperation and, 146–48; desire and, 143; future-orientation of, 135; honor and, 151–55, 188*n*14; individuals and, 140–56; and interdependence, 135, 150, 155, 169–70; intersubjectivity and, 145–46, 148–56, 169–70; materialism and, 10–11; natural and instrumental, 144–45; not a property, 139; passive, 139–40, 145, 157; peace and, 135; perception and, 141–42; plenary, 139–40; and public appearance/perception, 148–55, 157–61, 168, 170, 187*n*11; reputation and, 148–49, 152–54, 157–59, 187*n*8; social character of, 140, 144–45; sovereign and, 156–65; status and, 188*n*13; stereotype of Hobbes's concept of, 133, 135; temporality and, 135, 143, 146

Practical reason, 58, 95–96, 181*n*35

Predestination, 5

Prisoner's Dilemma, 185*n*15

Promises, 118–19, 184*n*5, 186*n*22. *See also* Covenants

Propositions, 30, 62

Prudence. *See* Practical reason

Public appearance/perception: ethics and, 116–21, 123–24; politics and, 142; power and, 148–55, 157–61, 168, 170, 187*n*11; sovereign and, 157–61, 168

Punishment, 120

Ratiocination, 59–64; advantages of, 30–31; desire and, 62–63; and practical reason, 181*n*35; problems in, 63; process of, 30, 59–64; truth and, 62–63

Reason: and agency, 35, 39–41; body and, 35–36, 42–44, 75; capriciousness of, 59; distinctiveness of, 44; ethics and, 35, 42–43, 113; instrumental, 54–59;

will and, 75–76. *See also* Instrumental reasoning; Mind; Practical reason; Ratiocination; Thinking

Reformation Christianity, 5

Religion, 97, 181*n*9, 185*n*21

Reputation, 148–49, 152–54, 157–61, 187*n*8. *See also* Honor

Response to stimuli. *See* Stimuli, response to

Responsibility, moral, 79–81, 103–5, 111, 125–29

Revolution, 128

Rhodes, Rosamond, 156

Rights, transference of, 167

Rogers, G. A. J., 70

Ross, George MacDonald, 32

Self-awareness: language and, 29–30; memory and, 8, 28, 32–34; sense perception and, 24. *See also* Self-consciousness

Self-consciousness: Cartesian versus Hobbesian views of, 33; of matter, 8; neuroscience and, 18. *See also* Self-awareness

Self-interest, 110–11, 130, 147–48

Self-knowledge. *See* Self-awareness

Self-mastery, 16, 75, 77, 89–90. *See also* Autonomy

Self-opinion, 98

Self-preservation, 4, 114, 126

Sense perception: change as element in, 25; common organ of, 46–47; definition of, 24; memory and, 25–28, 47; power and, 141–42; process of, 24–27; thinking and, 24, 30, 38–39, 45–46, 49

Servants, as power, 144, 147

Shared sovereignty, 163

Signs, 60. *See also* Names

Silverman, Kaja, 48

Singularity: of bodies, 93–94; of individuals, 12, 67, 156

Skinner, Quentin, 70

Social relations. *See* Collective; Cooperation; Interdependence; Intersubjectivity

Cultural Memory | *in the Present*

Gil Anidjar, *The Jew, the Arab: A History of the Enemy*

Jonathan Culler and Kevin Lamb, eds., *Just Being Difficult? Academic Writing in the Public Arena*

Jean-Luc Nancy, *A Finite Thinking*, edited by Simon Sparks

Theodor W. Adorno, *Can One Live after Auschwitz? A Philosophical Reader*, edited by Rolf Tiedemann

Patricia Pisters, *The Matrix of Visual Culture: Working with Deleuze in Film Theory*

Andreas Huyssen, *Present Pasts: Urban Palimpsests and the Politics of Memory*

Talal Asad, *Formations of the Secular: Christianity, Islam, Modernity*

Dorothea von Mücke, *The Rise of the Fantastic Tale*

Marc Redfield, *The Politics of Aesthetics: Nationalism, Gender, Romanticism*

Emmanuel Levinas, *On Escape*

Dan Zahavi, *Husserl's Phenomenology*

Rodolphe Gasché, *The Idea of Form: Rethinking Kant's Aesthetics*

Michael Naas, *Taking on the Tradition: Jacques Derrida and the Legacies of Deconstruction*

Herlinde Pauer-Studer, ed., *Constructions of Practical Reason: Interviews on Moral and Political Philosophy*

Jean-Luc Marion, *Being Given That: Toward a Phenomenology of Givenness*

Theodor W. Adorno and Max Horkheimer, *Dialectic of Enlightenment*

Ian Balfour, *The Rhetoric of Romantic Prophecy*

Martin Stokhof, *World and Life as One: Ethics and Ontology in Wittgenstein's Early Thought*

Gianni Vattimo, *Nietzsche: An Introduction*

Jacques Derrida, *Negotiations: Interventions and Interviews, 1971–1998*, ed. Elizabeth Rottenberg

Brett Levinson, *The Ends of Literature: The Latin American "Boom" in the Neoliberal Marketplace*

Timothy J. Reiss, *Against Autonomy: Cultural Instruments, Mutualities, and the Fictive Imagination*

Hent de Vries and Samuel Weber, eds., *Religion and Media*

Niklas Luhmann, *Theories of Distinction: Re-Describing the Descriptions of Modernity*, ed. and introd. William Rasch

Johannes Fabian, *Anthropology with an Attitude: Critical Essays*

Michel Henry, *I Am the Truth: Toward a Philosophy of Christianity*

Gil Anidjar, *"Our Place in Al-Andalus": Kabbalah, Philosophy, Literature in Arab-Jewish Letters*

Hélène Cixous and Jacques Derrida, *Veils*

F. R. Ankersmit, *Historical Representation*

F. R. Ankersmit, *Political Representation*